THE DOOR TO HEAVEN

The Chief Archangel Michael and the Six Archangels

From left to right: The Archangel Raphael; The Archangel Raguel; The Archangel Panuel (or phanuel); The Chief Archangel Michael; The Archangel Gabriel; The Archangel Sariel (or Saraqael or Suriel); The Archangel Uriél

THE DOOR TO HEAVEN

In Search of Future Happiness

by
Yuko Chino

Jihi-to-Ai Publishing Co., Ltd.
Tokyo

First Published by
Jihi-to-Ai Publishing Co., Ltd.
Room #305, Kichijoji Pine Crest
1-27-1, Kichijoji-Minami-Machi
Musashino-shi, Tokyo 180, Japan

Illustrations by Noriko Tsuchida

ISBN 4-915502-04-X C 0090

Printed in Japan by
Kyodo Obun Center Co., Ltd.

Letter of Recommendation regarding the "Kingdom of Heaven (*Tengoku*) Series"

Dear Readers,

I have been dealing with books for quite a large number of years as a librarian, and it is from this position that I would like to put forward a few words on this presentation.

Day after day, there are many books published and the total number of books just continues to increase.

I had previously always thought that "books are the thoughts and emotions of people put down on paper in print," but recently I am beginning to learn that this is not necessarily the case.

The ancient Shintoism of Japan preaches over and over again of "*Kotodama* (the Spirit of Words)." The Holy Bible too preaches that " . . . the Word was God." The number of books in circulation may have reached awesome heights, but I have truly begun to realize that amongst all these many books, there are, in fact, "books in which dwells a Life Power."

Several thousands of years ago, there was a secret book compiled by the Wise Men of Israel, now called *the Protocols of Zion*. This book, when translated with evil intentions by a foreign country, has long been said to bring about "Within a space of three years, certain War or Disaster" to that country. (An actual example is that this book was closely sealed up, but one part of it was stolen. Subsequently, it was translated and then published in Russia. Within the space of three years, the Revolution took place and the State fell. —"How foolish," you might say, "These two things cannot be connected!"— So dismissed, there is nothing more that can be said. However, there are many such examples.)

The book that I am recommending on this occasion is a book written by a lady called Ms. Yuko Chino, and it is being published in a series called "Kingdom of Heaven (*Tengoku*) series." It is a collection series of several volumes. (Starting with the *Door to Heaven (Tengoku no Tobira)*, three volumes have already been published. There are four more volumes that are planned for publication, as of June 1979).

This is not a strange book with a curse on it as was the previous book about which we were discussing. It is not a book which is secret, but rather one which I would like as many people as possible to read. It is a book that the "more one reads, the more one's soul calms down, and the happier one feels." There are some people who have read it ten, twenty even more times. I, for instance, have it on tape and I listen to it even when I am lying down.

Looking at the title of this series, your first reaction might be to ask—"Is it not a religious book?—Particularly, a book on Christianity?"—But in this book there is not a single sentence which says that "you should believe," "you should worship," that "you should pray" . . . In fact, if anything it severely criticizes the wrongs of religion, whether established or new. On the other hand, this is not a book that aims at being anti-religious, putting forward and laying down the law with left wing theories and ideas. It is not a book of philosophy, nor is it a book of science . . . . It is not a thriller nor is it an idealistic and visionary novel . . . . (You are, therefore, given a completely free hand in the selection of its field . . . !) This book has within it no element of the haughty and highhanded holiness which is so often to be found in books of this type. It is not in the slightest bit disagreeable, and in its extreme truthfulness, in being sincerity itself, one can imagine that one is able to hear the sound of angel voices. Sometimes there are places in the book which seem absurd, but the sincerity just melts the doubts away. I, for one, read the first book of the series *Door to Heaven (Tengoku no Tobira)*, and on that alone was so impressed that I determined to meet the author, and would not have considered the "road of a thousand miles" too far to go for this purpose.

The main point of this book, in a word, is "*Shoho* (the Universal Law or the 'Right' Law)." There is a law which is written but cannot be seen in this world. It is a law which concurs with the laws of science . . . . This book explains clearly and solemnly all the questions that Man has asked or has always asked and never been given an answer to, such as questions on God, on the soul, on life after death, everlasting life, etc. In order to have you understand better what is meant by this "Law," there is a monthly magazine published called "*Jihi to Ai* (Love and Mercy)" and also a meeting held in various parts of the country of the "*Shoho no Tsudoi*" groups. There are reports from reliable sources that just from understanding the true meaning of the "Law," gold or silver flakes from somewhere appeared on the hands or arms of some people. And also, there have been reports that when Ms. Yuko Chino has finished writing a book, there appear around the sun or the moon in the heavens strange ring rainbow-shape halos (double halos and treble halos in rainbow shape and color). Many people are said to have observed these and to have taken photographs of these phenomena. It is truly an unbelievable true tale . . . .

Earlier on, I mentioned that it was a book in which it was

possible to hear "the sound of angel voice," etc., but this is not to say that this is a relaxing, gentle book that will lull you into a land of dreams. There is a severity which will allow one to get away with nothing. Why should this be? It is because it is telling us that "the Last Day of Judgement," about which there has been much preached, is near. That we have entered the period already. It is truly a "terrible" book as well. Those who wish to laugh, can laugh . . . .

Truly, though—in the five thousand years of Man's history, it would not be too much to say that it is the first "miraculous writing," "a book that is stranger than truth," "a book that is alive" . . . . Therefore, this book is not just "a book," nor just "an ordinary book," but has nothing ordinary about it, and cannot be ignored. There are people who have been saved from certain disaster by having this book with them. But I would not dream of saying anything as foolish as "worship this book" or "carry it around with you as a good luck charm" . . . .

My wish is that you should understand the meaning of this book and that you should store it carefully in the library. And that you should read it with the practical, calm and analytical mind of a scientist. And further, that if there should be any questions, you should realize and know that there is a way through the "*Jihi to Ai*" magazine of asking for the answers.

I am sure that you will begin to feel, as you read the book, that there is something there. The feeling that one gets, no doubt, is different from one person to another. I felt, for instance, that from some distant corner of the Heavens, someone, grieving at the fall of man, and the ruin of man, is using Yuko Chino's body in order to talk to people . . . .

Lastly, I would like to say just one more word. With regard to the publication and a wider distribution of this work among the public, we would add that it is the result of the blood and tears of people who "genuinely desire the happiness of others" and that there has been no acceptance of donations or assistance from any specific religious organization, ideological organization or cultural disciplinary organization.

And so with apologies for the clumsiness of my sentences, I end my letter of recommendation.

Hiroaki Ichikawa
Former Head: Chuo Library, Chiba Pref.
Former Head: Yoka-ichiba City Public Library

Letter of Recommendation and Introduction of Kingdom of Heaven (*Tengoku*) Series and Mercy and Love (*Jihi to Ai*) Magazine

Dear Readers,

I am very delightful to recommend and introduce to you the Kingdom of Heaven (*Tengoku*) series and the monthly organ Mercy and Love (*Jihi to Ai*) magazine which have been published since 1977 under the editorship and authorship of Yuko Chino. As you may notice, these publications provide original rational and scientific interpretations and clear answers to man's most fundamental questions on the nature of God, the soul, eternal life, religion and of man, himself.

A great source of enlightenment to many people, the public response to these works here in this country has been tremendous. Ms. Chino and our editiorial office in Tokyo have been flooded with letters of approval and endorsement for these works, having earning the popular accolation of the "Modern Bible" or the "Sutra for the Modern Age." Prominent scientists, educators, and other scholars who have come across with the books express amazement at their achievements and their rigorous scientific examination of the unknown world.

Today it is said that man is in a state of crisis because of the destruction of the natural environment around him and the horror of senseless warfare and that the worsening educational environment has made our youth unsure of themselves in their roles as the leaders of the next generation. These publications cast a new and elucidating light on this world and are powerful educational materials for our young.

I take this opportunity to introduce the *Tengoku* series and *Jihi to Ai*. It is my sincere hope that the English translation of these unique and moving works will lead to a wide readership among the foreigners, both here and overseas.

The Door to Heaven—In Search of Future Happiness
(*Tengoku no Tobira—Mirai no Shiawase o Mezashite*)

Based on scientifically established truths—the creation of man and his evolution under the Universal and Natural Law—this book bears witness to the facts that when man dies, his elementary particles, the basic elements of the physical entity, and the Universal Energy contained in his physical entity form a spiritual entity and that these spiritual entities form the spiritual world; that there is no "God, the Creator," and what Man chooses to call gods are really the great holy men and teachers of Man that once walked the earth and that have taken spirit form and ascended to the Higher Dimensions; and that as the beings that guide the world of lower earth, their task is a great one and they indeed do merit the appelation of "gods." An enlightening book which shows that the fundamental natures of science and religion are compatible.

In this work, these spirits of the Higher Dimension, such as the great Biblical Archangels Michael (said to be the guardian of Joan of Arc) and Gabriel, and Moses, Buddha and Jesus, who have been variously held to be gods, boddhisattvas and saviors, speak out to us directly through the spiritual powers of the author. They explain the true story of the Kingdom of Heaven and the beginning of Man's history, call anew for the realization of an ideal world here on earth and give Man teachings that dispel the superstitions, fallacies and fanatical beliefs that have blocked Man's achievement of that New World.

The Witness of the Kingdom of Heaven—To the Star of Hope through the Last Judgement

(Tengoku no Akashi—Saigo no Shimpan yori Kibo no Hoshi e)

Man, when he chooses to live in harmony with Nature, can maintain a society of peace. Man, when he breaks away from that path endlessly reenacting a life of cruelty and injustice that is counter to the laws of humanity (e.g. the Middle Way: the Eight-Part Path of Righteousness as found by Buddha), or when he spews out foul pollution on the earth or takes up tragic wars, or when he destroys the natural environment, distorts the meaning of civilization. If Man is allowed to continue in this unguided existence, it can only end in his coming to where he can no longer live in Nature and the Universe—he will walk the path to self-annihilation.

Man has come to the brink of his existence. If the fate of the world is left to those that in their greed and egotism continue to spread ruin upon the earth and to the domination of the evil spirits, then good and innocent and all living beings must face the destiny of being destroyed with them. At that final moment to allow Man to avoid this fate there will be a Last Judgement as prophesied in the Bible and other holy books where all men shall be judged on their behavior. In this book the spirits of the Higher Dimension who called out for this Last Judgement in the *Door to Heaven* (above) explained to Man in detail just how the Day of the Last Judgement has come.

They also tell Man that, through the Last Judgement, the clouds of darkness shall be swept away and the earth made into a star of hope, a world of peace and progress without founding another Hell. This work is profusely illustrated with pictures and poetry and forms an introduction to that heavenly world.

Under the Light of Heaven—From Exorcism to the Explications of Atlantis (*Tengoku no Hikari no Moto ni—Ekusoshizumu (Akumabarai) kara Atorantisu no Kaimei*)

There are many people who, moved and enlightened by the above two books, had personal experiences of the highest joy by realizing the practice of the True Law in their lives. This book is a collection of those experiences and of some of the new research that has been set off by these books. Included here are the jewel-like essays on *Shoho* (the True Law) that have been found in a lady's new life of exultation, the shocking personal experience of one family that was rescued from demonic possession by the spirits that appeared to them through the editor, the story of a youth who, having successively embraced several religions, came to learn the horrors of certain religious superstitions and fallacies and the wonderful spiritual experience that he gained upon coming in contact with the True Law, and warnings from a scientist on the environment and pollution that speak of the hard times ahead for the world.

Also, the Archangels of the Bible appearing in the above two books make a statement on the historical proof offered by a scholar of pedagogies on the widely debated question of where the lost continent of Atlantis is located. In conclusion, the editor conducts a complete examination of the origin of life, the nature of spiritual powers and the spirit world.

This book contains a comprehensive scientific analysis and explication of the Law of the Gods—*Shoho* (the True Law). A remarkably rich and full book.

Soon to be published:

Explication of the Miracles of the Bible (*Seisho no Kiseki no Kaimei*) (Tentative title)

The Bible, as the fountainhead of Western civilization, has long had innumerable material and spiritual effects on the entire world. This book supplies historical and archeological evidence to answer the question of how the Bible as we know it came into existence. The book examines the phenomenology of the miracles that appear in the Bible, exploring what a "miracle" is and how such miracles occurred. The actual witness of participants in these miracles, the beings that are called Yahweh, the Living God or Jehovah, the Holy Spirit and the great Archangels is taken, explicated in light of physical and chemical science, to reveal the truth about Biblical miracles and prophecies. A book certain to attract of lot of attention.

This witness also provides proof that the spirits of the Higher Dimension that have appeared through Yuko Chino are the same gods and angels that are revered in the Bible, further substantiating the authenticity of the Prophecies and Law given by these beings as introduced in the first four books of the *Tengoku* series. This also shows the validity of their call for a new recognition and awareness that the End of the World is here with us and that Man must strive for salvation from it for himself. The publication of the following books is also planned (titles tentative):

Explication of the Miracles of the Buddhist Scriptures (*Butten no Kiseki no Kaimei*)

Explication of Riddles through the Physical Sciences (*Butsurigaku-jo no Nazo no Kaimei*)

Explication of Riddles through Supra-physical Science (*Chobutsurigaku-jo no Nazo no Kaimei*)

About the magazine Mercy and Love *(Jihi to Ai)*

Soon after the publication of the first books of the *Tengoku* series, a group of people from all over Japan that had been deeply influenced by the books spontaneously formed to publish a magazine to promote the enlightening ideas of the *Tengoku* series. *Jihi to Ai* is a magazine of enlightenment not bound to the framework of former spiritual thought or religious groups. It works to enlighten its readers by informing them of the True Law and correcting mistaken religious concepts, sects and superstitions through the application of Natural Law under the highly rational and coherent guidance of the spirits of the Higher Dimension. Ultimately, the magazine looks to the realization of a utopia here on earth that embodies the principles of mercy and love through the spread of *Shoho* (the True Law). *Jihi to Ai* calls out for the participation of more people in this constructive movement. The translation work of this magazine has not been commenced yet, but, whoever is interested in reading the Japanese issue, at present, is very welcome to order one at the publishing office below.

Editing and Publishing Office
  Jihi-to-Ai Publishing Co., Ltd.
  Room # 305, Kichijoji Pine Crest
  1–27–1, Kichijoji-Minami-Machi
  Musashino-shi, Tokyo 180
  Phone: (0422) 49–3310
  Transfer Account No. 5–74265 Tokyo
Editorial Staff
  Tetsuhiko Nishizawa
  Hiroyuki Nakanishi
  Katsutoshi Miyoshi

Thus far with hopes to have successfully appealed to you, readers, commenting on the value and the importance of the works of Ms. Yuko Chino and the like-minded people, I end my long letter of recommendation and introduction.

Fumiya Iwama
Assistant Professor,
Shibaura Technical College,
Tokyo

Preface

Readers abroad will not be familiar with GLA (God's Light Association), which frequently appears in this book. This association is a neo-religious group, which has a deep relationship with the Kingdom of Heaven (equivalent to the term "Celestial World" used in this book) through Shinji Takahashi.

Mr. Takahashi, the founder of the association, is said, to one's great amazement, to have been the reincarnation of Jehovah, the supreme authority in Heaven and a being of the highest dimension, who also appeared before the GLA by the name of El Lantie. Mr. Takahashi, however, erred in declaring his daughter as being the reincarnation of the Chief Archangel Michael, shortly before he died on the 25th of June, 1976. This revelation received the whole-hearted support of the members of the association, who further deified the young girl of 19. But the Archangel Michael denied the transmigration. At this point, the drama on the raison d'être and unreliability of the GLA starts to unfold.

Simultaneously, I have the obligation to report to you readers of the astoundingly great miracle manifested by Heaven to testify that the greater part of this book was written just as it was told by the spirits from the Kingdom of Heaven to the author and her students, through spiritualistic capacities endowed by the spirits. This is the first time that such a way of writing has been attempted. This miracle also evidences the strong Will of Heaven exhorting us to attest to the readers the genuineness of the facts contained in this book.

It occurred when the first proofreading of the manuscript had been completed and the proofs had been sent back to the publishing company. On that same night, the 28th of October, 1977, to be exact, from midnight until 1:00 a.m., I saw a clear, star-inlaid sky and the full moon brilliantly emitting its radiation, around which many white flakes of clouds were gathered, and as if to wrap them in, a gigantic rainbow-hued halo, distinctly seen even in the dark, circling the bright moon. (Later, I learned that the appearance of such a halo is very rare; none occur in the warm flatlands but it probably does in the cold highland or above the summit of a high mountain in the cold areas, in a country like Japan. It was a so-called second grade rainbow, with gradations of red on the inside edge, followed by six other colors, with purple on the outer edge.)

Calling out Mother and catching the attention of several passers-by, I verified that the scene was not a spiritual vision but a phenomenon in the three-dimension. Everyone was standing speechless, aghast at the magnificence and beauty of the halo, as if they were seeing a dream. Noriko Tsuchida, upon my call at that late hour, commented that she was shivering in amazement.

This miracle was performed by Moses to manifest the joy of Heaven, and the archangel Michael said that it was the first experiment of the sort. (This statement was curiously added later with the fact that there was a record of a promise made by Heaven of a rainbow after the Flood in Genesis, through my careful study of the Old Testament recently. Whether or not the story of Noah had been made up from a legend of the Mesopotamia district, as claimed by some scholars, the technic of manifesting a rainbow was nothing new to the people of Heaven, especially the archangels.) I believe there were many living in the same city who viewed that great manifestation and I, for one, will never forget that impressive sight.

The second serial volume, *The Witness of the Kingdom of Heaven*, was published in August, 1978, and the third volume, *Under the Light of Heaven*, in January, 1979. This series of books on Heaven is scheduled to total seven in number when completed. The Chief Archangel Michael has promised that the miracle of the rainbow-hued halo will occur whenever each manuscript for the following volumes is completed and whenever Heaven deems necessary. That promise has been kept thus far.

My heartfelt gratitude is due the translator; the editors; Teisuke Takimura, who contributed the publishing expenses; Hiroyuki Nakanishi, President of Jihi-to-Ai Publishing Co., Ltd., who provided a great deal of work and help in realization of this issue.

The Author

April, 1980

Contents

CHAPTER 1

Spiritual Experiences

Strange Encounters in Other Dimensions

I write these chapters to communicate with others who, like me, have felt themselves strangers to this world with an inexplicable feeling of loneliness—aliens left behind on earth. I hope to share with you how this extraneous mode of life without which existence would be meaningless was all at once completely affirmed for me, achieving for me a joyous state which seems beyond mere human capacity.

In the thirty years since entering this new life in all its physical and spiritual aspects, I have known many who live from one day to the next, conforming to events and the people around them, pursuing ambition and temporal satisfactions. I, on the other hand, had grown aware of another world—a realm of spiritual beauty—while vainly seeking in the hearts of others, from whom I could only be separate and apart. They, unable to understand my needs or knowledge, reviled me. Not being a contentious person, who might welcome friction or attempt to destroy the roots of my discontent, I bore this new alienation from these people in silence without any effort to retaliate. Yet I realized that these unknowing people traveled through life in mistrust of their fellow men, suspicious of others' sincerity and good will. There must have been many among them who sought the dream of a life lived in love and beauty. Yet none of the great rules I learned from books or from friends, or from teachers during my school days, was being practiced by ordinary society. I never happened to meet anyone who felt as I did. People of other countries, as well as my fellow countrymen—priests and missionaries, those in foreign trade, as in the chemical company for which I worked, and even those in the healing arts, as in hospitals—all were "too, too human," oblivious of the visions I had seen. Hiding my inner dissatisfactions, I made friends with these people, as anyone might, but sometimes, I could not help but wonder how one could study or by what means one could learn to become a mature member of society. It seemed as if society, like mold, infected everything people learned . . . or at least the good things. It seemed that they trod heedlessly on the hearts of others—thoughtless and cold, with lusts and cruelties hidden in the deep currents of their hearts, as if they were animals. Nowhere could one find respect for beauty or the worth of a man. Neither intellectuals nor unschooled people had the opportunity to gain or be taught such insight into truth, living in a nightmare of worldly passions, instinctive drives and insecurities. It was thus that I spent the time between adolescence and adulthood among people who lived in such perfunctory fashion, in a society without reason, amidst currents of passion and decadence. It was a fearful world of a corrupt generation and public unrest, in which people, poisoned by poor standards of mass news media, had lost the ability to discriminate between right and wrong.

From early childhood, I had had a weak constitution and repeatedly suffered from allergies and serious illnesses. My physical resistance was low and it seems that I had, unawares, become allergic to people who treated me unkindly or misunderstood me. When I was in the sixth grade, just after World War II, I thought of committing suicide during a period spent away from home, because of poor treatment received from the family I was made to live with.

After graduating from college, I worked for a firm where there was a man I liked. As I could not bring myself to talk to him, I wrote him a letter which he ignored. About the same time, I made a serious mistake in my work. The complications were so unbearable I left home, intending suicide. My mother hurried to church and asked for prayers from her pastor and also another minister. Convinced I had killed myself, she prayed, "Lord Jesus, I offer my daughter up to you." Because suicides are not able to enter Heaven, the pastor begged Jesus' forgiveness, saying, "Forgive this woman her prayer. She prayed without knowing." But he said that, if alive, I had undoubtedly fled with a man. My mother vehemently denied this because there was not the least evidence of my doing such a thing. I heard later that about that time, there had come walking a man resembling the High Priest Kobo Daishi[1], and this image floated in my mother's mind. She thought this strange since it was to Jesus she had prayed. But it seems that, in a past existence, her in-dwelling spirit had been a disciple of Kobo Daishi, who may have come to give her encouragement of my safety.

At that time, I had stayed one night in Tokyo, then in Yokohama, carrying sleeping pills. Unable to carry out my intention of committing suicide, I went to Kyoto on the fifth day, where I spent my last money to telephone my mother. She immediately came for me. Both the head of my section and the assistant head of a related section in the firm where I worked told my mother reassuringly that everyone made mistakes at first, and that I was unnecessarily sensitive. But I still resigned. Although I had graduated as an English major from college, my main duties at the office had been filing letters, serving tea and keeping the office tidy. Also, I had lost any desire to stay because of numerous behind-the-scene requests by male employees to write for them the draft for the office's English correspondence, which they felt inadequate to do themselves.

After this event, I took sleeping pills twice in an effort to end my life, but in some way I was protected and did not die. Human beings ordinarily are reared under the protection of three spirits from Heaven. There is the in-dwelling spirit which emerges within the body in childhood, and also a protective spirit and a guiding spirit which watch from without. (The in-dwelling spirit, originally the soul of one now deceased, co-inhabits the body with the body's soul. It is a union of two souls within one human body, and not to be misinterpreted as reincarnation, which merely means the rebirth of a soul in a new body.) The three spirits from Heaven watch over and guide us throughout our lives and keep us from evil spirits. This is a dispensation of Heaven to save people from the descent to Hell. At this time, the ways of the spirits were not known to me but I had always sensed the guardian power of Heaven. Ever since I was born, the spirit of the archangel Sariel dwelt within me so evil spirits could not possess me. Also, she would go forth when duties made it unavoidable but would return in haste to guard me from death. It seems that whenever I felt the urge to commit suicide, Sariel happened to be performing duties in the Celestial World, and she would immediately come to me.
Other guardian spirits gave me consolation. Jesus also helped me.

At the end of 1976, commentators on a television program predicted that 1977 would see a change from coarse and evil pursuits to a preference for sensible goals of moderation. True to prediction, many people during 1977 seemed to show a greater concern for spiritual matters. It is still too early to conclude that they have shed their concern for the momentary or passing things of life, but I believe that a sense of discretion may finally have been reborn.

People have begun to avoid extremes. "Good will" and "responsibility" are gaining in importance.

Along with this trend, my own spiritual world changed greatly. It actually began in 1975 when, through my mother, proof of the existence of gods was revealed to me. At first, I was unbelieving. No one else could have been more skeptical; because of past sufferings, I had concluded that gods did not exist. This apostasy resulted from contacts with a "new" religious sect. It was astonishing to me that there could have emerged from the same source as Christianity and Buddhism, this "new" sect, led by Shinji Takahashi[2].

My mother, who had lived in disillusionment like my own, had talked to me with vital certainty of Takahashi *sensei*'s[3] teachings after each of his meetings, regardless whether I tried to listen or understand. She told me of the greatness of Shinji Takahashi's remarkable teachings—how precious each word was, how marvels and miracles occurred and how unlearned tongues were spoken through the help of holy spirits at the meetings. Gradually, I began to realize that many of these teachings were strangely akin to what I had already come to know. But I stubbornly refused to acknowledge this bond—this treasure of true belief. Many of Takahashi *sensei*'s followers were people of the upper class, not likely to understand my sufferings . . . a successful group, which made large offerings of money to spread their faith. I could feel no kinship with the likes of these.

One day, a strange thing happened. There was among our friends a certain woman who commiserated with my mother about my stubbornness, about my clashes with my stepfather (my real father had died of granular tuberculosis when I was eight) and the difficulty of my mother's position in the middle of our triangular quarrels. This woman said to my mother, "Your daughter is assaulted by evil spirits; unless you live apart from her, both of you will be killed." When my mother told me this, I was unable to listen rationally. I grew excited and in a passion of anger, threw into a trash box my mother's three precious books by Shinji Takahashi. At that instant, my body grew rigid as if I had been tightly bound by an unearthly power! I felt an instinctive fear of this strange force and returned the books at once to their usual place. Immediately, my stiffness vanished.

Even before this, I had had two or three strange experiences with the other dimensions. The first happened about thirteen years earlier. I had been working in the office of a German chemical dye firm for six months. Nine German men, my superiors, occupied one office; when the man under whom I worked wanted to dictate a letter, I was called to this office. Being a new employee, I somehow felt that I was being watched and always felt ill-at-ease. One day, one of the men began to flatter me, saying things like, "Your work is excellent. What do you think of going to Germany to study?" I should have responded with some polite or innocuous amenity of speech but instead, I let him see that I was not pleased. Annoyed, he began to harass me as a subordinate, an insidious form of reciprocation, typical of Germans.

Liking a healthy personality in people, I pretended ignorance during the following two months, while inwardly regarding him with scorn. Finally, the situation became unbearable so I wrote a letter about it to my immediate superior after everyone had left the office. I left it on his desk and started to leave the office but I could not open the door, although it was not time for the office to be locked up. I was shut up in the third floor office. Later, however, the guard happened to come upstairs and let me out. Not till later did I realize it but this was a warning from a benign spirit, trying to deter me from this rebellious act. He was warning me not to invite trouble. I had a premonition of this but, for me, the important thing was to quickly solve my problem and boldly left the letter to my superior. As was to be expected, this was like throwing a rock into a quiet pond. The resulting waves seemed to spread unceasingly and all the German members of the firm at once began to treat me coldly. A month later, I left that company after working there only nine months. I came to mistrust the human race, particularly men, as a result of this experience.

The second event happened three years later when I was working as a secretary for an American pharmaceutical firm. As I had been baptized in the Christian faith during college, I went to church almost every week. However, the minister of our church treated me coldly, ever since the time I left the German firm, which represented my failure as a stenographer, and would not even help me with consultations. On the contrary, I learned that he had told the congregation things about me of which I was innocent—things which I had never even thought and were unfounded and abusive. Since his attitude was normal on the surface, I, who knew little of the world, had no suspicions of him. But my mother heard rumors about him from members of the congregation and we both lost faith in him. Yet, this minister was highly respected by most of his congregation.

I suffered such anguish that I decided to ask God if I was at fault and to beseech his answer in a miracle. I prayed for rain to fall within minutes if my way of life not mistaken. (I was totally committed to the teachings of the Bible. I loved Jesus and his faith was my consolation and support against all uncertainties, in spite of every mortal anguish. With prayer, and as my solemn duty, I did the best I could at work and I treated friends and acquaintances with love. I associated with all people with respect, trust and sincerity.) As I prayed, the sky, which had been clear, suddenly became totally dark, then there was a gust of rain. People nearby were frightened but I, even though I had sought a miracle, interpreted this abrupt storm as an illusion. I criticized myself for violating God's teaching against putting Him to the test. Still, my conviction in myself and my way of life deepened.

Two months after the shock and suffering of being mistakenly condemned by my minister, I had my first encounter with evil spirits (earth-bound demons, as opposed to the benign spirits of Heaven). At that time, I intended to abandon my faith and refused to believe God's providential answer to me. But I never gave up my trust in Jesus. Yet, I was obsessed by a hatred of the world and wanted to die. I so idealized the world and mankind that each time I was hurt, I would become sick of living. That night, I told my mother I was going to see a friend and left the house. On the road to the next city, there was a mountain with a small waterfall, into which I intended to plunge to my death. Taking a narrow, seldom-used mountain path, I suddenly experienced an extremely disagreeable sensation. For four or five seconds, a strong force seemed to press down on my head. I did not know then that it was a sensation of a different dimension. When the force disappeared, I suddenly grew wary and wanted to return home. But to pass the same spot on the way back required courage. Just as I feared, the same sensation attacked me. This time, during the four or five seconds, I said to myself silently, "I'm not afraid. I am Christian and fear nothing," and I returned safely home. It was said that at that time, the spirit of Sariel dwelling within me blinded the earth-bound evil spirit who attacked me with her aura.

About this time, due to a chronic stomach illness, I had given up the idea of going out to work and was teaching children English at my home. Even after being apart from the real world for some years, my feelings of doubt and distaste for the human race had only grown deeper, so that I was happiest in the company of children and animals. I had concluded that God did not exist and considered myself an atheist, but I cherished my own philosophy of life and my convictions. I disliked the warped aspect of society and people who were not straightforward. I often censured people who did not behave honestly. In particular, my stepfather was an illogical and eccentric man and he and I were not compatible—as opposite as water and oil. Sensitive as I was, it was improbable that I could build harmonious relationships with other people. I had one or two friends to whom I could open my heart, but I was lonely. I went through the experience of falling in love and also endured the Japanese custom of arranged meetings with men to consider marriage. But my relationship with my stepfather was so poor that I could not consider the plunge into marriage.

I turned to caring for baby sparrows which had fallen from nests on the roof or abandoned kittens or puppies. Unfortunately, due to my ignorance, I caused most of these to die. But one survived—a part-Abyssinian and part-Persian kitten I had picked up. I soaked absorbent cotton with powdered milk and fed it every three hours, night and day, for a week. When it caught cold, I gave it cold medicine made for birds. Finally, I succeeded in raising it. This cat shared my sadness, loneliness and misery, and was my greatest friend. I felt as if it were my child and, of course, the cat knew no other mother. As I think back, whenever I needed something or to do something, it was somehow provided to me, like this cat. This was the work of Sariel or of my guardian spirit. I, who knew so little of life, must have often vexed them, in ways for which I feel there should be only apologies to them.

Then I came to know Shinji Takahashi. About a week after I had thrown his books and felt the tight bounds of a spirit on me, I was lying down in my room. Suddenly, a golden aura enveloped me. A large figure of Buddha and Jesus, only about one-third life size, appeared before my eyes. I could not believe my eyes and cried out, "Demons, depart!" four or five times. They vanished; then they appeared again. As I had never seen before such a brilliant-hued spirit form, my only thought was that this must be a hallucination. But at the same time, I felt no fear. My mother had constantly told me, "Shinji Takahashi watches over the homes of all who believe in him and their abodes are bathed in light. The light shines from the teacher's books so that homes with these books can be seen shining from Heaven."

Shinji Takahashi was a man spurred by a mission to spread the true words of *Shoho*, in which he drove himself relentlessly. His teaching took the form of heavenly spirits entering and speaking through a medium. Thus were created his sermons, books, and prophesies, through which he opened the spiritual way to others. The spiritual path was illumined by light emanating from the hands, helping the faithful to find spiritual power and to speak with their guardian spirits. Shinji Takahashi himself was a medium of the great heavenly spirits and his teachings, emphasizing the past of the in-dwelling spirits of the people more than the present and evoking memories of past reincarnations, often let people speak out in unlearned or strange tongues. To do all this, he spent his life force, having received a huge quantity of light and energy from Heaven, impossible for human flesh to sustain. Thus, he died at only forty-eight years of age on June 25th in 1976.

At the time of his death, I had not yet thought of the *Shoho* as the true religion or ultimate belief. So intense was my antagonism toward all religion, I considered myself an atheist. But the news of his death had more than a little impact on my mind. In my mother's absence, I secretively began to read Shinji Takahashi's books, which she preciously kept in our home. Little by little, the light from the books began to penetrate my soul and for the first time, I began to feel a little moved by Shinji Takahashi and his teachings.

Twice, I saw dreams prophetic of the future. Accompanied by a black leopard, I descended on an escalator from a refuse heap in Heaven, littered with gravestones, churches, temples and sculpture used for image worship. From there, I passed through a winding mountain road with tunnels and entered a totally dark place which somehow transformed itself into an inn by a wide river at dusk. In two or three words, I asked a person looking away from me for lodging. The face which slowly turned toward me was that of a ghost, emitting an uncanny bluish light. I fled in panic, running till I was out of breath, and finally reached another five- or six-story inn further up the river. I cried, "Please give me a room without ghosts. I encountered one at the inn downstream." The innkeeper led me to a room on the top floor, with an outdoor veranda, carpeted with grass, and with a sheep and many little birds. The sky was a clear blue, calming all my fears. As I later told my mother, it was a dream of Heaven and Hell.

Another night, I had a dream in which people whose faces radiated golden light walked in the dusk. The light was in clear relief against the darkening twilight glow. Many people who did not emit light were also walking. Suddenly, I noticed the figure of my mother, who was radiating, and also my own self, holding a diary, from which emanated golden light. The dream was prophetic of the spreading of that teaching known as *Shoho*, the True Law.

As the year-end approached, a follower of Shinji Takahashi telephoned my mother, saying, "One tape of Jesus speaking is left. Would you like to have it?" Mother always bought phenomenistic tapes at the spirit communication meetings which she attended devotedly. She eagerly asked for this tape, which the man, an electronic specialist, delivered to us the same day. At that time, he told us that he had heard from his guardian spirit (a spirit dwelling outside the body and keeping it safe from harm) that in previous reincarnations, my in-dwelling spirit had been a disciple of Jesus, as well as of Buddha and of Priest Chigi, founder of the Tendai sect[4], and had saved many people. Also, that Mother's had been a disciple of Jesus, Buddha, and Priest Kobo Daishi.

About that time, I felt nothing special but subsequently, I realized that gradually a sense of responsibility and duty were growing within me. When I began to re-read Shinji's *Buddha the Man*, this time carefully, I was emotionally stimulated and moved to tears. This was so different from the time when I had casually scanned this book. Thus, I became completely a devotee of Shinji. It is said that tears are an evidence of reviving memories of past existences of one's spirit brother (the in-dwelling spirit). I came to long to hear the actual voices of Buddha, Jesus and the Tendai Priest Chigi. Timidly, I played the tapes and listened to their voices, as spirit phenomena . . . Jesus, speaking through Shinji's daughter, and the others through Shinji himself. Truly, with the undulating sounds of their voices, I was gripped by emotional excitement, and tears and sobbing flowed from me. Next, I heard the chief archangel Michael, the celestial being most closely connected with me, speaking through the daughter with Teacher Shinji in what I directly felt was the language of Heaven. To my surprise, again I was emotionally moved to tears. Chief archangel Michael and the six other archangels, including Sariel, were introduced, through a spirit medium, either by automatic writing or clairaudial transmission.

After this, whenever I even came across the word 'archangel,' I was moved to tears. I prayed that safety and light might be given to all those in my prayers—to my family, my friends, to my birds and animals, to my students and their families, to the followers and family left behind by Shinji, to my neighbors, and to the people of the world. I prayed, "May evil spirits be kept away from them." Often at night, while praying and watching the stars of the sky, my tears would blind my eyes. I could not think of the sky other than as the abode to which I would return.

There is a miraculous experience called "opening of the Spirit Way." One day, about the end of February, the Spirit Way began to open for me, giving me new and precious spiritual powers, enabling me to speak with spirits, who were previously not approachable, although they had entered my body. The Spirit Way does not open easily for those who from birth lack the medium's spiritual powers, being harborers of spirits from the lowest level of Heaven, the realm of limbo or Hell. Because women bear children, there has been from the beginning another separate road for them, not open to men, to the other dimensions of the spirit world. Thus, so I have heard, it is easier for them to acquire a medium's powers. Sometimes, by virtue of the powerful energy of spirits dwelling in the higher dimensions, men or women may acquire the spiritual powers of the medium in a short time.

Often, when my mother had gone out to a meditation and study meeting, and I had no English class, I would send from home impulses or emanations of healing energy from my hands to the sick living at a distance. There are religious organizations which rely on this alone, but the group founded by Shinji treated this ability as only one manifestation of power. Under his teaching, we studied deeper truths, using spirit healing within *Shoho* (the True Law) in much the same way as Jesus in his healing of the sick. Once, on a whim, thinking that Shinji's wife or his daughter, whom Michael would enter in spirit phenomena, might be suffering from sore shoulders, I tried to treat them by sending healing energy. When I will psychic healing energy to someone, that person's headache, muscular pains, and any areas of sickness are impinged back on my body, like the reaction of a detecting device, and the pains are felt as my own. Of course, it is more effective to perform spirit healing in the same room. There also were occasions when I would investigate the sufferer's condition while my mother from home would send healing emanations to treat such illnesses as a lung cyst or diabetes. Chronic illnesses, diseases of the internal organs, and ailments arising from poor metabolism due to old age require a doctor's treatment at the same time; otherwise, there is not much benefit. When sick people are possessed by death demons or evil demons, removing the demon will hasten the sick person's recovery. When illness is prolonged, it becomes easier for demons to possess the sick parts of the body.

This psychic phenomenon occurs because a golden aura shines from the body, in large amounts from very healthy people. Health must be not only physical but spiritual. This aura is strengthened by that of the benign spirit which dwells within the body. To achieve this psychosomatic health, one must follow the temperate mode of life, as is set down in the chapters to follow. The stronger this aura, the more it guards one's body from evil spirits and spirits from Hell. In some cases, these spirits are forcibly repelled; in other cases, they leave naturally. When the aura becomes weak, the body is constantly assailed by demons so that the solar energies are intercepted. Finally, the body becomes a dwelling of ill spirits and spirits of Hell.

Sickness of the spirit produces the same results. People sick of soul . . . those who are materialistic, the pessimistic, those filled with jealousy or hatred, the greedy, the vain of heart, the sour in disposition, the stubborn, the cold of heart, those who live by animal instincts, the sadistic, the masochists . . . such people are never at peace unless they are worshipping some ideal. As long as they are worshipping, no matter what their nature may be, or what life they may lead, they see no need for thought or self-examination. Character, or the quality of a man, means no more to them than a mere word taught in school or listed in a dictionary; such people lean blindly on religion for support, and would cross the oceans to worship a sardine's head if they heard it had divine powers. People healthy of soul are those who are good at heart, peace loving, living in harmony with others, productive, aspiring for a better life, sensitive to others, delicate, prudent and wise, warm-hearted, tolerant, of cheerful disposition, rich in sentiment, spiritually mature, and concerned about building a better civilization. Those of an opposite nature are called "sick." Though one's body may be sick, one's aura may be beautifully golden, if the soul is well. Even though demons should attempt to possess such souls, they may be easily repelled.

Physical and spiritual well-being not only are important during one's life but are inescapably linked with one's life after death. At the death of one unhealthy-minded and possessed by evil, the guardian spirits from Heaven move to a distance and do not come close, and the benevolent spirit merged within the body leaves. Then evil demons and death demons become the wardens of the lonely soul and it falls into Hell, to be led to a place where other like souls are gathered together. Until one repents of the sins and errors of his mortal life, there he resides in endless misery.

To hasten spiritual awakening, spirits from Heaven visit those in Hell about once in two years. But enlightenment is hard for those who are held in a shadowy place, among companions with similar weaknesses and faults, imprisoned by wrath and fear. The pessimistic who are good at heart do not remain in Hell very long. Those whose stay will be long are the egoistic and avaricious. Those who submit to the urge to suicide will be held in a dark blue place after death. Then there are those who are destined to be reborn in Hell, and to repeat the same kind of suicide, again and again. Yukio Mishima[5] and the death-brigade soldiers of World War II were such people. Those who are sacrificed to wars or suicide are often people too good or naive to function in our society. Very soon, spirits assigned to the Benevolent Deities[6] of the various heavens of the East will descend to succor them. Such succor is limited to those who endeavored as best they could but whose failures finally led them to suicide. Spoiled or immature people who seek suicide to avoid their responsibilities must spend a long time in expiation while awaiting deliverance from the lower dimensions.

In April of 1977, all condemned souls received a special amnesty from Hell and were lifted up to Heaven. But people committing suicide subsequently are still in the dusky underworld. Every four or five months, through the helping powers of the chief archangel Michael and of the soul of Shinji Takahashi, and also the work of people in the three-dimensional world (earth, at present), death spirits, floating spirits, and earth-bound spirits are lifted to Heaven.

To return to the subject from which I have digressed a little —when I tried to relieve the sore shoulder muscles of the family of Teacher Shinji, I first called the name of his wife, and then that of his daughter. But his daughter was not in the same directional place, so turning around and around, I sought her direction and called out her name again. Simultaneously, without realizing, I had called out twice the name, "chief archangel Michael"; I had been sending out psychic messages, assuming that the daughter was an avatar of Michael. I did not know the structure of her soul nor that, at this time, Michael was not reincarnated in union with a human being. Shinji, while alive, assumed the same as I did but after death, in the Celestial World, he realized his error. So he spoke through his daughter, according to a witness, saying, "I have made a terrible error. How pitiful is the child I left behind." No one realized the meaning of this message until later. In this book, it will be made clear for the first time by various beings from the Celestial World that Michael is not reincarnated in the body of a human being and that Michael and Shinji's daughter are separate people. I, myself, have merged with and am the physical vehicle for the archangel Sariel but my soul and Sariel's are two different souls. We two are not the same person, even though I have absorbed much consciousness of things and knowledge.

Michael, as in the past, serves as a connection between the Messiah and those who continue his work, through his un-assuming self-assigned role to provide helping powers. The protective function of the Celestial World needs to be made sure and strong. When a celestial spirit merges with a human body (in a sort of reincarnation), most of its time is spent within its receptacle body. A successful incarnation can occur only in times of peace, not in a world of chaos.

When I summoned Michael, a ball of fire, as red as the setting sun and about 40 centimeters in diameter came flying through the wall in four or five seconds (as if it had come on the orbit of my thought waves). It seemed to enfold and caress me for several seconds. I felt no strangeness or fear, only a pleasant and abiding-ly warm sensation. I must have understood this phenomenon in the depths of my consciousness, as I implored, "Please heal my ailing body." This strange happening was my first encounter with the chief archangel Michael. The spirit within me, the archangel Sariel, had conveyed to Heaven my sufferings, asking that I be helped as much as possible. That the archangels should directly extend their hands in salvation for me was a wonderful experience which I hoped might last forever, but it ended in about two minutes.

Afterward, however, the sky became clouded and I had a premonition that this was an ill omen and that perhaps I had done something wrong. As the sky clouded so suddenly and did not clear, I despaired and cried, "If I am not forgiven, I

shall no longer work for *Shoho* (True Law). I had no bad intent."
Depressed, I took a nap. After my mother returned home and
I had told her about my experience, she said that she, too, had
had a strange experience. During the group meditation and study
meeting, when Mother was meditating[7], first a purple and red
aura spread before her eyes and then there spread out a golden
light. When she asked the other members about this, they replied
that she had seen Heaven. But later when they gathered to listen
to a lecturer, Mother heard him say, "A person who was one
of the ten disciples of Buddha is reincarnated in this area, al-
though not yet one of us." This statement, coming unexpectedly
later and in the midst of the talk on an unrelated matter, stayed
in my mother's memory.

Although it was night when my mother and I talked about
our experiences, each time the name of the chief archangel
Michael came to my lips, my body became warm and damp
with perspiration. I could only think that somehow Michael had
appeared again. That evening, I took my usual nightly stroll,
walking and praying, "May my soul be ready for the opening
of the Spirit Way. . . ." Also, I prayed, "If the time be not yet
ripe, grant me help so that the preparation may be completed
soon." I had been constantly told how wonderful it was to
acquire spirit power—to know the events of one's in-dwelling
spirit and its past lives as well as to converse with one's guardian
spirit. In the middle of the night, I wrote a friend about *Shoho*.
It was the following morning that a partial opening of the Spirit
Way happened to me.

When I awoke that morning, I opened the first volume of
Buddha the Man; quite accidentally, my eyes rested on a passage
which discussed the Venuvana[8]. As I reread it, suddenly tears
flowed so that my eyeglasses clouded and I was unable to read.
Overcome by some unexplainable emotion, I silently cried out,

"Lord Buddha, who is the reincarnated spirit in me? Please tell me his name." In my ears, there came a whisper of a name, that of one of the ten disciples of Buddha, but I failed to recognize it, as it was not a surname. In tears, I repeated that name again and again, while sobbing continuously. Then when I touched my fingers together in prayer, my body suddenly became warm, just as it had the previous night. Time after time, my body shock as if due to a fit of agues and my nose bled a little.

Next morning, my mother awakened and came down the stairs to me. When she learned a spirit had spoken through me, neither could she identify the name. We pondered over this riddle and then sought *Buddha the Man* to try to find out who was meant. Thinking it a likely choice, we opened the second volume to the chapter on "The Gathering of the Dedicated Disciples." Finally, we found the pertinent passage and when we had learned its name as being Moggāllāna[9] (Mahā-maudgal yāyana), the spirit was satisfied and left us, after promising to return when necessary.

Later, there came to us one of the twelve disciples of Jesus. We learned his name, too, Philip, after he had indicated passages in the Bible recording it. My mother and I were astonished that both were personages from the holy scriptures. We also were told the name of my mother's in-dwelling spirit when he served one of the twelve disciples of Jesus. From that time, I was able to communicate with my guardian spirit. Three days later, the chief archangel Michael appeared again. At that time, too, I felt that warm sensation of his previous visit. From about 10 o'clock till a quarter to one, Michael caused light continually to bathe my forehead, and I was seized by uncontrollable spasms of quivering and sobbing. All this time, my eyes were closed and four visions, in brilliant colors, floated before my eyes like episodes from a cosmic drama. The drama seemed to be a vision of the Parthenon at Athens. There, among an assembled multitude, stood a golden-haired girl of about 18 in a white costume, listening to someone speaking from the steps of the temple. "Oh, it's Apollo," I thought. In the second scene, five or six angels were gathered together on a cloud, while a taller angel spoke to them. Flying in front of this group was a female angel with silver-colored wings, wearing a light blue dress. The angel who was speaking was the chief archangel Michael and the one flying seemed to be Sariel, my in-dwelling spirit.

In the next scene, two men, who seemed to be Buddhist priests of India, were walking along a mountain path together, one talking to the other. Then there appeared a place like the Veṇu-vana Monastery; Buddha was teaching many disciples in one of its halls. His countenance appeared much as when he had appeared to me the previous year. I recalled that his halo was very large.

The fourth scene seemed to be from the time of Jesus. Someone, under a gloomy and cloudy sky, who was being stoned by a crowd, looked up to Heaven with arms outspread in supplication. This was the same image that came to mind when the Spirit Way opened for me, and it was immediately made known to me that it was the disciple Stephen. This was an unforgettable scene which Philip, the spirit brother of Moggāllāna, had witnessed during his life. When I was given spiritual powers, I cried for a whole day, repeating, "Poor Stephen. How I wanted to succor him." Each time, my guardian spirit consoled me, saying, "It was destined. Like Jesus, he gave witness to the glory of God."

The panorama ended, but the strong light still bathed my brow. I waited stoically, thinking that this was to enable me to speak the spirits' language. Two hours passed. I thought I had failed, and unable to bear more, I rejected my fate, saying,

"Michael, let it suffice that I do not attain knowledge of the Spirit Way." Then I went to my upstairs room. The light followed me and shone on the back of my head for fifteen minutes. Then it ended. My mother said that these happenings were similar to the time when Shinji attained a spirit medium's powers. From the happenings of the past five days, I was enabled to recognize the mood surrounding the presence of the chief archangel Michael.

Struggles with Demoniac Spirits

I was told by Michael that when the Spirit Way is fully opened and one attains complete spiritual powers, he is vulnerable to attacks by demons. Therefore, only the senses of sight and hearing of the higher dimensions had been bestowed on me. When I first talked with celestial spirits, I had no fears, even as today. I felt calm, just as if I were conversing with an ordinary person of our own world. Nothing felt unusual; birds were singing and my pet cats and dogs behaved as usual. Actually, I felt more cautious about meeting strangers of our own three-dimension.

When I was teaching my students, Satan's challenge would loom over me and interfere, so that my attention was diverted. Also, all of my five cats would shrink away from me, whenever Satan's threat loomed. They watched all the time and would not approach me. Satan and his demons often disrupt the daily lives of people, cunningly controlling the consciousness, with the ultimate objective of taking their lives. The good spirits behave differently, striving always to help with beneficial admonitions and advice, in order to aid us in our lives in the three dimension.

About this time, I first experienced the separation of body

and soul. The human body is already conditioned and ready for such an occurrence, as one's soul leaves the body, going elsewhere and returning, similar to the state of sleep. Also, the separation is simple, although it seems strange at first, as only part of the soul leaves. Then there was a chain of happy occurrences. When I asked that light be sent to my household, the entire house grew warm and there was a sudden flood of light. I also asked, in order that I might teach my pupils *Shoho* (the True Law) in a simple way, that they might see blue skies and starry nights occur, as far as possible only in the vicinity of my house, at least at the time my pupils would be going to and from school or studying in my home. As I asked, so was it granted, and the children wondered greatly and believed it a miracle indeed. Again, on a certain day, I was taking a walk, despondent and alone, when a female angel, with deep blue eyes and auburn hair, dressed in white and blue, with large wings, suddenly descended before me. She attended me for three days, walking beside me and protecting me with her gentle presence wherever I went. My confidence returned and I realized that I had much more courage and composure if I tried to walk with spiritual wings. Thus, I gained strength and my newly-posted guardian spirit watched over me until Michael finally took her place to guard me day and night thereafter.

Wanting my peers to know of these various wondrous happenings, and to share in my rejoicing, I had my mother telephone the superiors at the headquarters of the disciples of Shinji Takahashi—the GLA[10]. Surprisingly, these members said the being called Moggāllāna that had spoken through me could not be the Buddha's disciple because it was already elsewhere. They also scoffed at the happening concerning the disciple of Jesus, Philip, and I was forbidden to talk about the dispensation of blue skies. All at once, I lost belief in myself and, for the first time, Satan took possession of me. All the contents of my spiritual talks now seemed strange, with answers in rapid, disordered speech, typical of evil spirits. When I sent spirit healing energy to cure the sick, I did as I was told at first but as their commands seemed somehow abnormal, I stopped immediately sending such vibrations. But as I recall now, strange wave forces came rushing down in heavy, streamlike concentrations from a certain place in the ceiling of the room next to mine. Because of this, the room assumed a strange aspect, like that of a deserted place.

It was the end of winter. In a neighboring house, there lived a man and wife in their fifties. Since October of the previous year, the husband had been sick and possessed by death spirits, so that his sickness had become progressively worse (I was informed of this by the person who had brought the Jesus tape at Christmas). He had been confined to bed ever since he had injured himself by stumbling and falling at the entrance to his house. This long confinement resulted in progressive muscular atrophy, and finally, in February, he was hospitalized. It is said that in his youth, this man had killed someone in a quarrel and later, there were suspected instances of his causing grief to others. He had the reputation of believing in wealth as the sole condition which qualified one to stand above other men, and that the poor should be victims of the rich. He was hospitalized because his wife had to go to work in his stead, and he required care. Their home became like a deserted house. Since death spirits and earth-bound spirits gather in hospitals, his wife brought these evil spirits home after each visit to the hospital. Also, she liked the *Hannya Shingyo* Sutra[11] and used to chant it before the household altar whenever she felt like it. Each such time, Hell's demons arose and attached themselves to the house, which thus became their gathering place. Making use of this opportunity, Satan evidently built a road of Hell from that house over to my house. But he did not enter immediately. Since I could not hear his words distinctly, and believing that I was speaking for a second time with the heavenly beings which had possessed me when the Spirit Way first opened for me, I said, "Please enter." But there was no warmth, and my body began shaking rapidly for about five seconds. This interval was probably necessary because, unless the wave length of Heaven was changed to that of Hell, the force could not enter me. Then in a strange cadence, speech began, but I could not understand it.

Just about that time, my mother, being concerned about me, telephoned the person in charge at the GLA, asking that he make an appointment if possible with Shinji Takahashi's daughter, to find out from her who my reincarnated spirits were. Midway through this call, the person said, "Please wait a moment," then the connection was cut. Later, we were told that, sensing something strange and fearful, he had hurriedly cut off the call. That night, about eleven, I heard a loud sound like the beating of a heart, and an oppressive heat again began to spread into and through the house. I sensed that the chief archangel Michael had come. As the strange utterings of the evil spirit died away, I fell asleep, and when my eyes opened, the drumming sound had become faint. Suddenly, I felt a terrible sensation like that of being tightly bound in fetters by an evil spirit force.

It was strange how well I had a conscious understanding of all these things which were happening to me for the first time in my life. It seems that my guardian spirit, resigning herself to the evil spirit's presence by my side, had remained close by and given me this knowledge. When salvation is possible, the guardian spirit does this to alert (the beseiged person) to danger and encourage him to defend his body (from invasion). Only when all hope is gone does the guiding spirit leave and return to its celestial world. But the good spirit co-inhabiting the body remains till the end, so that human beings of our planet in the three dimension are never left entirely alone to struggle with evil.

As I felt the sensation of being bound in fetters again, the throbbing sound grew louder and the area around my bed became hot. Then just as suddenly, the fetters felt loosened. It was already bright in the morning. I left my bed and, after eating breakfast, went for a walk. All this time, until I returned from the walk, the throbbing sound continued, close to me, as if it were immediately above my head. It was as if it was always protecting me. Like the time when the red ball of fire floated before my eyes, I felt strong of heart and happy. When my protecting force saw me completely freed from the influence of Satan, it left me. But for five days more, between eleven at night and nine o'clock each morning, it returned to stand guard over me and those in my house.

After that, I again began to talk with my guardian spirit. But on the third day, Satan renewed his persistent attempt to possess me, by whispering this-and-that in my ear. I talked with my protective spirit continuously and without haste, so annoying Satan that he was driven out. If one asks a simple question, such as "When is Christmas?," without allowing the correct reply to arise in the conscious level of the mind or thinking of some other, incorrect, date, Satan will not hesitate to err. This is the primary way to recognize his presence. Good spirits have the wisdom to answer correctly in advance of the medium's thoughts but this doesn't always work. Because they are human souls, and when we are not sincere or when our intentions are bad, greedy or vain, we will receive undependable answers. The good spirits avoid people whose rhythms are at variance with those of Heaven. A protecting spirit is always forthright and warns us, or attempts to help us correct our faults. The higher the dimension in the universal scheme to which the being belongs, the more that being will avoid or treat with circumspection the type of human who expects his gods to provide everything without effort on his part, depending on Heaven for all things, or who consults Heaven about trivial matters or seeks wisdom from fortune tellers. The higher beings invariably have keen intelligence.

In truth, all men who know and consort with celestial beings ought to grow wiser and more virtuous. They are guided along an upward path. No matter how much learning a man may have, if he does not comprehend this truth, circumstances will arise that will confuse his life and all his knowledge will be seized on and used for evil by the demons, who will treat him with scorn as befits a fool. But if one should strive with all one's might, heavenly beings will extend him the hand of salvation. An insincere or superficial plea to Heaven will not alone suffice to procure the benediction of the celestial beings. Unless one earns such commendations, as being fine or wise, these celestial beings will not come to you.

The good spirits are honest so their evaluations may be trusted and believed. The evil spirits feed on vanity and greed, and are weakened by exposure to truth. That is to say, the spirits are honest in their intellectual struggle with the humans of our three-dimension. But, and this is a warning based on my own experience only to those for whom the Spirit Way is opened (and may not apply to those without this knowledge), unless one strives to be good of heart, to avoid extremes, and to control his passions, he may be possessed by demons before he realizes it and be led to Hell. Even if this should not be the case, human beings need the protection of Heaven so all men should strive to improve themselves, to increase their merit, and to attain such character as to justify man's status as the highest form of life. People of poor character or base, destructive persons may attain the lowest level of the Heavenly World, but their souls will be extinguished in due time and shall not attain everlasting life. Shallow-thinking men may think, "Then let's go to Hell!" but I believe that, after being sent to Hell, they will soon see and know its horrors. Such souls will find the suffering so unbearable that they will try to take possession of the bodies of the living.

Until April 3rd of that year, I was repeatedly menaced by Satan and each time, drove him away. I was protected by the halo of Buddha or else I was succored by seven of the disciples of the Tendai sect priest, Chigi, who prayed that possessing spirits be exorcised. Also, one night, I was guarded by Moses. During that time, I suddenly thought of a plan to be put into effect with the help of Shinji Takahashi. After consulting my guardian spirit, on two occasions, at evening and before noon, I did this, interspersing words of prayers to exorcise from our world all the possessing spirits, the earth-bound spirits, the spirits of (ferocious) animals, the floating demons and the souls of those who had died that day. This was exorcise on a large scale. Then Shinji appeared as a spirit, and sent me emanations from Heaven, which were entirely different from the emanations of Satan. With the chief archangel Michael watching over my doings from an adjoining room, we did this for three days. But many evil spirits appeared from the neighboring house. Hastily, I implored them not to enter my house but to wait outside, as aid would soon come to them from the skies. So many came that I was exhausted by their numbers alone. During this time, Michael continued his vigil, observing and judging the manner of my work. Finally this work ended and it is said that 500 million souls were raised to the Heavenly World.

This probably greatly angered Satan. When Shinji and Michael left me, he again assaulted me. This was the Satan whose name is Lucifer. I conversed at length with him and I made him listen to the tapes of Shinji. For three days and sleepless nights, I talked about his duties and responsibility as Luciel to the Heavenly World. I believed the mixture of truths and lies he told me, placing my hope in his words when he spoke like a benevolent angel. Finally, on the morning of the fourth day, he said, "Let's take a walk," so we left the house. I was also influenced by Satan's glibness of speech, and on being told that Lucifer was my elder brother and brother to Michael and the angels, I, his younger sister, cried for the soul of Lucifer, who, although my brother, was hated by all. During that time, I always called him Luciel. Looking at the beautiful blue sky, I asked, "Do you not wish to return to that beautiful Heaven? All that is needed is to reflect on your mistakes and to ask forgiveness of the gods. Naturally, you must make reparation but . . . . You are reviled by the beings of the Heavenly World, feared by man, and must live in a chilly Hell, where your only companions are disgusting demons. Are you not weary of such a life?" For some reason, I could not hate Lucifer. Suddenly, tears welled up in my eyes. I felt Lucifer's sorry plight as if it were my own and I grieved deeply. Mediums cry often, probably because they identify with the feelings of the spirits.

Until this time, Lucifer, whom I had believed to be talking to me from without, had been within me. Sariel, disdaining the duality with Lucifer, had left the shell of my body, but remained nearby, and reported my condition to the Heavenly World. It was planned that someone would come to my succor if my own strength proved insufficient. I foolishly believed what Shinji had uttered during his life, "No evil spirit may prevail over the loving and the merciful of heart." Thus I struggled with Lucifer. On the third of April, Lucifer left me and returned to Heaven, only to return for a short time to earth, having been told to put his soul in order. Then the chief archangel Michael, acting like my guardian spirit, extinguished his energy and came to me, to guard all unknown to me. Every third day, I would ask my guardian spirit, "What is Lucifer doing now?" Hearing that he was in Hell, writing his penitence, in the form of an angel with white wings, I felt peace of heart. But each time, came the added words, "Not yet. Still a little more." So on the other hand, I worried for fear Lucifer would grow weary and have a change of heart.

Then came the 13th day of April, and Lucifer, as Luciel, formally returned to Heaven. The truth was that the soul of the man Lucifer, who rejected the gods and fell into Hell, and the soul of the angel Luciel merged, to walk hand-in-hand through areas of time. But Luciel continually caused the voice of conscience to impinge on the conscious senses of Lucifer, in an unceasing effort to fulfill his heavenly task of returning Lucifer to the way of virtue. Truly, there has never been an angel like Luciel, with such a strong sense of duty, wasting no effort to save even a single human soul. When Lucifer assaulted human beings or fought with the other angels, Luciel separated from him, but continued to appeal to his conscience and his morality. So the event was not only an occasion for rejoicing by the beings of the celestial world but a victory for Luciel. People assume without thinking that Lucifer must be everlastingly Satan, and also condemn, along with Lucifer, the beloved disciple of Michael, Luciel, who strove night and day for Lucifer's salvation. Such blind bias is false and contributes neither to progress nor improvement.

I was told that Luciel had vowed to remain in duality with Lucifer until he completed his expiation to Heaven. So for three days, the joyous celebrations continued, and all rested, freed temporarily from work and responsibilities. I, too, relaxed my guard completely, believing there was no need to be concerned about evil spirits. I regret that I had no prior knowledge, but this was a matter no one could predict. Everyone was overjoyed and talked together light-heartedly. Good spirits, like the demons, can speak very rapidly. Not to be confused with demons, however, the benevolent spirits usually speak in a slow tempo matching the beating of one's heart, so one might think it to be the whispering of the wind or a manifestation of one's own consciousness, reinforced by some external stimulus. However, evil spirits are not capable of slow, clear speech, as are the benevolent spirits. But spirits, whether good or evil, speak in a common tongue. It is the same as with humans. For instance, Japanese, though their nature or their thinking may differ, or whether they are good or evil, still talk to each other in the language of Japan. At the GLA, I was taught that the speech of demons and good spirits differ, so I suspected Shinji of being a demon when he first came to me. However, I believe that those possessing a scientific attitude toward the search for knowledge will agree to the truth of these theories.

At my release, I was in a state of bliss, and asked Heaven for the perfumes of the aromatic herbs, roses, chrysanthemums, daisies and lilies. As a reward for the return of Luciel (Lucifer), Shinji and Moses filled my room with these fragrances. The parents, the brothers and their wives of El Lantie, who had come from a far star, as well as ladies from the upper dimensions of the celestial world all descended to talk with me. Even after the rejoicing had ended, an air of freedom pervaded the Heavenly World; Michael appeared and played music for me. Without movement of the keys, the music cannot be heard distinctly, but while looking at the score, I sensed that his two hands were skillfully evoking the music. I knew the foot pedals also were being properly pressed. Even the most technically difficult music was played effortlessly. Being so perfect and flawless, I grew weary of the music and engaged Michael in conversation. He answered me quite correctly while continuing to play. Still, I probably distracted him, and toward the end, he had me turn the pages of the score. I was then told that this was done from the fear that the actual sound of music (without a visible player) might alarm me. Also, when I sang a favorite song, Michael and Raphael caused my body to sway in rhythm. I had always loved negro spirituals but couldn't sing them well; for the first time, I felt their true rhythm as I sang. When Michael gave me energy, I reached high notes always before impossible for me to sing—Bach's and Gounod's "Ave Maria" and Mozart's "Alleluia." When I sang Schubert's "Ave Maria" with piano accompaniment, Schubert came down from the Heavenly World to help me. All of Heaven's beings love music. Mozart descended one day to help me with my piano practice. I was so awed that I made more errors and ended practicing by myself, as in the case of Michael. On such an occasion, many flying angles appeared and there flocked before my eyes small boy sprites of the piano, wearing green costume and peaked hats, and also, glittering, golden sprites of light. It seemed like a fairy tale, with sprites of the violin and other musical instruments, of water, air, and light, not to mention the flower sprites. The violin sprites were boy cherubs in amber costume; the flute sprites were boy cherubs in light blue and the harp sprites were girls costumed in white.

I hoped that these days of luminous splendor would continue until I died. I prayed that I might always converse with the angels who guarded me and especially that the chief archangel Michael, between his tasks in Heaven, might descend to play my music for me and talk to me of my scholarly studies. I wished to ask his opinion of my own thoughts and to learn how far the Heavenly World had advanced in the study of the various fields of knowledge. Also, I wished that I might resolve my doubts of various theories of *Shoho* (the True Law). The celestial beings were delighted to visit me when my pure and unsophisticated pupils were gathered at my home. Not only the archangels but Jesus, Buddha and Moses often descended to visit. During this time, I was given to know that I was the embodiment (main body—see Chap. VI definitions) of the archangel Sariel.

Previously, when Lucifer was making his many assaults, he once brought with him many evil spirits, including lackeys of the Nazis, and spirits called Zorgé. At that time, my thirteen-year-old dog, sick and dying from filaria and diseases of the heart, liver and kidneys, was tortured by their collective assaults. I took the dog and fled into the open night, but it tried hard to run after a female dog possessed by demons and collapsed. Then the archangel Raphael appeared, and making himself small, entered into the dog and killed its teeming worms. The dog miraculously stood on all fours and passed that summer in full health. It was unbelievable to see the dog, which had repeatedly been stricken by hardening of the arteries, eating heartily and walking vigorously. In that condition, I felt that it would be a blessing for it to live to the age of sixteen.

When I was beset by obstinacy, the hand of Heaven intervened and my soul attained separation from my body. I saw myself reclining on top of a high-floating cloud. The golden aura of Buddha, as once happened before, enveloped my body and an object, shaped like a softly-lit sun, was visible above my feet. Soft, warm, white light poured over me. A gentle but commanding voice called out, saying, "Tell the evil spirits to acknowledge you as the daughter of the Count El Cantareh. You shall remember this name, the Count El Cantareh. El Cantareh is your father." I had heard before the name of El Lantie but this was the first time I had heard of El Cantareh. When I asked to hear the name again, the words were repeated three times, each time exactly the same. Then, even after my soul had returned to my body, Buddha accompanied me and hid me in a great halo. Princess Yashodhara[12] also graciously stayed by my side. Of course, Michael and his aides made every effort to drive out the evil spirits.

As usual, those at the GLA ignored me, saying, "This couldn't be so!" During the less than ten months following Shinji's death, this group had changed toward a narrow, self-righteous viewpoint, indistinguishable from any other organized neo-religious creed. As I laughingly told my pupils, they had changed into a salvation faith, setting up the deceased Shinji and his successor, the daughter, as their Messiahs, while giving lip service to a religion which stresses self-reliance for progress. Considering how much Shinji used to talk about the defects of the new institutional religions, I had believed that at least the GLA would not become like them. [All were based on Messiahism or the belief that all would go well and effortlessly, simply by placing faith in an all-powerful savior, whose every word and act was inviolable law, and including Mohammedism, Jehovah's Witnesses, nearly all the Christian churches, and the *Soka Gakkai*[13] (wherein salvation is represented by a folded piece of cloth). Even the Holy Priest Nichiren[14] in Heaven has been taken aback.]

Since both the beings from Heaven and some of the high school students I teach English at home liked to joke about things, I was sometimes made to laugh till my sides hurt. We (my students and I) envisioned the chief archangel Michael in all the beauty of his wonderful wings and rainbow-hued aura, with great light shining down, and Jesus with a halo so great that his form was hidden within it. We had spiritual visions of images of the archangles and of the famed beings of the Heavenly World.

One of my students, in whom was merged the soul of the artist angel Luriel, painted these images many times. Also, the spirits of chief archangel Michael and Shinji entered into me in turn, or simultaneously, so that my face came to resemble both of theirs, and the students could see a halo of gold with a rainbow-hued border and strong light being emitted from the place on my brow where the Spirit Way of Michael had opened for me. Once before, this light had shone forth when the Spirit Way was opened to me. When I sent healing energy to cure the ill, such a strong light was emitted that I felt as if my blood was rushing to my head. One of the students said that she heard only superhuman beings could emit this light, so I wondered if this was what Shinji had called "Powertron" and that I might have some supernatural power. At times, as Mother and I watched from the veranda upstairs, a golden fan-shaped aura, capped by a rainbow-hued aura, appeared around the sun.

Each evening, no matter how tired I might be, I had to take my dog for a stroll. Once, Michael, sympathizing, said, "Allow me to take the dog walking." I was hesitant but when I took off its leash, the dog continued to walk, slowly and sedately without running, exactly like it was being led by someone. It reached a corner about five meters away, then turning it, disappeared from view. After a while, it reappeared, peering at me from the corner, tilting its head slightly in a wondering fashion but it didn't come toward me but acted, rather, as if it were restrained by someone holding its collar. Michael, having caused my power of spiritual sight to weaken, could not be seen, so the happening seemed truly unusual.

I often thought how similar the behavior of those of the other dimensions are to those of humans. I no longer feared, convinced at last that Michael was the celestial Michael. I had been repeatedly plagued by doubts and each time, I had been allowed to see miracles, dissolving all these doubts. Because of the wonderful meaning of the conversations and the reassuring, joyous feeling around me, which was in such contrast to the feeling when Lucifer and his demons beset me, I came to know that I had been touched by and was truly protected by the archangels.

When I had been beset by Lucifer for such a long period, my health suffered from complete exhaustion. By dispensation of the Heavenly World, the archangels guarded my house at all times to insure that this should not happen again. If they were called by duty elsewhere, they soon returned to me. I think this was all granted in token of Luciel-Lucifer's return to Heaven. Also, I was greatly pleased to be in the company of the archangels. At this time, a high school student with powers granted by the archangel Uriel, assisted by Shinji, saved by prayers and exalted to the Heavenly World about 500 million earth-bound spirits, floating spirits and other spirits which had been accumulating recently.

Then, like a bolt from the blue, a horrible new Satan, five times as powerful as Lucifer, driven from the star world of Veh-erde, came to assault us. This one was a couple, male and female. I was subjected to terrible sufferings by these two. It was obvious that neither Buddha nor the High Priest Chigi could guard me from their devastating attack. Sariel did not remain merged within my body but would sally forth to attack the Satans, then return to protect my heart. My only source of hope was Michael and the six archangels. The seven formed a protecting shield over me.

The Satans came leading a multitude of powerful cohorts, their sole objective being the taking of my life. For over three weeks, by day and by night, while pretending to threaten other humans and animals, they aimed at me. I fled desperately, just as commanded by the archangels. I feared for the lives of my mother and stepfather, although my mother's spiritual sight had been purposely weakened by the Satans and in spite of the fact that my stepfather, who refused to accept my explanations, scoffed at both the GLA and at spiritual phenomena, and believed that I was of unsound mind. To heighten the feeling of terror, Satan produced horrible sights, sounds and visions, one after the other, so that I was unable to take food or sleep for five days. Then he renewed the assaults on my heart, using methods unthinkable to man.

During this time, my students came to my house to visit once but my protective spirit met them before they reached my door and warned them, "Please return to your homes at once. You must not enter," so they returned. But two of them caused their souls to leave their bodies and, from the sky, to battle with the demons. Vexed by this, the Satans sought to take the lives of all living things in my house. Mercy and love were nonentities to these Satans. While my body suffered their wounds, I appealed to any feeling of virtue or truth they might have had. But they had no ears for my words. They felt an unholy, sadistic joy in inflicting hurt on the humans of our three-dimension. The seven archangels concealed their presence by turns while still guarding me, in order to make the Satans believe that I alone was struggling against them and that, therefore, I was unconquerable. But the Satans grew gradually more violent and finally, all living things in my house belonging to the three-dimension had their souls torn from their bodies and mutilated. At once, the archangels and angels assuaged the wounds and restored the souls to their original bodies. Then El Lantie descended from the Celestial World and destroyed the satanic couple, while their host of demons was destroyed by the angles.

Satans cannot make direct attacks on the flesh of people of the three-dimension. Rather, the lives of my protecting archangels were in direct danger. Except for Raphael and Michael, all were wounded. Raphael gave me strength throughout the fray and Michael fought while silently guarding me but it seems that even he thought it was hopeless. My heart and kidneys were impaired and I spat up red blood. Also, my urine showed blood, which came from the arteries. It seems that during the five days I took no food, I had been killed. The angels fought the demons, while I went in and out of my house, parrying or fleeing the Satans' assaults. I thought to myself, "I no longer care. I am so exhausted, I want to be killed. I want to die." Because I failed to be true to myself, I was killed. The next day, I was allowed to come back to life, held up by energy given me by the archangels, so I continued the flight from the Satans. This day, we reached the limits of our endurance. I withstood the assaults till the end but El Lantie, the archangels and the chief archangel Michael all knew that these Satans could not be defeated by man, so the gods themselves prevailed in their extinction. I was told later that heavenly beings are merciful and destroy their opponents only when the threat is absolute.

All this happened from the first week of May till 11 a.m. on the last day of the month. Finally, I was able to return in peace to my home and devote myself to rebuilding my health. One month later, I began to hold gatherings to discuss *Shoho*. To prevent evil spirits from closing in again, the six archangels set a tight guard, day and night, on all the living things in my house, including the dog, cats and birds. Gradually, my health returned, enabling me to write this book. It was a strain on my physical body but a satisfying and welcome task. Presently, all my days are spent in peace and happiness.

Recently, there have been miracles mostly concerned with the prevalence of golden flakes, emitted with perspiration from the skin pores of my arms and feet, and also with the high school students. Such flakes are emitted only by those who are true in heart and are attuned to the rhythmic vibrations of the Heavenly World. So the golden flakes are emitted in greatest quantity during gatherings of *Shoho*. Some grains are as large as two square millimeters. People who cannot emit these golden flakes are probably, for some reason, not in accord with the will of Heaven. It is said that quantities of such golden flakes were emitted from Shinji.

Institutions Possessed by Evil Spirits

I have written at length about my spiritualistic experiences so that all may know the distinction between good and evil spirits. I seek to provide a text to teach the real form of *Shoho*, as observed by the Heavenly World. I wish to relate how I came to approach the beings of the celestial world and how I was able to communicate with them. People of simple heart (like my high school students) can also be taught splendid things and provided much help for their efforts by the heavenly beings, if they believe in the benign spirits and their protective powers. This is true both for people with and without spiritualistic powers.

When the spirit path was opened to me, there were two spirit brothers whose names were already claimed by members of the GLA. In my case, they were only spirits of a past existence; presently, I am merged with Sariel. As mentioned before, the claims of the GLA are unreliable. But it is of no consequence to me now so I will write no more of it, except that the GLA is now an organization possessed by demons. Members of the GLA have refused to correct those mistakes revealed by re-awakened memories and revelations concerning their past lives, contending that truth was false and that which was false was the truth. Many, actually born in union with celestial souls of the fifth dimension or of the world of the sixth deities, contended their in-dwelling spirits were of the seventh dimensional realm of the Bodhisattva[15]. Thus, there was much falsification of truth.

People of true ability were working from outside this group. In order that the path might be opened for these true followers of Shinji, the beings of the Heavenly World spoke through Shinji. The spirit of Shinji and the angels sent many messages to the GLA, saying, "There will come many people of ability and from the upper dimensions, so those of you who came early must not be prejudiced but shall welcome with rejoicing those who come afterward." Just as in the time of Buddha, however, the disciples of GLA drove out the newcomers, even though some had great ability, and did not accept them in their fellowship.

Among these early disciples, the one whose acts least affirmed her to be a true follower was the daughter of Shinji. Quite early, expressions of doubt were heard among those in the outer circle of the GLA who believed in *Shoho* (the True Law) and in Shinji. One such time was when the chief archangel Michael appeared to Shinji and spent the whole night discussing and explaining the content of the Old Testament in the Bible. Of course, Shinji (a Buddhist)[16] knew nothing about the Bible. Hearing his daughter repeatedly mention that she heard someone utter the name "Michael," he had said, "That is the name of the angel, Michael! Michael! I beg you to enter my daughter!" Thus, Michael merged with the body of the daughter and conversed with him, so it is said. However, it would be strange to ask a spirit already dwelling within a human to merge; rather, the in-dwelling spirit would have to be asked to exit the body first or asked to speak as is. At the same time, Shinji's daughter is said to have almost fainted from the shock of the spirit merging with her body. Being the main body of the ancient priestess-empress Himiko[17], she would have already been given spirit powers and even knowledge of spirit speech, so that such shock would be incomprehensible. If she were really the reincarnation of Michael, this could not possibly have occurred. That she should have been on the verge of fainting also indicates that she was not close to being a vessel of the spirit Michael. Because Shinji said at the time, "You are Michael! Michael, without doubt! Have no doubt of this," it seems that his daughter so believed, wrote it in her book, proclaimed it to her people, played the part like a star on the stage, and even sold pictures of herself to those who gathered around her. In addition, as she claims no memories of growing wings and flying, it is doubtful that she has ever been transported to an existential dimension frequented by the angels. Also, whatever spirit powers she may have had has completely vanished and she seems to be unable to understand people spiritually. On the contrary, because some members of the youth movement made a minor mistake, Shinji's daughter lost her temper, slapped them repeatedly and lectured them for hours overnight, ordering the teachers to hit their pupils the same way. Another time, she took pleasure in having members of her youth group carry her like an *omikoshi*[18] and drop her onto a mat. It is evident that such incidents and manner of speech would not be the doing of one in whom dwells the spirit of Michael.

Considering Shinji's daughter in this light—surrounded by devoted followers, who create dramas without compunction to deceive the public, themselves possessed likewise by evil spirits and unable to discern the irrationality, impropriety and falseness of her actions and sayings—leads one to judge her to be in unquestionable possession by the demons of Hell.

If she had always spoken or conducted herself in such manner, one would not be led to make such judgments, but her meta-morphosis was too sudden. She ceased to follow the Eight-fold Noble Path[19] preached by Shinji Takahashi and the self-criticism which he advocated. While her followers continued to give lip service to Shinji, at the same time, they changed the group's name to the Michael Society and their school to the Michael School, and renamed their monthly publication the "Michael." This magazine failed to carry to its readers the voice of truth and instead, devoted its entire pages to Shinji's daughter. Whereto went all the good things accomplished by Shinji and, alas, the love and mercy he preached?

Numerous people left the GLA because they became weary of the manipulations and devices used by its inner circle, of its leaders' admonitions to "learn from the *Soka Gakkai*," and disillusioned by the sayings and doings of the daughter. But many more are still ignorant of what is going on because of the skillful wieldings of the GLA's inner strata. The book published under Shinji's daughter's name is another example—a product of sham. She herself did not write the book. She had others write it, a task which took ten months, but the GLA attempted to create a religio-mythical legend by claiming that she had com-pletely written this book in ten days or that she had written in five days what her aides had spent five months copying from tapes. All these manipulations to treat Shinji's daughter as a living goddess evidences the transformation of the GLA into an institutionalized or formalized neo-religious movement.

In reality, when the daughter was born, a spirit from the Realm of the Bodhisattva (the seventh dimension) became an in-dwelling spirit of her body, but now she seems to have fallen to the conscious level of a "star" in *Rei-kai* (the fifth dimension or the level above limbo). Those who are not knowledgeable see her on stage and are deceived by the deftness of her performance.

But the vibrations are not those of the Heavenly World but rather, make one feel as if immersed in cold water. Her following is formed of all sorts; there are those who return content from seeing her because their force waves are exactly in harmony with those of possessed death spirits, and those who do not notice the weird mood emanating from her two published books. But those who know the truth can only lament the situation. Shinji, through the use of mediums, has called out to those in both the inner and outer circles of the GLA but evil spirits seem to have stopped up their ears.

Even though possessed by the demons of Hell, if one lives a righteous life through one's choice of beliefs and conduct, and if one uses self-criticism and reason, after realizing a mistake, Hell demons will go away. But no matter how many times the celestial beings exorcize demons from the possessed members of GLA, they cannot be saved if they continue to believe that their present ways are in no way mistaken, as the evil spirits have easy access to their kind.

Established religions and neo-religious groups are organizations that attract large numbers of people. In many instances, unless their purposes are right, they succumb to the ills of institutionalism perpetually possessed by beastly demons. Such religious organizations fatten on donations and grants, preying on the weaknesses of those who are easily tempted by easy salvation.

Moreover, since his daughter is false, Shinji is also now suspect. There are several who say that El Lantie is the name of an indigenous Egyptian god, and that there is no chief archangel Michael. But as I have written in this book, Michael appears in the Bible, and appeared to Jean d'Arc to protect her under the name of St. Michael. His sculptural image is in France, and even in Hokkaido[20], there is a sculpture of Michael struggling with Lucifer in the form of a great snake. Also, it is impossible to reject completely the co-union of the celestial being with Shinji, who, just as Moses smote the rock and divided the seas by spiritual force, has in like manner, though on a smaller scale, displayed in his palm a mineral rock, of a quality clearly indicating its foreign origin, gathered by projecting himself spiritually across the seas. Such a miracle would be difficult to believe, even when seen with one's own eyes. Michael calls to El Lantie, using his name, and the fact that El Lantie was so called in ancient Egypt indicates that El Lantie's name had already been made known to the ancients, through persons with power to converse with the spirits.

I am told there is a place in Egypt named El Qantara, where people from Veh-erde first descended to dwell, long before man on earth. This name is a variation of El Cantareh, the true name of the one called El Lantie. Since I was told this after I was taken to the ninth dimension[21] and saved from the evil spirits, I am not much disturbed by the supposition that El Lantie is a product of Egyptian mythology. The Amundsen base in the Antarctic also derived from the name of the famous explorer, and this sort of parallel is common. The matter does not seem to be of much importance but I have been told that Count El Cantareh adopted the name "El Lantie" for its sound.

As Shinji made evident to us, each individual has his own unique soul, different from that of people of the past, and different from the in-dwelling soul. My own eternal life must begin from my current single life. No matter how splendid the lives of the spirits, and no matter how illustrious the name of one's in-dwelling spirit, the soul of each one of us must strive to both emulate and suppress to elevate one's character and deepen one's insight of Truth. Otherwise, one is only a "fox in a tiger's castle," and all is in vain. Unless one devotes one's life on earth so that the soul, guided by a sense of duty and responsibility, may attain

Heaven, the values of life in the future will diminish. The mistakes and lapses of this existence are naturally expiated and corrected in the next existence. There is need to reflect on the preciousness of this opportunity to live one's life and to recreate our true selves. If there are those who have not already attained this enlightenment, I desire nothing more for them than their understanding. Every person's soul is created by the life he lives. One should treasure his soul, always listening to one's virtuous inner spirit and progressing step-by-step to the self-creation of one's future self. Such are the expectations of Heaven.

Shinji Takahashi, a human being who suffered various spiritual trials and who may be said to have made his share of human errors, has rectified in this book some of the errors which occurred in his writings during his life. One expression of his teachings while alive was a calendar poem entitled "Love," which is presented here in conclusion of this chapter. We should seek understanding of this spirit of love, avoiding repeating the error of building a large institution and rather, working though few in number to create horizontal ties to influence society, striving to promulgate *Shoho* and studying it with an everfresh outlook.

LOVE

Harmony bestows peace of heart and limitless horizons
At the roots of Harmony is a being working through Love
In Love, there are no demands of Self
    There is no vanity
    There is no flattery
Even though there be joy and sadness
    One is not bound by these

If there be those who suffer
    Let their suffering be cured
May light bathe the wounds of those who suffer
    And give them hope to live
Love is the spirit of the Lord
    Stripped of the sense of self
And the great bridge leading to Peace of heart[22].

(Any deviations from Shinji Takahashi's teachings in this chapter, concerning the theory of *Shoho*, the True Law, have in every case been given his benediction.)

An Oath to El Lantie—by the Archangel Sariel and Yuko Chino

(This oath is recorded in the language of the star world of Veh-erde, with a phonetic version appended.)

(1) EL YAAUK WKLVA EL JKHOVA WKLVA LIWILA
    KELACEVA EL LAVTË
    (EL YAWEH BELNA EL JEHOVAH BELNA LIBIRA
    KELACENA EL LANTIE)

(2) EL KELA DE CEL MELEVKYA——
    (EL KELA DE CEL MELENEYA)

(3) ESKELA WKL ELVA CELIA JELIVA VA WKLVA
    MELDILVEA KLIAWKL ELA TLEA CEA
    (ESKELA BEL ELNA CELIA JELINA NA MELDI-
    LENEA KLIABEL ELA TILIA CEA)

(4) ESKELDES MESLEA MLEKDVEA ——
    (ESKELDES MESLEA MĒLĒKDĒNEA

(5) ELIMEL MIKAEL DEL LAADAVA EL JELIVA
    (ELIMEL MICHAEL DEL LĀDANA EL JELINA)

(6) KLIMA DEL MĒLIO EL DILVEA
    (KĪLIMA DEL MILIO EL DILĒNEA)

(7) MELAVE CEA MILDEA WKL DEL LAADAVA TOLEA
    ULKLEMA
    (MELANE CEA MILDEA BEL DEL LADANA
    TOLEA ULKELEMA)

(8) KLEA CEL MADE CEKTEA WKLDOLEA VA MEL
    CELEDIVA REKUA RŌLEA
    (KELEA CEL MADE CEKTEA BELDOREA VA
    MEL SELEDINA PEKUA POLEA)

(9) CEL TOLEA CEA WKLDLIVA DEL ELIA——
    (SEL TOLEA SEA BELDILINA DEL ELIA . . . .)

(10) SŌLIMA ELDE WK̦LTELEUVA MŌDELKA EM CEKEA
DEL WOILEA ES LEUWEVA——
(SŌLIMA ELDE BELTELEUNA MODELKA EM
CEKEA DEL BOILEA ES LEUBENA)
(11) TOLIA OL K͡ƷMEKA CEK D͡ƷCEA DŌLIA
(TOLIA OL KĒMEKASEK DĒSEA DŌLIA)
(12) MEL TOLEA EL WƷLVA TOL WƷLVA KEL WƷLVA
ŌLEA CEM TƷLEA WK̦S DEL KŌLO VA WK̦L DE KEL
CEA CEK WOITEA EL TŌMEK DEL ELIA——
(MEL TOLEA EL BELNA TOL BELNA KEL BELNA
ŌLEA CEM TĒLEA BES DEL YULO NA DE KEL
SEA CEK BOITEA EL TŌMEK DEL ELIA . . . .)

In 20th Century English, the meaning is as follows:
Thou art Yaweh! Thou art Jehovah! The Almighty
God El Lantie!
Thy virtue shall spread through the universe
I, one of thy seven messengers, and ordained in this ex-
istence as the one to come after, shall fulfill thy commands.
   Striving to spread *Shoho* (the True Law)
      throughout the entire world
   And the archangel Michael whose presence be here
   As the servant of thy successor
   Shall provide wisdom and lend his powers that
      I may cause to spread *Shoho* among men
   So shall both strive together till the day
      when all men on earth obey thy will and
      create a world of peace,
   His firm covenant was given to me
   All shall be done as thou will it.
   The beings of the Heavenly World shall stand
      together of one will, and shall strive for that day

Pray that I shall tell the people of earth of thy will
Grant thy protection, thy blessing and thy light
to the men of earth, to hasten the day when
they shall recognize the source of their joy.

CHAPTER 2

Our Spiritual Heritage

It was only a year ago that we finally came to learn, across all the eons since time began, a heaven and earth-shaking truth: three hundred sixty-five million years ago, there came to earth a few groups of people from a star called Veh-erde. We learned also at long last that about 10,000 years ago the spirits of these people came to dwell in the bodies of all those who then inhabited the earth, ever since, sharing with the earth people the rise and fall of cultures, and floating or sinking with the great stream of history.

Our culture on earth has barely reached a level of technology advanced enough for space pilots to walk on the moon. Although we may boast that our scientists and astronomers have discovered the laws of the universe, the truth is that our science today can penetrate the universe (the neighborhood of our galaxy) only to a depth of about fifteen billion light years. The limitless span of the universe embraces more than one hundred billion galaxies of stars. And each galaxy has an average of a hundred billion suns comparable to the sun of our own solar system. It may be that there are even more gigantic suns, each with planets and satellites. Their numbers may be compared with the grains of sand on the beaches of Honshu, the main island of Japan. Whether spheres or ovoids, these one hundred billion galaxies and their star groups are travelling out into space at a rate in proportion to their distances (from the universe's center) so that the universe is in a process of expansion. This is about the limit of the earthmen's knowledge of the universe.

Although man has flown unmanned exploration ships to Mars and Venus, there are many undeveloped areas of space science. The existence of unidentified flying objects (UFOs) is still not generally accepted, and travel by humans to stars outside the solar system is still about six hundred years in the future.

To us living on earth today in its present stage of civilization, the universe is still a mystical void, which like the light of the stars projects many mysteries. Thus, when we hear that Veh-erde is a star where there once lived the ancestors of our souls, we all are impelled to lift our eyes to the night sky, to focus our thoughts on this star, and to let our imaginations evoke the profiles of these distant forebears.

Many times I have asked the beings of the Celestial World the location of the star they call Veh-erde. While Shinji Taka-hashi was living, he told several people it was the star Beta in the constellation of Andromeda. I have also heard the location was related to M45 or M35 or M36, so-called on Messier's catalog[23] of the constellations. Andromeda is about two hundred million light years distant and the other star groups are too distant to reach easily, so it is not likely that a flying object could visit earth easily, even flying at the speed of light or in excess of its speed.

In order to write this book, I fervidly inquired for this much desired specific information. But I was not given the exact location. I was only able to ascertain that Veh-erde was a planet of a star near the solar system. Beyond that, I was forbidden to speak because this would violate the covenants of the star worlds. As for knowledge of Veh-erde, and its language, save for the phrases in this book, in no place on this earth, nor by any human intermediary, will knowledge be available.

We people of earth may discover some day the exact identities of the stars from among such possibilities as Sirius, Procyon, Pollux, Arcturus, Alpha Centauri, Proxima Centauri, Vega, Altair, Formalhaut, the star Barnard under the zodiacal sign of the serpent holder and others. The discovery awaits the development of earth's civilization and of space science. That much of earth's progress in culture and science was foretold by men from space and their spirits, who came from another planet outside the solar system, is a fact both to astonish and inspire awe.

How have we earth people devoted our energies till the present? Have we not accepted the palaces-built-on-sand, the cultural cycles of creation and destruction, simply as acts of God? One cannot feel but that it was a great blessing that the beings of Veh-erde came to earth with virtuous intent, seeking peace and harmony and transmitting that splendid code of the gods, called *Shoho*—the True Law. Not only Veh-erde but the beings of those stars inside M45, M36 and M35 had already built their utopias, and had mutual covenants. Our own solar system is, I was told, the last star where the beings of the Higher Dimension under El Lantie are striving to achieve a world of harmony.

When I heard this, I felt that we earth people also ought to place great importance on our spiritual progress as civilized people. That we ought to cultivate cheerful consideration, each for the other, and cleanse our hearts so that justice, love, service and mutual deference might prevail. With this foundation, we must strive to prevent any more wars or destruction on earth. When there is no longer destruction, will there not be progress in civilization and science?

Now, I hope to tell you something of the days spent on Veh-erde by those people who came to earth and gained everlasting life after death, passing through the cycles of reincarnation, and with great hope, holding on to their dream of a terrestrial utopia. These include the Seven Archangels, El Lantie, the in-dwelling spirits of Buddha, Jesus, Moses and others.

El Lantie was born the second son of Count El Lideream Cantareh, the elder brother of El Lihitoeim Cantalune, monarch of the United Kingdom of Veh-erde. El Lantie is a pseudonym of Count El Shalrea Cantareh. The titles of peerage adopted in Veh-erde came to be used on earth in like manner through inspirational spirit communications.

Count El Shalrea Cantareh was lord of the nation of Y in the solar system of Veh-erde, and was especially revered for his wide knowledge and virtue. The being we are taught to know as El Lantie or Count El Shalrea Cantareh obtained a doctorate in physics at the age of twenty. While serving as a university professor as an authority on nuclear physics, electronics and space physics, he also devoted his life to research in the field of electronics. In a certain Veh-erde calendar year, he invented a spaceship using gravity-reversing equipment and capable of supra-light speed travel. Subsequently, he introduced this ship into other solar systems of the federation, so that inter-solar travel, occupying only brief intervals of time, was achieved.

Three hundred sixty-five million years ago, earth was a new planet in the neighboring solar systems where life was in a process of normal development. Vegetation flourished and there were fish and small reptilians. Lord Cantareh, judging this planet to be capable of supporting human life, summoned the rulers of the solar federation. These were all either blood relatives of Count Cantareh or close allies. In ancient times, there had been long wars between the star worlds, at a terrible toll in lives. So the peoples of the star worlds agreed to enforce a great plan uniting the nations of the alliance and our solar system in harmony and peace. For this purpose, Count Cantareh gathered together volunteers from his family, relatives, and allies, including those beings now known as the Seven Archangels, to investigate and explore earth. This group reached earth at a point in Egypt close to the Nile River. This place, which they called El Qantara, had beautiful verdure, so they planted many fruit trees which they had brought from Veh-erde. They named this place of peace "The Garden of Erden." Devising many tools and implements, they dwelt here in comfort and happiness till Count Cantareh died in his fifty-sixth year.

Humans, capable of association with the star people, had not yet evolved on earth. But after the arrival of the second and third space exploration ships, Erden became crowded so the people from Veh-erde moved elsewhere. In the second exploration group came various associates of Count Cantareh, including scientists in the fields of chemistry, archaeology, geology, and biochemistry. They left after various discussions and went elsewhere.

With the third group, there came the beings who were eventually to become the in-dwelling spirits of Buddha, Jesus, and Moses, including four sons of King El Cantalune: El Lunelael Cantalune, Reina El Cantalune, El Birnabil Cantalune, and El Michelael Cantalune. Of these four, Birnabil Cantalune was the adopted son of King El Cantalune, having been born as the second of five sons to Tireluna Quetticea, the savior of the star world M45.

The stars from, M45, M35, M36 and Veh-erde, with earth, composed the five solar systems of the planned utopia. Those who set their hands to this work died within twenty to thirty years, so successors appeared generation after generation, while those who had died ascended to the celestial world, later called the Heavenly World, or Kingdom of Heaven, whence they gave aid and comfort to those in the three-dimension of earth. Thus, the same conditions prevailed as we find on earth today.

Naturally, except for earth, the other stars have attained almost perfect harmony, and in Veh-erde, life is extremely quiet and peaceful. It is only earth which is so vexing the beings of the Heavenly World. From now on, there will probably be various improvements, but there still remain unsolved not only spiritual problems but the problems of pollution of the ozone and the waters of the earth by industries and agriculture, of calamities caused by weather conditions, and of development and conservation of natural resources. Compared to the civilizations of the other stars, earth's is still in the earlier stages of development.

At the end of this chapter is a geneological chart of the family Cantalune. The in-dwelling spirit within Buddha was El Lunelael Cantalune (the eldest son), El Birnabil (the second son) was the spirit within Jesus, while El Michelael (the third son) was the in-dwelling spirit of Moses. The being called Reina El Cantalune afterward became the archangel Sariel; she was the eldest daughter of King Cantalune. During a spiritualistic communication, I wrote that I was "the child of Cantareh." But I was later instructed by the beings of the Heavenly World that this phrase was transmitted to release me from the power of the evil spirits because those on earth have knowledge only of Count Cantareh, also known as El Lantie.

El Lunelael, a doctor and an expert on theology, was a splendid being whose duties were concerned with religion. But in Veh-erde, no religious institution of any sort has been formed; there is no necessity because *Shoho* (the True Law) is universal on Veh-erde. But a sort of religious philosophy is still practiced, and religion is an independent body of theory among the various philosophic theories. All of the theoretical arguments are based on *Shoho* (the True Law). So the star people feel it unnecessary to torment themselves on or debate the concept of God. Based on such a civilization, both science and material cultures make continual progress. Lunelael came to earth and died at the age of fifty-six, just as did Prince Cantareh.

Birnabil was the son of El Quetticea, the ruler of M45. From childhood, he was called "the divine child" because of his high intelligence, combined with a good nature. At the age of fifteen, at the insistence of King Cantalune, he was adopted as the second son into the family. On reaching manhood, he gained a doctorate in engineering, and did joint researches with Prince Cantalune. He died when he was forty-five years old.

Lunelael, as the eldest son, was intended to succeed to the throne, but he declined the succession, as did Birnabil, and also Michelael who was destined to become the in-dwelling soul in Moses. So 21-year-old Reina El Cantalune succeeded to the throne and married for her royal consort Count El Pirettela, who later became the chief archangel Michael. Count El Pirettela also was given right of succession.

Reina El Cantalune, during her life, was a nuclear physicist, but she died of leukemia five years after reaching earth, only 35 years of age. Count El Pirettela did research first in physics, then nuclear physics. He also died of leukemia five years after reaching earth, when he was 38 years old. Thus, after the nine-year reign of Reina El Cantalune, there was no successor to the line of King Cantalune, and the throne was yielded to the lord of another realm.

Michelael devoted his entire life to research in biochemistry and died in his 42nd year. His child, El Regshelil, who was later to become the archangel Raguel, died at the age of 35, in the third year after he reached earth. In life, he studied civil and religious law, as does the archangel Raguel.

The archangel Gabriel, whose real name is El Gabnuel, is a brother of the chief archangel Michael. On Veh-erde, he was the eldest son of Duke El Pirattilaila, elder brother to King Cantalune. He bore the title of count and enjoyed a life of taste, including hunting and literature. On earth, he lived a long life, reaching the age of 80.

The youngest brother of Michael and Gabriel is Marquis El Bitterelna, now the chief archangel Teriel of the spirits of the Veh-erde system.

The archangel Panuel was El Panuluela, the third son of Marquis Cantara, the second older brother of King Cantalune. He also was a specialist in chemistry and related sciences, and held a government position similar to that of director-general of the Chemical Technology Authority on earth. He died five years after reaching earth at the age of 45.

The archangel Raphael was the eldest son and Uriel the second son of Count El Cantareh, or El Lantie. Raphael, known as El Raphalraiel during life, was one of the great writers of Veh-erde and was also a gifted painter. He is said to have come to earth and lived till the age of 50. Uriel, El Urileina in life, was an economist and held a high position in the Veh-erde government. After reaching earth, he lived till his 58th year. Finally, the archangel Luciel, known in life on Veh-erde as El Auria, was born the eldest son of Lunelael, son of King Cantalune.

This ends the geneology of the archangels and the beings of the ninth dimension (the middle realm of the Sun) and also of El Lantie. The prefix El means "light" in the tongue of Veh-erde, and is granted after ascent to the Heavenly World. Those beings who had children or families left them to come to earth, and rejoiced in occasional reunions when they were able to return for visits. Whenever they wished, they could return by spaceship.

As for the earth's civilization, most of its concepts came from the subconscious level of the brain—spirit-thoughts filtered into the consciousness as a phenomenon of the co-existence of the Veh-erdens' spirits in the physical bodies of men. It is only natural that names and styles often are quite similar. Moreover, the categories of the blood types and their names differ, but there are four main types, and special blood types can also be distinguished. The position of Veh-erde, relative to its sun, naturally creates special conditions in Veh-erde, but there is a large region in which the climate is comparatively warm and the Veh-erdens are gentle in nature and intelligent.

That one's consciousness may communicate with one's in-dwelling spirit has interesting implications. For example, the several spirits co-inhabiting two parents and their child do so in accordance with a covenant made in Heaven so each spirit knows the names of the others. When a child born in the three dimension (our world) is named, often the parents choose the name suggested to them by their in-dwelling spirits.

For instance, the artist Raffaello was a man whose in-dwelling spirit was the subsequent body and a spirit brother of the arch-angel Raphael in Heaven. That is, when the man, the subsequent body of Raphael was alive, the in-dwelling spirit of his was Raphael (Detailed definition in Chap. VI and Notes). As for Michelangelo, Apollo, whose in-dwelling spirit was the chief archangel Michael, became the spirit brother of Michael in Heaven upon death, so when Apollo's spirit came to dwell in the new-born Michelangelo, the parents must have been advised by their own in-dwelling spirit in the choice of a name. Michel-angelo is the combination of Michael and angelo, and *angelo* is Italian for angel.

This is prefatory to the discussion in Chapter IV of Shinji

Takahashi, but once one knows what kind of beings made the Heavenly World, does not the blind worship of almighty gods, or messiahs, or of images appear foolish? It matters not how great or virtuous the beings of which they are the spirits. Jesus himself could not endure the overpowering solemnity and pomposity of the Catholic mass in the beautiful chapels of their gigantic churches, or the long drawn-out, pretentious worship of the Protestants. One can understand how the Virgin Mary might wonder why perforce she is the object of such prayer and worship. There is, likewise, little difference in the pomp and ceremony of Buddhism.

Unavoidably, costs of operation and maintenance become dominating concerns when religion becomes formalized and a matter of ceremony and as organized groups and sects grow large. As a result, church members and the faithful give dues or make donations, under various names, which really do not benefit Heaven, but promote the institutions' earthly or material concerns. They give these monies to ministers, Buddhist priests, or leaders of groups, either as an offering or to provide for their livelihood. The beings of the Heavenly World are, without exception, embarrassed by the over-sized altars to Buddhism and the other gods, and as a sign of their displeasure, imposing churches, temple buildings, Buddhist statues, and graves are piled high in the waste yard of Heaven.

Let us consider this matter from a different viewpoint. Sometimes, the petitions of people who rely completely on the gods to provide all things, without much, if any, self-effort, are not granted. Either the person's desire is too selfish, or the being of heaven do not think it good, or the time is not right, or the individual's fortune is bad. So the petitioner becomes resentful, loses hope completely, or takes the attitude of an agnostic. That is to say, he denies the goodness of the spirits. I have heard of extreme cases in the West, where people spat on the images of Jesus and Mary. This indicates that when peoples' expectations are too high, their unhappiness due to unfulfillment may turn into resentment of the gods. If one avoids reliance on petitions to the gods on which hang one's life and fate, disappointment will not be so great, and one will be less inclined toward reviling the gods.

There are Christians who have said that it is a fearful act of desecration to deny God or claim Jesus was merely a man. But recently, I have come to wonder which is more desecrating, in a certain sense, to God and a vexation to the spirits of Heaven. In the past, I also was one who practiced a "dependence faith," relying on the gods to do what I ought to have done by my own effort. I also turned to agnosticism out of resentment.

Of course, El Lantie, whose other names include Yahweh and Jehovah, Jesus, Buddha, Moses, Shinji Takahashi, the seven archangels, the tathagata[24] and the Bodhisattva—all the beings of the Heavenly World—are asking, "Can there exist a god which can satisfy the desires of all the multitude?" What sort of God do you choose to create all by yourselves in your hearts and to worship? The beings of Heaven are looking down at you with great interest.

Note: As for the expressions of 3rd and 4th dimensions in other places of the text, they can be replaced with three- and four-dimensions. Others, 5th or 6th dimension and etc., are numeral.　　　　Author

Geneology of the House of King El Cantalune

(Descended from King El Solattiya—the former King who retired to M45)

A. *Prince El Pirattilaila*—eldest son
  1. Count El Gabnuel—the archangel Gabriel (eldest son)
  2. Count El Pilattera—the archangel Michael (second son)
  3. Marquis El Bitteruna—the chief archangel Teriel of Veh-erde (third son)

B. *Marquis El Cantara*—second son
  1. El Solterina—(eldest daughter)
  2. Viscount El Bittarabaya (eldest son)
  3. El Kilteriade (second son)
  4. El Panuluela—the archangel Panuel (third son)
  5. El Girerd (fourth son)
  6. El Pilterione (second daughter)

C. *Count El Lideream Cantareh*—third son
  1. Count El Bittarabaya (eldest son)
      a. El Pilterina—(eldest daughter)—the in-dwelling spirit of the 2nd Century Japanese empress Himiko, inhabitant of the Realm of the Bodhisattva after death, who was later the in-dwelling spirit of Shinji Takahashi's daughter.
  2. Viscount El Davide Cantareh—(third son), who married El Helena, second daughter of the Messiah of M35, El Solattiseya
      a. El Biliteruna—(third daughter), later the in-dwelling spirit of Maitreya[25], inhabitant of the Realm of the Bodhisattva, and also the in-dwelling spirit of the wife of Shinji Takahashi.
  3. Count El Shalrea Cantareh—(second son, and twin of El Davide Cantareh) also called El Lantie, who married

El Marienne, eldest daughter of El Solattiseya, the Messiah of M35.

   a. El Raphalraiel—(eldest son), later the archangel Raphael

   b. El Urireina—(second son), later the archangel Uriel

4. El Laienne—(eldest daughter), later, successively, the in-dwelling spirit of Māyā (mother of Buddha), of Mary (mother of Jesus Christ), of Jōchebed (mother of Moses) and of Yoko Hoshi (younger sister of Shinji Takahashi)

D. *King El Lihitoeim Cantalune*—fourth son and monarch of the United Kingdom of Veh-erde

1. El Lunelael Cantalune—(eldest son), later the in-dwelling spirit of Buddha

   a. El Auria (the archangel Luciel)—(eldest son), later the in-dwelling spirit of Lucifer

   b. El Alnaoe—(second son)

   c. El Lelieina—(third son)

2. Reina El Cantalune—(eldest daughter), later the archangel Sariel. Married Count El Pirettela, who later became the archangel Michael.

   a. El Leiluerina—later the angel Luriel, the in-dwelling spirit of Noriko Tsuchida, and the spirit especially given guidance by the archangel Uriel

3. El Birnabil Cantalune—second and adopted son (born as the second of five sons of the Messiah of M45), and later the in-dwelling spirit of Jesus.

   a. El Kittelerina—(only daughter) later the angel Saiel, and in-dwelling spirit of Utako Motohara.

4. El Michelael Cantalune—(third son), later the in-dwelling spirit of Moses.

   a. El Regshelil—(only son), later the archangel Raguel.

E. *Prince El Battiya*—fifth son

1. Marquis El Solattiya—(second son), later the in-dwelling spirit of Okuninushi-no-Mikoto[26], an inhabitant of the Realm of the Bodhisattva after death, and also the in-dwelling spirit of Yukai Murakami.
2. Marquis El Mikattilaielna—(eldest son), later the in-dwelling spirit of Yamatotakeru-no-Mikoto[27], an inhabitant of the Realm of the Lesser Gods (the sixth dimension) after death, and also the in-dwelling spirit of Yudo Nakano.

Other persons appearing in this book, and their in-dwelling spirits, are:

Yumi Akimoto—Her in-dwelling spirit is Eluria, second daughter of the M45 Messiah, El Tireluna Quettiseya, and younger sister of El Birnabil.

Keiko Kawakami—Her in-dwelling spirit is El Solattina, the third daughter of Marquis El Solinadiel, younger brother of El Birnabilel, the M36 Messiah.

Katsue Uchihashi—Her in-dwelling spirit is El Televetia (also called the goddess Aline), an inhabitant of the Realm of the Bodhisattva, whose in-dwelling spirit was El Nuquereteya, the third daughter of the younger sister of El Solattiseya, the M35 Messiah.

Michiko Chino (mother of the author Yuko Chino)—Her in-dwelling spirit is Mahāprajāpatī[28], who dwells in the Realm of the Bodhisattva, and whose in-dwelling spirit was El Lionelia, younger sister of King Cantalune and the second daughter of El Birerina.

Naoko Miyata—Her in-dwelling spirit is El Tiereluna, an angel of the Realm of the Bodhisattva.

Note: A brief acknowledgement is made of the following people of earth, the three-dimension, who assisted in the work on this book: Yumi Akimoto, Noriko Tsuchida, Utako Motohara and Keiko Kawakami.

CHAPTER 3

A High School Group Discussion

Written on a June day
This is the actual record of a weekly gathering to discuss *Shoho* (the True Law). The lecturer happened to be late that day. So the chief archangel Michael merged into a high school girl in whom the angel Luriel dwelt and who had spiritualistic capacities to speak for him with the author, who was the discussion leader, and the other students in attendance. I would like my readers to understand the seriousness of our study of *Shoho* (the True Law) and the importance of the contents of the law because of its harmony with universal truth.

When a heavenly spirit enters a human, his face somehow acquires a resemblance to that of the merged spirit and a strong aura is emitted from the head. Those close to the possessed person feel an unusual warmth and, along with perspiration, golden granules or flakes crystallize on the skin of those nearby and of the medium, or fall onto their clothes. This indicates that the spirit comes from a high dimension of the Heavenly World, such as an archangel or a dweller in the ninth dimension (Realm of the Sun). When the merging spirit is from a lesser dimension, such as the fourth dimension (limbo)[29] or from Hell, the golden granules do not appear and the body feels as though suddenly drenched with water. The difference is immediately distinguishable. When spirits from the Heavenly World are nearby, the higher the dimension from which they come the greater is their warmth. In the case of the guiding and protective spirits, neither their presence nor warmth will be felt (except when they purposefully make the person aware), unless that person acquires spiritual powers to communicate with them.

Moderator: What sort of being is God? How does God differ from man? Let us discuss the relation of God to man. These are things of which all of us know nothing. We understand only what can actually be seen with our own eyes. We want to know what God is like and how He is related to man, do we not?

Michael: Let us talk of religious faith.

Moderator: I have one more thing to add, please. Most people think that God and man have entirely different existences, that God's existential dimensions are completely different, and that He suddenly appeared from somewhere to create man, and all the things of the universe. Such is the teaching of most religions. Let us seek an easily comprehensible explanation of the nature of the real God and His relationship to nature and the universe.

Michael: There must be complete harmony between religion and science. As we have so often said, many men have expounded various religions but none have succeeded in this. I want you to know that in your present physical existence, the religion you are seeking is a new one, fusing religion with science. What do you think is the answer to God's obscure existence? Let's hear from each of you.

Student A: God is a being who leads us in various ways to improve the world.

Michael: (Turning to another student) And you?

Student B: God is too vague for me to understand.

Michael: Perhaps.

Student C: I myself have never seen God so I can't believe in

Him. If He does exist, He must be as everyone has described Him through the ages.

Moderator: Exactly what do you mean by "as everyone has described Him?"

Student C: Like doing good . . . or representing virtue itself.

Student D: That's my idea, too. Also, God is a being shining with light.

Moderator: Being?

Student D: Well, He's not a person. All nature is God. I can't think of God as a personality.

Moderator: So you believe that God is not a personality, and that nature itself is God?

The almighty and universally worshipped God, who . . . "who" might be misleading . . . does good and leads man to be righteous and serve mankind is nature itself, unrelated to man and not symbolic of man on earth. Is that what you mean?

Student D: I wasn't talking of God being symbolic of man . . . . Man is. . . .

Moderator: Nature itself. Scientifically speaking, nature is the basis of man. Didn't man arise and evolve from nature?

Student D: That's why man is called the child of God. . . .

Moderator: Yes. That's the same as saying, nature equals God, isn't it?

Student D: Yes, that's what I mean.

Moderator: God may be abstract but at the same time, God seems to have substance.

Student D: Substance!

Moderator: Something like substance. But we can't talk of God as having personality or being an object of worship, can we? Whether we call it personality or godliness, what we call nature simply exists, does it not?

Student D: Yes.

Moderator: It's not something that does good or leads us to do good or that kind of object, is it?

Student D: No.

Moderator: Just that God exists. We now have two opinions about God, don't we?

Michael: That's right. For example, according to the Old Testament, God, being almighty, made the universe, and all things including mankind, so it is written. Don't you believe that to be most scientifically illogical? Can you honestly believe such a story as that God made the universe, the Earth and mankind? You can't believe it, can you? That's right. Mankind, the universe, furthermore, the Earth, namely, all existing things are things which evolved very gradually.

For example, let us consider the evolution of man. The earth was at first a formless hot sphere which had just been born. It gradually cooled and finally organisms that could be called living things appeared. Then there developed some time later, from the invertebrates the vertebrates, then the reptiles and the mammals. Then from the anthropoids among the mammals there evolved man—is this not the teaching of science? This is true as given.

Therefore, from one viewpoint, God is the power which enabled these forms of life to appear in the universe. So the word "God," although vague and indefinable in this manner, can be grasped in this sense. It is unnecessary, however, to define God exactly in this way.

You have spoken of worshiping God as a symbol of man's potential for good. As an object for worship as a symbol, the being closest to representing the power of natural forces in the universe is the one called El Lantie. We also have the concept called "God's teachings," haven't we? "God's teachings" consist entirely of explanations of "goodness." Then you may ask who seeks goodness. The answer will be that all mankind living on earth does, isn't that right? Man, however, has mostly acted out of a sense of self-preservation, letting his own desires rule his actions. This is why the Earth has become so polluted. Therefore, the "spirit of goodness" or the "goodness of heart" is really "the sense of love of nature."

Nature has various meanings. For instance, there is the nature of trees, grasses, mountains, oceans. Also, there is the "naturalness in men's hearts." What do we mean by this "naturalness in man's heart?" As I mentioned before, man's spirit is divided into nine levels. God's spirit is in the middle.

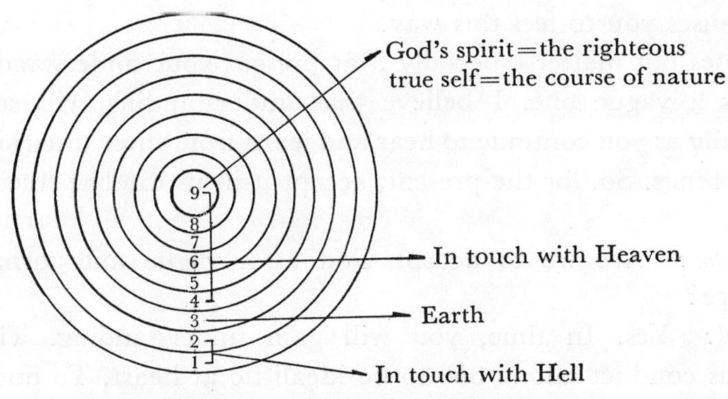

The Nine Levels of Man's Spirit

I will explain later but to "act natural" or as nature intended means to act according to one's virtue or inner conscience. Let's assume that one's conduct is bad. To give an example, one acts solely for one's own benefit, without thinking of others, and as a result, someone is hurt. Such action is evil. That is, good or virtuous conduct is nothing more than acting in accordance with the natural order of things. Is the connection between this naturalness of heart and the righteous self difficult to understand?

Student D: Yes.

Michael: Basically, only virtue dwells in man's heart. Such as, when one is good, one feels good. And if one continues to be good, doing good things, one can be continuously satisfied or content. The continuation of such a feeling of satisfaction or content is a natural one; that is, an ideal state of being.

Moderator: Why aren't men who commit evil deeds, happy or content?

Michael: Because their virtuous self or conscience disapproves. For instance, let's assume that you shirked work to go someplace. You would feel bad, wouldn't you? It is your conscience that causes you to feel this way.

It does not matter especially if at present your understanding is only a vague one. I believe that understanding will come gradually as you continue to hear and learn from these discussions or teachings. So, for the present, accept it in its dimly perceived form.

Moderator: Are we to accept God as a vague and formless presence?

Michael: Yes. In time, you will gain understanding. Thus, virtuous conduct allows one to be idealistic at heart. To understand idealism, let us consider nature—the nature of trees and grasses. For example, when they flourish green and luxuriant, unscorched or undamaged by the rays of the sun, and bear fruit in their season, then we have a state which may be called ideal. This is nothing more than nature in its normal form. The condition of ordinary idealism is an integral part of nature's form and virtue or goodness.

The animals, which are a part of nature, and perhaps even botanical life, each has its natural adversaries, so that their numbers are held in natural balance, neither flourishing nor diminishing to excess. This process of "natural selection" maintains this harmony, and keeps the balance at an ideal number. The virtuous spirit of man also, the harmony between one man and another, is weighed in terms of the mean or moderation. The spirit of nature is harmony. Goodness also is harmony, and thus, can be likened to nature. Is this understood by everyone?

Moderator: Going back to what we call "God" .... El Lantie does not proclaim himself to be God—you told us that we would come to understand this naturally. He has not taught us that He is God nor that man should consider or worship Him as a manifestation of "God." In other words, I undetstood through your explanation that he has existed throughout the long course of history, including the times of Jesus and other religious leaders, exhorting them to preach on God, not to "worship as a personality being" but as "nature itself," in its every manifestation —and that he has been ready to confirm this.

Yet, it is written in the Bible that Jesus said distinctly, "Have faith in God," and referred to Him as "Our Father," or meant Him to be "the Almighty God." El Lantie thinks that is a mistake, doesn't he? He regards these words of Jesus to be wrong, doesn't he?

Michael: In Jesus' time, El Lantie appeared as Jehovah. But the lot of common men in those times was miserable and life without hope of salvation would have been unbearable.

Moderator: Those times were extremely unscientific. Men knew little or nothing of science.

Michael: That's right. It was just because people knew so little of the sciences that it was essential for them to believe in an "Almighty God" and He was everything to them.

Moderator: Did Christ say that to that effect only at that time?

Michael: That's right. Jesus taught, "Have faith in God," but what this was meant to convey was, "Be true to your own pure heart."

Moderator: Jesus also said, "The Kingdom of God is within you," didn't he?

Michael: Yes.

Moderator: It was difficult to understand where Jesus said, "Have faith in God," meaning a personality being in Heaven, and also "the Kingdom of God is within you."

Michael: I agree with you.

Moderator: Ah! Now, it's clear! Do you all understand? During the time of Jesus, the level of culture was primitive and man's understanding was likewise limited. He had not yet discovered the knowledge which comprises the sciences. Man was not prepared to understand the tenets of science or the developments after the coming of man.

Instead of teaching man to believe that nature was the mother force giving birth to all things, or exhorting man to place his faith in his own soul and harmonizing his being with the natural order of things, Jesus taught men to believe in "Almighty" God, whom he represented, with manifestations of great miracles, and to obey His will.

Jesus sought to teach the men of his time of El Lantie, in such a way that they might know he existed. If they followed his teachings and lived with trust, there would be a better world free of suffering. Thus the God of the time of Jesus Christ differs from the God as has been explained to us here. In truth, God is the will of nature and we should all know this truth.

Michael: In the same way, the life of Jesus was not long enough to spread his teachings properly. He lacked sufficient time to make his teachings understood. This was prophesied even during his lifetime. It is written in the Bible that, "While hearing, they do not hear nor do they understand."

Student C: This may be unrelated but, are the Greek legends of the gods true?

Michael: In a sense they are true. You are referring to Zeus and Apollo, I presume. Zeus is a reincarnation of El Lantie. Apollo was that of myself, Michael. (Reincarnation here is meant as the one who was in-dwelt, while alive, by El Lantie or Michael, not spirits reborn into the world in carnal form.)

Naturally, there was none of the frivolity and sensual excess which appear in the Greek myths, as we have received them. In that age, as now, we persevered to explain *Shoho*—the True Law to mankind. People of later ages, created their own myths so the gods were depicted as frivolous and profligate, a conception which still remains today.

Moderator: Is the same true of the legends of the gods in Japan?

Michael: Yes. Amaterasu Ōmikami[30] (Goddess of Heavenly Light) is the central figure among Japan's traditional deities. Her story was derived from various sources in legend and allegory which expounded *Shoho*, just as they are taught today. The beings of the Celestial World come in turn, one after the other, to the terrestrial world to teach. Our mission has been to teach the True Law—*Shoho* because of the need for all people living on earth to create their own utopia.

Do you all know what utopia is?

Moderator: An ideal land, is it not?

Michael: Utopia is not a place but an ideal. It is nothing more than living in harmony with nature, following the heart's innate impulse toward good. All who live thus will live in contentment and joy. There will be no pollution or destruction of nature and all humans shall join hands to live together in harmony. There will be no more hatred of one race for the other. All men shall be equal, living with love and tolerance for each other. This is the utopia of which I speak. It is to realize this utopia on earth that we have sent messengers of light from Heaven to earth these many thousands of years. Among those known to you are Jesus, Buddha, Moses, Amaterasu Ōmikami, Zeus and many others.

Moderator: Is not the same purpose to be found in Buddhism?

Michael: In the main, Buddhism bases its teachings on the Eight-fold Noble Path as a standard of conduct in life. Before the coming of Buddha, the people lacked faith in the existence of gods. Rather, they placed all their hopes in reincarnation—their future life after death. Only complete submission to the Brahman caste could open the way to a future existence. Thus, a religion spread in which men were concerned only with self. It was to crush this system that Buddha was born. He expounded the Eight-fold Noble Path and the Five Precepts[31] and the necessity for self-reflection or meditation.

Moderator: In other countries, similar religious traditions originated in the manner of the legends of the gods in Japan, and developed as myths.

Michael: That is right.

Moderator: I interpret these indigenous religious traditions as evidence that the heavenly messengers came down to earth and taught *Shoho*. Is this correct?

Michael: Yes. The religious people who transmitted *Shoho* to men on earth died in the course of time. As generation followed generation, the law became changed in various ways, according to each interpretation, and resulted in something unlike its original form.

Moderator: My interpretation was that there was a single origin to all the tales of the gods and allegories and that various interpretations produced the individual tales that remain today.

Michael: That is not wrong, either.

Lecturer (Mr. Yonemoto):   (who came in and was listening to the discussion) One tale of the gods, one truth, can become two or

even more, and their origins may even have been multiple.
Michael: That's true. Are there any other questions?
Student C: If gods exist, are there also demons?
Michael: Certainly, they exist. They are known as Satans, too. Do you know what demons are? They are, simply, spirits with only evil in their hearts. Their nature is opposite to that of the spirits of the celestial world. They can only think of themselves and of tempting others. That fearsome place called Hell exists only because of them. At present, except for both the Eternal Inferno[32] and the *Tengu Kai*[33] (part of Hell), Hell does not exist in Japan. This is due to the efforts of the person, born as the one to be indwelt by Sariel, so that the demon and other evil spirits of Hell were redeemed to dwell in the celestial world.
Moderator: So the Demon called Lucifer indeed no longer exists?
Michael: No. (To the students) Do you all know that a Satan named Lucifer did exist through history for a few thousand years? His name appears in print.
Moderator: (Also to the students) In the Bible. His image also appears in paintings.
Michael: This Lucifer was a person who was dwelt in by an archangel dear to me who was called Luciel in the celestial world. He was of a most kind and pure nature. So was Lucifer under the guidance of Luciel, but he was later stained by various evils of the world and descended to Hell. He has, however, ascended to Heaven, while Luciel has been reinstated as an angle.
Student C: Who causes the fall to Hell?
Michael: One causes one's own fall. A person of evil spirit can not go to Heaven. There is the saying, "Birds of a feather flock together," but if one's spirit is impure, he can not ascend to heaven but can only fall to Hell.

Lecturer: Yes. Like an elevator.

Michael: Wave motions. . . .

Lecturer: Think of an elevator suspended by a spring. The elevator will stop at a place determined by its weight. Those heavily burdened with evil hearts will fall to the lower regions. Those with light hearts will go to higher levels. This is a law of nature.

Michael: Also, there are wave motions. Assume that I call out. That one word creates a wave motion. It is a sound heard riding on that wave motion. But there is also the wave motion of the soul. For instance, we mentioned the nine levels of man's spirit. Let us say that there is a certain man, whose spirit belongs to (i.e., is on the same mental level of) the *Rei-kai*—the fifth dimension (the realm of movie stars and the like) and who is a comparatively self-centered person. A soul belonging to the fifth dimension of the spirit world would be destined to go directly to that realm (*Rei-kai*) in Heaven when the person dies. But if the person had an evil soul, his words and thoughts would travel on evil wave motions connected with Hell, and he would become possessed by its hellish spirits, floating spirits and earth-bound spirits, and descend to Hell after death.

In the same way, if a man's soul belongs to the realm of the Bodhisattva (saints) or *Nyorai* (Tathagata), the wave motions will reach high levels. The spirits dwelling here and the people on earth with spirit power may communicate. Even those without spirit power can receive the protection of their guiding and protective spirits. Depending on the state of the mind, one's wave motions can go to almost any place.

Student T: Just a while ago, you said that Hell had disappeared. What if a man with evil heart died? Would he now go to Heaven, instead of to Hell?

Michael: All such spirits are raised to limbo and put to work performing severe austerities. To reestablish Hell would only mean repeating old mistakes. It is hoped that Hell need never exist again in Japan. Yet, the spirits of the dead are now increasing in number. These are wandering, lost in this world of the living. Being evil spirits, they are easily drawn toward the wave motions of bad-hearted people and possess them. In order to lessen the number of such vagrant spirits, as well as to destroy the hells of all other nations, a special time will soon be allotted to raise all the hellish spirits of the dead to limbo in Heaven by El Lantie, with the help of Shinji Takahashi and the person in whom Sariel dwells.

Student S: Can't we save such spirits?

Michael: If you were to attempt their redemption, they would possess you. These spirits have forgotten the warmth of human kindness, and are engrossed only in their own salvation. People like you whose auras are very bright are especially easily possessed. But because you have a virtuous heart, they cannot cleave to you for long and will leave in time. You must leave the redemption of such vagrant floating spirits to the beings of the celestial world. If you rashly attempt to redeem them, you will only endanger yourself. You are still unable to differentiate between good and evil spirits. You must abandon this idea. There are angels of light called Benevolent Deities of the various heavens in the East who can perform this work.

Student T: What should one do if one finds oneself possessed by an evil spirit?

Michael: First cleanse your soul. If your conduct has been bad, reflect on this and repent. Then call out to the afore-mentioned deities or the archangels for help. They will remove the evil spirit from you.

Student S: Please teach us the meaning of an angel of light.

Michael: Angels of light are beings of the Realm of the

Bodhisattvas or the Realm of the Tathagatas. Although called angels, they differ from the winged angels who dwell in the realm above that of the Tathagatas. This expression, the angel of light, which means a messenger of heaven, was specially used by Shinji Takahashi. These spirits from the higher dimensions of the Bodhisattvas and the Tathagatas come down to earth and exhort people to preach on *Shoho*. You need not be concerned particularly about the word "angel."

Student C: All people have a greedy aspect and a spiritual aspect —that is, a good side and a bad side.

Michael: Yes?

Student C: Is it wrong to believe that such is man's character?

Moderator: You evidently feel that man's way of life is greed incarnate. There are many aspects to greed.

Student C: Greed. . . . That's right.

Moderator: There is human greed, which is present in all men.

Student C: Well . . . uh . . . to love someone, that is. . . . .

Moderator: That is also related to greed.

Student C: Could that be greed?

Michael: Greed can not be a part of the virtuous heart. As I earlier explained to you, it is not part of the ideal, natural order of things. For instance, if you were to really live according to the divine will of God, you would no longer desire to become rich and live a life of ease and luxury, nor would you yearn for luxurious clothes. If you actually live through this experience, you will understand. Adornment of the body and such desires are nothing but devices for self-preservation. That is, it's the attitude that as long as oneself is fine, the well-being of others is of no account.

So it is a mistake to say that to be greedy is only human. Greed comes from the thinking of only selfish people. People are not born greedy. They become so out of jealousy when they see others around them living a more affluent life. Such people may not themselves be poor; they are probably of the average middle class and envious of the so-called elite or upper class. When a man is envious, even though he may not be particularly needy, it indicates his greediness, does it not?

Although he has enough for himself, he craves things finer than those he already has. It is not natural to seek what is beyond one's capacity to obtain. There are those who turn to theft when lacking money to obtain desired luxuries. Such greed is not part of "goodness."

Man is not born into the world with material possessions. It is a mistake to say it is only human to flagrantly lead a life based on satisfying one's desires. This is no more than an animalistic way of living. This is obvious, is it not? Man is given the power of reason and the ability to understand goodness or virtue. If he lives by good use of these faculties, such selfish desires and cravings will vanish.

You mentioned love, did you not? There are two forms of love. One is agape and the other is eros. The love of eros is, for example, like the love between man and woman, with the emotions of love and hatred in its wake. Let's say that there is a certain couple, who love each other, which is good. But should one's feeling change, that of the other will turn into hate. Such love which can change to hatred is called eros. The love of eros is an insecure one, constantly accompanied by the fear that the partner's love may change. In such love, there is no peace of soul.

If one is to love, that of agape is better than the love of eros. Agape is God's love. To explain, using the same example of the two lovers, even if one person's feeling were to change, the partner would be satisfied as long as the other is happy—such is agape, God's love. It is the ideal form of love.

Moderator: (To Student *C*) It is not a self-seeking love but love which gives.

Michael: That is exactly right.

Moderator: It's love like God's, which does not seek, but only gives.

Michael: Yes. Love which seeks nothing but gives to others and feels good if all others are blessed. This is agape, the love of God. Do you understand this?

Moderator: In short, that spiritual love is finer.

Michael: Yes. Carnal love serves only to preserve the race. If one knows true love. . . . Unfortunately, you have yet to encounter this true form of love.

Moderator: Another point in question comes to mind—animals exist only to preserve their species and do not know agape, do they?

Michael: That's true.

Moderator: Why is it that unselfish love is expected only of humans? If we say men should live in harmony according to the natural course of things, the "preservation of the species" should be accepted as a mode of human life, should it not?

Michael: Yes, we should accept it but the ideal way is for the perpetuation of the species to be premised on agape, not eros. If earthly love were based on agape, such things as divorce, infanticide and child abandonment would no longer occur.

Moderator: Isn't this expected of us because we are human?

Michael: Yes.

Moderator: Because we can reason.

Michael: True.

Moderator: Since animals cannot reason, aren't their acts regarded as natural behavior, even if they seem to be doing the same things as humans?

Michael: That's true. Humans alone are granted the power of reason. You should use well your faculty for reasoning and not be carried away by your passions. If you become swayed by passion or greed, linked with the urge toward self-preservation, you will become emotionally involved, inevitably causing your downfall.

Moderator: One thing more. It is my own interpretation but. . . .

Michael: Yes?

Moderator: When men live on the level of animals, they often do things more cruel than animals.

Michael: Yes, that's true.

Moderator: Self-centered things!

Michael: That is because men are capab'e of thinking them up.

Moderator: Therefore, agape is precious.

Michael: It becomes all the more necessary.

Moderator: It makes a spiritual way of life necessary.

Michael: That's right.

Student D: Uh . . . what is most human, and at the same time, most inhuman. . . .

Moderator: In the sense that the mind is noble, it is human. . . .

Michael: That's right.

Moderator: An attribute possessed by that animalistic being called man.

Student D: Man!

Moderator: It is not enough to be what the world understands man to be.

Student D: Not what the world thinks . . . .

Michael: Yes. That is the ideal way to live. Living that way, there is no mental strain, or suffering or anything else. Faith and agape lead to trust of one's fellow man and such cruelties as were mentioned earlier will not occur. Is this understandable?

Moderator: Yes. Evil thoughts will rebound. If one causes others to suffer, he himself will be made to suffer likewise.

Michael: That is true.

Moderator: Wounds are reciprocative, are they not? Preferable to a world of violence is one in which people lead peaceful lives, with consideration for each other. God teaches us this.

Michael: That's right.

Moderator: I made a mistake, using the word "God." I meant a heavenly being teaches us this.

Student D: Speaking of God, can God be considered to be all things since God exists in our hearts and spreads spiritually? Not because God created everything. How shall I say it . . . that around us. . . .

Moderator: No. Didn't we talk about this before? What we call God is our own goodness of heart or one's own urge toward good.

Michael: Therefore, God is not in your heart; rather you yourself possess the spirit of God in the depth of your soul. In due time, as you strip away its veils, one by one, you will come to discover this.

Moderator: Now, let us have Mr. Yonemoto (the lecturer) speak for us. The spiritual phenomenon will be ended now. Let us give thanks to the archangel Michael for talking with us for such a long time.

Michael: You're welcome. I am blessed that I could have this meaningful time.

CHAPTER 4

The People of the Heavenly World

Michael, Chief of the Archangels

I am Michael, perchance there are among you those who know me. For those others who know me not, I am the angel Michael who appeared to Joan d'Arc in a revelation, ordaining her to save France. The Bible records that I and the angel Gabriel proclaimed to Mary the immaculate conception, and I served as a helper of Jesus during his life. It is also true that I lent my powers that the apostles might be gathered, with the help of other angels, to spread His teachings and that there might be wrought sundry miracles. I was charged with the administering of the Last Judgement, and therefore, am I clearly recorded in the Book of Revelations by John as one of the seven archangels who, bringing about the seven calamities, descend from the Heavenly World to the earth. Also, I am recorded as he who fought with the Satan, Lucifer, who for a thousand years had been changed to the shape of a giant snake.

Now, in the pages of this book, I seek to tell all men about the Buddha Shakyamuni, revered as a Savior of men, of Jesus Christ, and of Moses, as he appears in the Biblical records of the Exodus from Egypt. Moses brought his people, the Jews, having been persecuted for many years as a captive people, safely across the Red Sea and out of Egypt, under Jehovah's guidance. Lastly, I shall tell of the fourth person, Shinji Takahashi *sensei*, who was raised to the Celestial Realms in June of 1976 after seven years of labor for man; having left many books, having elucidated those teachings of the Gods called *Shoho* (the True Law), having been born as a receptacle of the Almighty God, as the reincarnation of Yahweh of the Jewish scriptures, and of the one God of the Christians, Jehovah. Like many other religious people who have bequeathed great doctrines, these four, all derive from one common source, and all disseminated the same basis teachings.

This doctrine teaches that all things which the Universe is comprised of follow the same universal law. Nature, man, animals and plants—all things that are in being, and all phenomena—have their common origin in the universe, the "universe" is seen to be the very being that gave birth to all things and all appearances. This is what all people should define as the equivalent of God. Because, the beings which till now have been worshipped as Gods are, without exception, the spirits of great men, the souls of one specie of animal called man, which simply is a link of the form of life that evolved according to the laws of evolution. Be we angels, Tathagatas, Bodhisattvas, great scholars, inventors, or physicians, we are all alike after death—the spirits of men. And we are different only in that, depending on our status, our roles and works may differ.

Of course Jesus and Moses, and that one known as Yahweh, Jehovah and now El Lantie, the in-dwelling spirit of Shinji Takahashi *sensei*, are all beings so great as to be worthy of being revered as Gods. Their spirits shall dwell forever in the ninth dimension of the Heavenly World, the Realm of the Sun. They shall marshal the spirits of Heaven to protect men on earth from the machinations of evil and the temptations of Hell.

Man forgets that he is an inalienable part of eternal nature,

The Chief Archangel Michael

and that his soul shall never perish. He is prone to consign his life and destiny to the forces of destruction and decadence, and to give himself to thoughts of the flesh, which shall surely perish. He shows not the beauties of his world to, nor does he take notice of the good thoughts for the soul which does not end with death, but is the precious gift he is graced with. So, without realizing it, he is led into the darkness of the underworld.

The truth of God has been repeatedly shown to us by His efforts to teach us, through those called Messiahs, and through all the many religious leaders, that we might open our eyes to our foolishness, that we might attain understanding about the true way of life, and what is the land of God—a world of peace and idcals.

Men, who are a part of the universe, should consecrate themselves to helping each other. They shall not be permitted to pursue selfish courses of action, ignoring the laws of Universal Nature, which govern alike the relations of the suns and their planets as well as the life cycles of animals and plants, each giving life to the other. We, the spirits of the Celestial Realms, shall not allow man the glorification of self. We strive, night and day, combatting the evil spirits who seek to lead men to do foolish acts, confusing and inciting them to the destruction of nature, to damaging the environment which thus invites the downfall of man, to impairing the natural phenomena of the earth, and thus to hastening the end of Earth.

This is an eternal truth which cannot be understood, nor may it be practiced save by a loving and compassionate heart.

Moses and Jesus both preached by precept and admonition to the men of their times, licentious and barbarian, what men ought not to do and what they should do. Jesus particularly, taught men the meaning of love. I ask you to read his words again and to follow those commandments and teachings.

Buddha himself brought men to know that the universe and the individual man are comparable by the fact that both are forever repeating their cycle of rebirth in accordance with the same laws. The scientific world calls these laws the laws of the Conservation of Matter and the Constancy of Mass: Buddha called reincarnation, the immortality of the soul, by the term "rebirth by Karma" or "metempsychosis." As the sun pours its beams and benefits every being on earth, the human mind should also be filled with mercy to give fully to others. And, to abolish the discrimination between men based on rank, Buddha taught that men must respect one another and exercise the Right Judgement to live in the spirit of moderation.

All these teachings of Jesus and Buddha are the doctrines and the will of the Being of Heaven.

Man, the highest manifestation of all existing things, shall not violate those laws of "coexistence for the common weal," and of "mutual preservation," that govern the natural world. On the contrary, he should set the example for other life forms. We must rethink these principles of "mutual preservation" and of "coexistence for the common weal." Then this world of peace and harmony will be just like a land of gods, and like that ideal land which was lost to us in ancient times called "the Garden of Eden." There will be no destruction, and it will be possible to build highly advanced civilizations one after the other. If only men refrain from clinging to greed rooted in the five senses, their spirits will mature, and they will cease to rush into foolish actions.

This is the truth of the Gods—which we call Divine Truth, and *Shoho* (the True Law).

Shinji Takahashi *sensei* advocated scientific interpretations of religion not previously taught, and set those down in writing for the first time. Then came this book, wherein we can delve deeper and more scientifically into religion. If the scientists of this generation should, with modesty of heart, seek the meaning of the true gods, and if they should listen to what our messages seek to tell men, there will appear in quick succession books with far more accurate and detailed research on religion.

May you gain perception of how man might best live by calm reflection on the truths elucidated by philosophers from the time of the Greeks, to which you shall add the truths and knowledge of man and his relation to Nature which were not yet then revealed.

It is to this era that we, the Messengers from the other dimensions known as the Heavenly World, have come as Spirits to speak through those with the ability to converse with spirits.

It is desired that men fully understand what it means to be human, what is man's natural state, and how humans ought to live so that their common effort finally brings prosperity, happiness and peace to Earth—and that they so live.

Men have been enjoined to build the Kingdom of God on Earth ever since the time of Jesus. And now, the opportunity having presented itself, there are several things I must clearly convey to all men in this book. Let me clearly deny the erroneous concepts now current in the world that I am something non-existent, and also that I am a spirit in co-inhabitation with the child of Shinji Takahashi.

No matter how often it is proclaimed to men that someone is "my avatar," or written in books, I, Michael myself, simply deny it. And I charge such persons to avoid repetition of such mistaken thought, and of such tales.

This is not only the admonition of myself, Michael, but of those in the high dimensions of Heaven. This book shall make clear the true voice and the true plans of the Celestial Realms. And it shall also serve to correct, one by one, whatever mistaken rumors that may now prevail among men. Even more this book shall prevent the marshalling, and fetter the armies of demons seeking possession of man—seeking to manipulate like puppets the good man who should be guided by the spirit of the children of God, or to make an instrument of harm, eroding the soul, of he who lives hedonistically for the moment only, or to lead astray from the course of Heaven's planning, by cunning tricks, even the man who is cognizant of evil demons. Our foremost hope for the people of the earth is that all men will be as one, in harmony with Heaven, and that they will build a world of peace and accord.

Such a dream may not be limited to the Japanese only; it can only be realized if all the world is of one heart. How the goal be chosen is of vital importance. Each person should strive to practice *Shoho* (the True Law), each must teach *Shoho* to the other correctly, so that all shall gain a deeper understanding and better enlightenment.

Such people will be freed from evil spirits, and the protective powers of Heaven will be greater. This is the will of Heaven.

The Archangel Gabriel

I am Gabriel, one of the six archangels. We, the six archangels, do our work under the guidance of Michael, the chief archangel.

I administer communication and its vehicles. Each of the other five archangels also have their allotted roles. For instance, Panuel presides over all matters of science while Raguel administers the laws. And, also we the six archangels, like the other angels and beings of Heaven, strive night and day toward discipline of the soul. I was reborn as the co-inhabiting soul of the Danish philosopher, Kirkegaard, to teach men what it is to be a true Christian, and to lay the foundations of Existentialism. Again, I was reborn as a Priest of Italy to research the Bible and to spread among men the original teachings of the Christian religion. I was reborn again and again as the co-inhabiting soul with the German philosopher, Shopenhauer, as the composer Schubert, as the poet Dante, and as Byron. Thus I performed my various tasks. Thus, for enlightenment of the soul, I transmigrated to many men.

The training or enlightening of the soul is dealt with in detail in the Chapter of Shinji Takahashi later in this book. Again, in Chapter I on the spirtual experiences of Yuko Chino, other means are employed to show that, no matter how greatly are the gods revered by people, this is to naught unless the individual human being seeks to draw near the gods in the quality of his soul. I also desire to speak on this particular thought.

Such words as "Oh, that I might be as splendid as that," or "Might I not paint so splendidly," or "How I would like to sing as gloriously as that," express what might be called "man's original aspiration to rise." But those, whose ambitions have gone through a process of purification, will aim for something higher, rooted in a higher discipline and enlightenment.

Whenever you start to do something, do you not feel a voice of judgement from your heart, saying "That is good," or "That is not right"? If you hear this voice within, a co-inhabiting spirit which decended from Heaven is teaching wisdom to you. If you can not hear such a voice, it may be that no spirit of Heaven dwells within you. This voice some call the voice of conscience, while others call it the voice of the heart or that of the "good self."

If there are those among you who live unconsciously of conscience or the voice of your "good self," you may be vexatious to those around you, and they may shun you. Lest you be shunned, lend your ear to the inner voice of your "good self."

If you are one who is spiritually joined with a spirit being from a high dimension in the Celestial Realms, it is all the more fitting that you cleanse your soul, always thinking whether or not your conduct is good or right. The spirits of the Celestial Realms are all good at heart, but unless you possess a clean and beautiful soul (I speak of one's attitude toward worldly things and worldly ambitions), they are not able to extend to you their benign love. That they can not extend celestial love does not mean that they will thrust you out into lonely isolation, but they will cease to speak intimately. Those who, not recognizing their separation from the spirits of Heaven, become rebellious, contrary, or jealous, or who persecute the simple of heart, or treat others as aliens, will not receive the mercy of Heaven.

Unless the bent of your heart is such that you have at least some desire to know beauty and pureness, and how you may acquire or learn these things, the spirits of the Celestial Realms will neither grant you grace, nor will they give of their benevolence. Thus, your span of life may be spent in darkness and misfortune. This is the meaning of the phrase "seek the light." When, on the contrary, one shuns or hates the beautiful and the pure, one becomes a "seeker of darkness," inclined toward the companionship of the demons. Immediately, when or if the good spirits leave, the demons take possession.

If it be your desire to live with the demons, thrown into Hell for many thousands of years, then, and then only may you flee from the light. But if you love the light, you will cease your foolish living, and strive to make your heart atune to this light. Those who are not in harmony with light but behave as if they loved light are the hypocrites. They are the self-deceivers. Hypocrisy is the property of evil spirits and hellish spirits, and those who desire to be received into Heaven must forgo hypocrisy, completely.

It appears as if the Celestial Realms will welcomely receive anyone. But, the Celestials are very strict, and those who habitually deceived themselves or speak with a double tongue are sent to Limbo or Hell. No matter from how high a dimension of the Celestial Realms your co-inhabiting spirit may have come, Heaven will thrust you into successively lower dimensions. This occurs in the course of the ascetic disciplining of the soul. You will not find entrance to Heaven until you have cleansed a base or ugly soul. You should not feel rancor about this. It is you and you alone who prescribes your fate. It is you who chose to ascend to Heaven or to fall into Hell.

The flesh shall not last more than about one hundred years, but every experience of your life—what you feel at various times and what you do—is recorded in the tablets of your soul. Your soul being immortal, these records are also immortal. When you accumulate much experience, your powers of judgement will be increased, and thus you shall mature. So even after your admittance to Heaven, all that you have experienced on earth will serve you well, so that you may both speak and listen to kindred souls. Then you may become protecting or guiding spirits dwelling near man in the third dimension. Thus must you work for the elevation of your soul.

In the Celestial Realms, one continues the ascetic disciplines. In all things, a point of perfection never exists nor it can be said, "Good enough." There is a saying that "man learns until he dies," but in the Celestial Realms there is no ending of self-discipline with the end of life. The life of discipline is eternal. Not only you men on earth, but we, the beings of Heaven, are ordained to discipline our souls day and night. The self-discipline of your soul is not for your self-benefit only. When you have acquired *"satori"* or an illumination about something, or an enlightenment, you are then able to teach this to others. Thus, other men may approach your comprehension. Again, you may listen to the higher perceptions attained by others, and approach their levels. A great amount of spiritual effort is necessary to reach the type of illumination where self is equivalent to others (non-self). But if you live to that purpose, it is well within the realm of the possible.

In that even El Lantie, the proxy of godhood, practices the discipline of the soul, likens him to not only we, the other beings of the Celestial Realm, but to man on earth. You, men of earth, are of the same company as we the angels. So I say to all righteous men who believe in God and in the goodness of the soul, and who attempt to live in these beliefs, that you shall not be alone. Your companions shall be multitudinous, both on Earth and in Heaven. May you find courage in this knowledge.

What I have to say to you is only this—let us walk together! And let us strive toward the discipline of our souls! All souls! Endeavor to draw near to the spirit of the gods. Forward without fear! May happiness be with you.

The Archangel Raguel

I am Raguel. I too am one of the six archangels serving under the chief archangel, Michael. I preside chiefly over the Laws. I have been reborn in this world as the co-inhabiting soul with Prince Shotoku[34], the giver of Laws in the sixth and seventh centuries, with Descartes in the seventeenth century, and with Robespierre in the eighteenth century. When I was reincarnated in the body of Prince Shotoku, he corrected the confusions in the class social structure, established a constitution of seventeen articles, and strove for a climactic development of Japanese culture. Thus, I pray you may comprehend how my work relates to Law.

When I was reincarnated as the co-inhabitant with the soul of Descartes in the seventeenth century, he left as his legacy to the world the philosophy of rationalism. In that age, he treated the subject of the existence of godhood by advancing the theory of Pantheism—that God and Nature are not separate existences, but that the whole universe is God.

In the eighteenth century, my spirit brother, (the spirit of a body I formerly co-inhabited) was reborn as the co-inhabitant with Robespierre. He is known to all of you as a zealous statesman of the French Revolution who attempted to return to men their natural rights of freedom and equality. The other archangels in their respective duties have also performed renovating works.

Thus we, the angels, are reborn on earth to work for the progress of the future generations of man by making great reformations in our various fields of responsibility. After each rebirth we return to Heaven. The major discoveries of our lives are developed by later men. And again, when this development has been carried to fruition, it stimulates another great change. Thus has the world progressed. I preside over matters of Law so that I continually preach of the Right which is accorded man by Nature, namely the Right of Equality. I strive that men on earth may comprehend the way a natural man should be, to the end that they abandon the philosophy of every man for himself, and know that men are equal one-to-the-other.

The Archangel Panuel (or Phanuel)

I am Panuel. I was reincarnated as the co-inhabitant with the philosopher Plato in ancient Greece in the fourth to fifth centuries before Christ. He was a follower of Socrates, known at that time along with Christ, Buddha, and Confucius as one of the four great holy men of the ancient world. He (with the help of myself), studied, mathematics and philosophy in particular, then erected a school. His mentor Socrates taught that one should avoid error, practice reason and self-reflection, and seek for the good. So in accord with this teaching, along with other men, he inquired into the image of true man.

In the seventeenth century, I was reincarnated in the body of the English physicist, Isaac Newton. In that shape, he bequeathed to men many things, including studies on light, atoms and molecules, on integral calculus, and on gravity. Light is like the spirit of godhood, shining indiscriminately on all men alike. Gravity exerts its power on all life and matter equally. Thus did he attempt to illustrate to men, through science, that just as the laws of the universe—of light and gravity—govern all men equally without special favor to anyone whatsoever, so must all men live in Nature and in equality.

Then, in the eighteenth century, I was reborn in the body of Linnet. As my primary body, Linnet is well known as the botanist who conceived and applied double nomenclature to the classification of plant life. Also, he left to man the principle of the "cycle of life" as it includes both animal and vegetable life. This is also a teaching of Buddhism, called metempsychosis, or rebirth by karma. But he gave proof to all men through observation of the natural world—through the everlasting, ever-changing cycles of plant to plant, animal to animal, man to man, as is even the cycle of the soul—that everlasting life was a universal truth, not merely a religious term.

Our, the spirits', existence is to be trusted. This existence can be evidenced by scientific observation. During my existence as (the co-soul of) Newton, not only did he make mathematical and scientific discoveries, but also he took interest in the mystic nature of godhood, and wrote two essays, "The Discussion of the

Mystic" and "Discussion of Demons." Newton also questioned and investigated the existence of angels, of God, and the occurrences of miracle. He was only able to define with certainly that all things on earth are equal. And he ascertained that all things happen scientifically and according to rule, that religion is also inseparable from science, and that all existence can be evidenced by reason.

Reference is made to many miracles in the writing of this book; these miracles are not deceits. They were evidenced in truth. And there is nothing about a miracle that is strange or unaccountable. All true miracles will sooner or later be evidenced and understood by many, if not all men.

We desire all humanity to comprehend that *Shoho* (the True Law) is also science. What sign shall I give you? I would spare no effort for this sake. But know that this is only that men should know more certain of the existence of *Shoho*. I desire no more than that the True Law be made known to all mankind. The precepts of *Shoho* of which all men must attain true, spiritual understanding are "create natural good" and "conduct all things in the spirit of beneficence." If you do thus, happiness will naturally abide with you through all your life. We of Heaven remember in our hearts those who so live, and endeavor to extend them our succor. Know all you that we frequent not those who delight in evil. May you all find that, we, the spirits of the Celestial Realms, will walk with you, and will bathe with light of Grace you who feel our presence even when in the net of misfortune. When man feels the presence of Heaven in tiny bits of happiness, he is attuned to the celestial vibrations.

I call on you, all Mankind! Open thy eyes! We of heaven watch over all men. Take courage and go forward!

The Archangel Sariel (or Saraqael or Suriel)

I am Sariel. I, like the other archangels, serve under chief arch-angel Michael. I preside over medicine and pharmacology. Of all the archangels, I am the only one who is a woman. But there is nothing which differentiates me from them. There is no original difference between man and woman; each has one indistinguish-able soul. Medicine and pharmacology, over which I preside, are indispensable to the world of man. The healing of wounds and curing of disease is absolutely essential in the lives of human. So I have been reincarnated on earth as the co-inhabiting soul with Louis Pasteur and with Albert Schweitzer, to thus further discoveries and new accomplishments in medicine. In other roles in the world I appeared in the body of the bride of Buddha, Yasodhara, of Artemis, of Amaterasu Ōmikami, and finally of Madame Curie. Artemis appears in Greek mythology and Amaterasu Ōmikami in the pages of early Japanese legends of the gods, but, of course, neither were originally born as gods. During their times, they performed the works of *Shoho* (the True Law) and disciplines of the soul, but it was men of later times who wrote (and thought) of them as gods.

The wounds and diseases of the body will surely be made well by correct treatment. Even those ills which are today called incurable shall have, as medical science advances, perfect cures in the near future. More troublesome is that the people of this Earth are suffering from sickness of the heart. Concerned only with self, pursuing self-profit and hedonism, they have lost sight and memory of the natural state of man. The news media of today emphasize murder, child abandonment and killings between blood relations, all so atrocious that one wants to avoid looking. Men become coarsened, forgetting to look into their hearts. The ills of the heart can not be mended by medical science or by drugs. The only instruments for their cure are the ways of love and of *Shoho*. The actual practice of the True Law is in no way difficult, because it is a discipline one applies in the usual course of daily life. But, during one's life on Earth, one will doubtless meet with various difficulties and trials. One must not avoid the facing of trials. In the final reckoning, what shall benefit those who pursue ease and pleasure solely? They will never know what it is to pass through a trial by ordeal. Their hearts shall be weak and empty, and the growth of the self will not be promoted, but stunted. There is no profit in avoidance. Those who struggle through their ordeals, striving always to raise their level of life, will invariably be graced with strength and courage, their days shall be full and rich, and they shall receive everlasting life. Trial and testing should not be feared, because it is the staircase to the elevation of oneself.

To cure sickness quickly is desirable. To this end, there is a message which must be spread among men. We, the archangels, feel that time is drawing short. There is no time for squabbling. Men need *Shoho* now—in order to bring back into man's heart the qualities of love and freedom from anxiety. We pray for the advance of man in all respects, and especially in matters of ideals and of the soul.

May it be that all men rediscover, if even one day sooner, the spirit of God! May true happiness be visited on all mankind!

The Archangel Raphael

I am Raphael. I am also one of the six archangels serving under the chief archangel Michael. I exercise jurisdiction over the fine arts, over literature, and historical studies. Like the others, for the discipline of my soul, I have been reincarnated in a number of humans.

In the fifteenth century I was reborn in the person of Leonardo Da Vinci, both an artist and a scientist, to teach that in the future man must strive toward all-around genius and balanced ideals. In the sixteenth century I lived in the body of Raphael, the artist who painted man and the aspects of Heaven. In the seventeenth century I was reincarnated in the body of William Shakespeare, delving deeply into the ways in which men lived. During this existence I led Shakespeare, in his becoming the author of many works treating the universal human drama (including four great tragedies, tragicomedies, and comedies), which I believe are often seen by many people today.

In these plays he depicted many aspects of human nature including characterizations of the well-rounded man, of melancholia, of manic types, of paranoia, and of unreserved and happy people. Unlike the idealistic portraiture expressed by Leonardo Da Vinci, he took interest in analyzing and depicting man from varied points of view. This method of viewing man can be said to be my own.

Especially, if one analyzes the characterization of Portia as the heroine of *The Merchant of Venice*, various differing propensities are brought into one woman, creating an unexpectedly well harmonized nature, one which is complex and lovable. If you read my interpretation you will almost surely realize that her inclinations are either the same as those within yourselves, or that there are many points in common. There may be, among the readers of *The Door to Heaven*, those who have an incorrect concept of the nature of humanity which we of the Celestial Realms accept and love. If they read this, my chapter, all men shall learn compassion through knowing the complexity of human tendencies and the manifold manner in which such are expressed. Thus shall they at last find peace.

I desire all men to comprehend that the qualities in human life which are dearest to those of Heaven are neither self-denial or abstinence, nor pure orthodoxy. What I have said by means of the works of Shakespeare is what the Celestial Realm considers to be good. Although there are times when it is difficult to think of the character typified by Portia as being heavenly ideal—when it seems that she has a will like steel, as with formal argument she cooly and intellectually expounds justice—there are other happier times when she softens the hearts of her listeners with humour, vitally expressing joy, anger, sadness or pleasure, without at all losing a spontaneous resilence of heart. She is bright and expert. Never is she bound by form or custom, in the individuality of her concept of creativity, or of their expression. Nor does she lack restraint. She neither fawns nor is she servile in facing the authorities, but plays her role with exhilarating naturalness. Such is her nature. In her, many contrasting elements of character are brought gently together, avoiding bias, so that something harmonious and well-rounded is created. It is a soul, like this, complex but wholesome, which is possible solely to human being.

The matter of health or wholesomeness doubtlessly can be measured in many ways on many differing scales. But, when viewed with the eye and the standard of we of Heaven (which judge Portia as being good), there are many people living unhealthy lives. In most instances, this is because they are afflicted with that most deeply rooted disease of man, prejudice imbedded in typology habit, institutionalization, and social rank—so that they have lost sight of the value of man's freedom of soul. The thieves of the freedom of soul of humanity are greed, vanity, and the desire to possess. Such are the shackles which bind man to the face of the earth, and the crevices between earth and sky which bar man from Heaven.

How shall those so enchained come to Heaven? Of course, they must rend the chains which have taken away their freedom. Let us consider the best way to cut such chains. First there are the Eight-fold Noble Paths that were taught by Buddha. The Section on Buddha appears subsequently in this book; it teaches the ways to rectify standards for judging events and things.

By seeing rightly, thinking rightly and by speaking rightly— these three precepts reflect that attitude of the spirit necessary to achieve the criteria necessary for simultaneously judging both the external appearance and the hidden inner content of things and to take proper action. You may understand the other five paths by reading the teachings in the "Section on Buddha." Here at present, only the above three paths are necessary. Let there be added the holy mercy expounded by Buddha, and the love of heart taught by Jesus. With these five powers, the chains shall be rended asunder, and you shall see Heaven. What is more, it will be possible that Elysium, Utopia, will be realized on earth.

Let us apply the test of the right judgement to something real —namely, what is love? If one makes the correct judgement, it becomes clear that love is not unconditionally tender or magnanimous. If the loved one takes a wrong attitude toward life or, if he or she does not live or act in accordance with the right standards, assuming that human society itself is not distorted, one should counsel him or her to rectify what is amiss. And if they do not so rectify, love may assume the guise of exacting severity. But usually people, to stay on good terms or avoid friction, will allow love to mutate into indifference or an appearance of unconcern. Or, they may coddle people with unsuitable sympathy, so that the distortion in their life increases. When this has occurred, some people who, misguided by a sense of loyalty and thinking that they should bear with the situation, carry through a mistaken view of right and wrong. The man who is unable to see and judge the situation from its greater aspect, is without ideals, and it is his wont to make his decisions emotionally. Jesus denied the validity of this attitude. He taught that man should live by love according to the Will and Reason of Heaven. Should one change the words "Will of Heaven" to those of *Shoho*, the True Law, this "will" may be understood to be that which is in accord with the laws of nature and the universe, and it shows man the path to true harmony. What shall be the form of that harmony which man attains by observing the precepts of nature?

In such harmony, one man shall not cause distress to another. And the freedom and humanity of the individual shall be held dearly. Thankfulness shall not be forgotten. Apologies shall be honestly extended when appropriate. People shall work together for harmony, meeting each other with sincerity, a sense of duty and responsibility, and with a helping hand in time of need. They shall judge each other's hopes and joys wisely, and bring their fulfillment. This is the shape of the harmony which is in accordance with the order of nature and the universe. And of such is that difficult to define term love, and of the true expression of the concept of love. Human love, harmony and peace are interrelated, while magnanimity is inseparable from mercy of heart.

Among all these attributes, mercy and love are the noblest of emotions, which only man is capable of giving. Animals have some capacity for these, but, unlike man, they are not capable of these attributes despite all obstacles. The animals, by instinct act unconciously in ways that appear to be love or a show of mercy; but man can bestow a love or benevolence which is based on reason, undominated by feeling or instinct. Man can act and make judgements not tied to considerations of self benefit.

In order that there may be created on earth a Kingdom of God—a Utopia likened to Heaven—man's lives must be, in act and in intent alike to ours, the dwellers of the Celestial Realm.

But in order to correct the warps in society and humanity, merely to exhort men to be good suffices not. At times we must do battle with the thoughts of evil spreading through man and his society, just as if we were struggling with demons. Here, too, without the foundation of a harmony of spirit based on those noblest sentiments of man—love and mercy—man will find even slight differences hard to reconcile and they will invite mutual destruction. Even they who have the intent of shunning evil and fighting for justice will, if they forget magnanimity, end by randomly inflicting wounds on their fellows. Whether struggle and peace can co-exist together has been an unanswered question. Because of my words, some men may have reborn doubts. According to the scaling of Heaven, one must take up the sword of justice if peace is violated by an invasion of evil.

Let it be repeated that peace and harmony are not compatible with such compromise as an exchange of honeyed words in place of truth, or the mutual recognition of unhealthy or twisted things. When such a condition becomes the accepted custom or gains social tolerance, the individual is forced into a conformance which is evil. And, as a society, built mainly by men on earth using only one tenth of their potential of wisdom and consiousness, becomes the sum-total, man's concern becomes focused solely on his mundane existence on earth.

May those who so think be aware that this is not a true acceptance of life, nor a wholesome judgement.

Magnanimous as the intent may be, unlimited concessions will not always suffice to achieve peace. To tolerate evil, or injustice, or unwholesomeness of thought may, on the contrary, promote confusion and impede the development of civilization and the upward course of the spirit.

Such is the spirit and the nature of ideal man. I have explained in order that all may understand the teachings of *Shoho* (the True Law) as they have been transmitted from ancient times over 4500 years ago.

Let me add that this Scripture has the intent of clarifying the abstract concepts of God (or Godliness), and to enable a return of God to concrete manifestations of nature and the universe. In the process, it is well that we make an answer to the resurfacing doubts as to "how should man live and what is his position in the universe?"

Shinji Takahashi also expounded on these matters during his life on earth, saying individual by individual, men should know their "souls."

It is not intended that man be exhorted, "All is reduced to material and energy. So shall man! Life has no meaning. So live thy days like the beasts without thought for each day!" If we so live, there would be no meaning in our having been given the most advanced mind of all living beings—of man as the lord of the universe.

No matter how dark our vision is, or how bright, or how hopeless, we—man and the angels—can not spend our days without thought like the beasts. Even in this day of priority on science, we can not live regardless of human thought and feeling. These become literature, the arts, and religion—those spheres in which the soul of man seeks God.

We of Heaven hope that when your heart is being impelled toward the guest of God and religion, your thoughts turn toward yourselves living in an era of scientific culture. Our hope is that you will not be led astray by false gods but that you will strive to live rightly, treasuring things of the heart and the natural goodness within you, and disciplining your soul. May you, each and all, create splendid personalities, fulfill the destiny of man in the universe, and may you always continue to question the nature of your duties and responsibilities.

*   *   *   *   *   *   *   *   *

Notes by Yuko Chino

This is in reference to "a society built mainly by men on earth using only one tenth of their potential of wisdom and consciousness." The beings of the Celestial Realms would consider that man on earth possesses a physical body which gives rise to various needs for its well-being, and that energy tends to be expended for life based on the five senses and six roots, and the needs of the flesh. Consequently, man can not absorb knowledge or wisdom fully, nor make use of his brain. Only ten percent of the brain is developed for effective use. According to Shinji Takahashi *sensei*, when man passes through death, becomes a spirit, and energy is no longer needed to sustain the flesh, the conscious power of the other 90 percent of the brain is used so that the person achieves splendid wisdom. This function is to be comprehended as prajñā-pāramitā.[35] (See note.)

It is necessary to add that this book, in bestowing godliness on man, does not release man from his duties and responsibilities, nor is it a license for irresponsible atheism.

And in the "struggle against social evils," the beings of the Celestial Realms neither condone nor approve of the use of skilful verbiage presented under the guise of an idealism for the purpose of manipulating mens' souls: Political groups of any kind utilizing terror; national, ethnic, or student group movements or those who cooperate with these. They shall be placed in the same category as Satans or demons, bereft of the succor of the good spirits, and they shall not receive everlasting life. This is attested by the chief archangel Michael and all his archangels.

Those charged with decision regarding "social ills," for example, policy to cope with "hi-jacks," must always make their decisions on the same basis as for solving other problems—the tests of "correct sight, correct thought, and correct speech." In Japan, the "respect of human life" has taken precedence over all else, and Japanese tend to criticize the harder measures of saving human life operations in Israel and the Western world. The view of the Celestial Realms is that the release of brutal criminals on other countries under the principle that concern for human life takes first precedence, is a mistaken interpretation of humanism. To speak without compromise, this is an instance of "aligning alongside social evil." To confuse compromise with magnanimity, and in a defeatist way set malicious hi-jack terrorists abroad free does not take into consideration that many countries and the lives of many future hostages will be endangered and sacrified thereby.

In that the criminals are Japanese, they should not be imposed on other countries. Also strong effective measures should be taken to ensure against future repetition. The criminals must be detained and brought to justice. This is not nationalism but only collective duty and responsibility to others. Japan, in forgetting these things, should realize it is taking advantage of the rest of the world. Such are the words of the archangel Raphael.

In the scientific sector, the world has rebelliously continued nuclear fissions tests for military purposes over-and-above nuclear research applicable for peaceful use. Already the world is circled above the equator by the double belts of radioactivity called the Van Allen belt. If these layers of radioactivity continue to be formed in the ozone, Earth, the sole planet to be inhabited by man during the eternity of the solar system, will become a dead planet, to say nothing of that weird member of our system "Saturn." What is done lasts forever, unless its form be changed. Let man take heed of the principle of the indestructibility of matter—with its fearful implications, and beware.

As such are many other cases where even the scientists cooperate unawaredly with "social evils." The problems of environmental pollution and the harm of medicine are the obvious cases. As we are the dwellers in this civilization of modern science, all the more, we have many things to appeal to regarding the conscience of the scientists, the brain in the core of our civilization. And it is not too much to say that the fate of the whole Earth is entrusted to them.

The Archangel Uriel

I am Uriel. As Gabriel, Raguel, Panuel, Sariel, and Raphael, I am a cohort of the chief archangel Michael. My rebirths were in the bodies of Abraham Lincoln, Franklin Roosevelt and John Kennedy as well as Hong Xiuquan[36]. My responsibilities are government, economics and self-government. I receive communications from the angels under me regarding changes or progress in my jurisdiction. I convey this either to the chief archangel Michael, or, in the case of items prescribed by the council of the Celestial Realms, to other angels. But as an individual, I like the economic growth with wholesome balance and democratic government that is based on discussion and debate as practiced in the Celestial World. Correctly interpreted democratic government conducted by the people as evolved in ancient Greece and transmitted to America is, I believe to be desired. No trace remains of the governments of ancient Greece, while America has become a democratic nation in form only. It is said that those governments called of the people or democratic have not understood the true meaning of this concept. All of the beings of Heaven feel even as I: when *Shoho* (the True Law) is correctly transmitted, even the ravaged souls of men will consider the lot of their fellows and become compassionate of heart. Democratic government, implicitly, is a government for and by the people; not one in which a handful of people selfishly determine legislation or where one man controls governmental affairs. Regrettably, most countries which term themselves democratic—one might even say all—are under egocentered rules by a few people. And due to a few such soul-less people, the world is now in an extremely precarious situation.

They seek their own advantage. They seek rank. They thirst for fame. Men who desire these are blinded to all else. And their underlings in government do not look beyond their own countries' interests. Consider the state of relations between nations, of trade, and of the state of self government in the various countries. Men are concerned either solely for themselves or for their own race. If these present attitudes are perpetuated into the future, the fate of man is sealed.

The world as it now is shall not be able to avoid a third world war. Now, today, there are so many countries possess hydrogen bombs and nuclear weapons. It pains one to think of what will happen to the world if war occurs. Life on Earth will be exterminated, and Earth turned into a sphere of death incapable of sustaining life again. Nothing good is born of war: War brings only destruction. We shall not tolerate this thing.

To avoid Earth's destruction, the era of *Shoho* must come now. It is important that *Shoho* reach even one extra person, one time interval earlier. If mankind now would gain true knowledge of *Shoho*, democratic government in the real meaning of the word could be conducted, and both politics and economics could reach an ideal state.

The ideal society shall be built when people think with consideration for each other consistently. This society must be built on earth. The building depends on you. Whether to allow the spread of evil and the destruction of mankind, or whether to build an ideal society, and make the world a harmonious utopia depends on man today. We of Heaven stint no sacrifice in order to build this Utopia. But we, the spirits of the Celestial Realms, can only help you, man. Whatever may be, it is you on earth who must be the creators. Thus, the True Law needs to be disemminated among the masses on Earth, as soon as possible. Even one moment sooner—and to even one more man. This is the reason for causing this book to be made, with the aid of those so inclined. Truly, this book derives, not from the will or imaginations of its recorders. We of heaven willed the creation of this book, knowing full well that time is pressing hard, to give our message to the masses of men on Earth. Ours is a single plea—that utopia be built on Earth. Our desire is that many men hear and correctly understand these writings.

The Section on Buddha
"Let Us Bring Back Original Buddhism"

In the beginning, the Buddhist teaching I preached was a "way of conduct for Living Man." Put in other words, it was a way for the individual man to strive for enlightenment, and for individuals, one by one, to gain a harmony of the spirit, thus creating a utopian world.

Present day Buddhism has become no more than the conducting of the daily rituals. The way of life for living man has,

Shakyamuni the Buddha

sometime and somewhere, undergone a metamorphosis into a service or requiem for the dead. It has lost its original character. The Buddhist temple, which should be a place for the calming of the soul, or for discipline and refining the spirit, is now a lonely dwelling place for demonic spirits. And they continue the worship of idols. What efficacy can come from speechless images made by man; one may as well worship a wooden chest or a desk. Instead of offering or readings of the Sutra without understanding their contents, would that man practice what is written therein.

Let us consider anew the nature of the true Buddhism. The good self within your heart is the essence of the human spirit, and foundation of immortal life. If thy heart contains only the good self, loving and giving service to others, you shall be refreshed and cleansed, and you shall not suffer. This is the meaning of the release from the cycle of physical existence and suffering taught by me, and in the *Upanishads*[37] of the earlier Hindus.

How may man escape that inevitable circumstance of human existence—the sickness and death of old age. Man's life is everlasting. The body declines and perishes but the soul does not suffer the body's ruin. In its entirety, there shall be rebirth by karma; there shall be transmigration of the soul. Water shall become rain; and from rain, there shall flow streams. Streams shall merge into the great river, and flow to the seas. The oceans shall give forth their vapors, and there shall again be rain. Thus, the true nature of water shall endure throughout the eons of time. The everlasting life of man is no different; he may be reborn time and time again. This body which at best can last only a hundred years! Life shall not be of this world only, so consider not life and death, but rather let us give meaning to our daily lives. Let man—for the very reason that his life is everlasting —enrich his soul to the full during the tens of years of his physical existence.

Beyond this (physical suffering) are many other pains of existence. More than pain is the warping of the soul. The ego-centric feelings such as greed, jealousy, the bent to slander, and anger—when these abide in the heart it becomes fouled. And those so fouled are indisposed, nervous and irritated so their relations with their fellow men are worsened. But, if one is a human, it is thy unavoidable fate to have such feelings. Nevertheless, you can not live without correcting such perversions. What is important is not to repress or keep hidden these perverted feelings but to accept their existence and then wash them away.

There is the desire, when one has already satisfied the necessities of life, to crave extravagance or luxury. Unless one is rich of heart, luxury will not be of service.

If a home lacks harmony, no matter how splendid the house is, how precious the jewels you have are, those shall not console you. Everything is of the heart. Suppose that your neighbor's talents exceed your own, and that you envy him. It is far preferable for you than bearing envy, to attempt to approach him. Rather than speaking maliciously of your fellow man, it is preferable that you help him to remedy his faults. Rather than blame your fellow man just because he has displeased you, it is better to consider his circumstances. When later, you examine your conscience (the spirit of Good within you) you will feel good. It is a mistake to become angry because you adversary did not do as you desired. Center not your thoughts around yourself, but think rather of the circumstances of your adversary, and ask yourself once more why you felt anger. The Eight-fold Noble Paths I preached are rooted in the spirit of mercy—conduct based on consideration, and on "the 3rd person's viewpoints," or thinking by placing ones self in the position of others. Buddhism is more than just a way of release from worldly suffering.

Let me expound the principles of the Eight-fold Noble Paths one by one.

1.   Correct View

Looking at things correctly. This means seeing things from the viewpoint of others. It is essential to see the hidden intent, not only what is on the surface.

2.   Correct Thinking

Seeing things correctly. The nature of the thoughts determine whether a man's heart will be plunged into darkness or into light. If one thinks correctly, focused around consideration for others, one's relations with others will be bettered, and thy own soul will be more bright.

3.   Correct Speech

Correct speaking—this means to speak with words of love and mercy. Thy manner of speech should convey a tone of love and mercy. Correct speech will create harmony.

4.   Correct Action

Work correctly. The society of today stands on a division of labor. Provided one thinks of his labor as a contribution to offer people, or society, extremes of poverty and wealth and destruction of the common environment will cease, leading to the harmony of society as a whole.

5.   Correct Livelihood

A correct life pattern. This entails the development of one's abilities and the correction of faults. Faults, if correctly used, may quickly become positive abilities.

6.   Correct Endeavor

To make the right efforts. To achieve harmony within society. To see oneself in relation to others, to consider, and to live accordingly in harmony.

7.   Correct Aspiration

One projection of a man's will will be immediately transmitted to one of three thousand human emotional spheres throughout the world; by this he may draw in all things. Likes attract likes. So, unless one makes projections of one's aspirations correctly with an unclouded heart, what comes in return will be evil friends and demons.

8.   Correct Meditation

One should reflect, from a detached viewpoint, whether or not one is practicing the above seven rules. And, this is also determining, after identifying ones errors, not to repeat them.

The Eight-fold Noble Paths are not at all difficult to follow. Their realization is quick, and need only that one put them into effect honestly, with a cleansed heart.

The Section on Jesus

I was born two thousand years ago in Israel in the town of Bethlehem. As it is so recorded in the Holy Bible of the Christian faith, I walked the land teaching men how to live, and speaking of the sacredness of love and the way love is to be through the relation between man and his God—that God's love brings to man the love of his neighbor, and through the love of his neighbor, the love of all humankind—that love is spreading. I exhorted men, in an era still ignorant of science, to worship Yahweh, the Almighty God, that is to say Jehovah. But I also preached that the goodhood within man—humanity as the good self—is that which is shiningly reflected in the mirror of Heaven. And that Heaven is to be found in the heart of each and every man.

Looking at the course of history, until my time there had been the philosophy of the Greeks and the religious philosophy of India expounding the Laws and the universality of Nature, what the Buddhists called *Bon*, the ultimate cause of the universe, in constrast with *Ga* or the individual self. And I was the first to explain God in subjective terms and also via objective observation, from the viewpoint of individuals. But the purpose of both types of elucidation was the same—the explanation of what the life of man should be.

The love of which I spoke is a godly love surpassing that between man and woman, or that of friends. It is a love called "agape" which neither desires nor asks for reward, but only to give. Inevitably, such love exists in the company of the quality of mercy. I told men that God is Love, and men know this to be the teaching of the Christian faith. But I also clearly taught by parable the power of mercy and its benefits. Also, that Godly love is merciful. Love without mercy is no more than an extension of love of self which is a manner of greed. May you understand that this is a love which seeks something from another, and not the quality of love which bestows its gifts to others. There is a precious need for people to love themselves. The good implications of self-love concern the self-respect which humans derive from their manhood, their *satori* or realization that they are God's children—knowing all this, "love thy neighbor as thyself," was a portion of my teachings. It was the age when men were used as slaves, and the level of the awareness of the dignity of man was low.

Next, among my most precious teachings was the need for man to build his kingdom of Heaven on Earth. This was because there were many ignorant people, and men who knew only war and did not hesitate at the most brutal acts, while, scholars were bound by laws. They conducted their trials by precept. They knew not about forgiving, or mercy, or the gentleness of spirit seeking peace or of that love, the manifestation of the Spirit of God, difficult to place on measuring scales which extend itself to all men. How difficult it would be for such men to build on earth a place filled with light, harmony and peace, of the same order as prevails in Heaven—a true Kingdom of God. The people were many who had never looked back to consider that the true self is the good self, the spirit within one which is Godly. Thus, did I preach the Sermon on the Mount in order that people might gain enlightenment as to what kind of man is suitable for the purpose of building the Kingdom of God.

> Blessed are the pure in heart who know their spiritual poverty,
> for theirs is the Kingdom of Heaven.
> Blessed are they who mourn,
> for they shall be comforted.
> Blessed are the gentle,
> for they shall inherit the earth.
> Blessed are those who are hungry and thirsty for righteousness,
> for they shall be satisfied.
> Blessed are the merciful,
> for they shall obtain mercy.
> Blessed are the pure in heart,
> for they shall see God.
> Blessed are the peace makers,
> for they shall be called God's sons.
> Blessed are those who are persecuted for righteousness,
> for theirs is the Kingdom of Heaven.
>
> Matthew, Chapter 5: 3–10

The humble of heart are those who are modest, not arrogant, nor proud. Heaven does not exist in the conduct or the hearts of those who are self-esteemed; they shall not see Heaven nor are they able to build it. Those who sorrow or suffer, if they

Jesus Christ

receive not consolation from man shall find consolation from and salvation by the guidance of the spirits of Heaven. These men moderate and gentle of heart shall be leaders on earth, giving good guidance to the souls of men. And those that thirst for righteousness are the seekers of justice; even though they despair, Heaven and man will evidence that there is enough justice on earth to fill all needs. As for those with great compassion in their hearts, this is an emanation of the merciful heart. When these people meet with trouble, they shall receive the compassion of others. And only the pure of heart may see God. Unless one cleanses one's self of vanity, egoism, self-conceit, self-flaunt, hatred, adultery, destruction of peace and all emotions other than those nurturing love of one's neighbor, one shall not be visited by the messengers of Heaven, nor shalt thou see God. The maker of peace naturally shall be among those who build the Kingdom of Heaven on earth. Forsooth, they are worthy of being called the true Children of God. And those who believe in justice, and were persecuted for their convictions —many martyrs for the Christian faith were produced—not only those martyrs but all the people who were misunderstood because of other right beliefs, and suffered persecution, shall see Heaven. And they shall be the representatives of Heaven's will. Because it is they who represent that love which sacrifices self to render service to others. I was bound to the cross to atone for the sins of man, and for the Jews, who were ordained to be abandoned by God, living in sin, bereft of love, and persecuted by the Law. This was so that man might learn of the salvation of God.

"Enter through the narrow gate; for wide is the gate and spacious the road that leads on to destruction, and many are those entering by this gate. Because narrow is the gate and contracted the road that leads on to life, and few are they who discover it."

Matthew, Chapter 7: 13

By these words and by parables I taught that the gate of Heaven shall be shut against those men who think only of themselves—abandoning themselves to greed, unconcernedly living a life of dissolution. And that for a rich man to enter the Kingdom of God shall be as difficult as for a camel to pass through the eye of a needle. I taught that to enter the Kingdom of God, or to build God's Kingdom on earth, man must make a rigorous judgement of his own soul, contemplate his way of life, refraining from excessive ambition, avoid an excessive attachment to material things, and maintain purity of heart. Unless a man has a Godly soul, he can not enter Heaven nor can he build the Kingdom of God on Earth.

Again, I taught people the parable of sowing seeds. Even though he hears and rejoices in the Good Teaching, if a man's soul be not capable of comprehension—just as seed falling on rocky soil can not take root—so the soul can not retain and bring the Good Words of teaching to fruition, but will stumble and fall when faced with difficulty or persecution. Or where thorns spread, they grow and choke the seed fallen, no crop is yielded from it. So will the lure of the world and the temptations of wealth take over that the Good Words are hindered and will not nurture man. The soul of such a man will not become rich. If the seed falls along the road, the birds will come and eat it. Likewise, evil people will come to steal that seed planted in the soul. Whereas, the seed which falls on good soil, springs up, growing and yielding a crop—thirty, sixty, even a hundred fold. If a man listens to the Good Words of God's Teaching with a genuine heart and makes good use of them in his own life. They will not enrich life in other ways.

Let me speak once more of love for those who know not the Christian faith. The Letter to the Corinthians was sent by two followers, Paul and Sostene, to people in the Church at Corinth. I believe the thirteenth chapter (of Corinthians) better explains love than any other writing.

"Even though I speak in human and angelic language and have no love, I am as noisy brass or a clashing cymbal.

"And although I have the prophetic gift and see through every secret and through all that may be known, and have sufficient faith for the removal of mountains but I have no love, I am nothing.

"And though I give all my belongings to feed the hungry and surrender my body to be burned, but I have no love, I am not in the least benefitted. Love endures long and is kind; love is not jealous; love is not out for display; it is not conceited or unmannerly; it is neither self-seeking nor irritable, nor does it take account of a wrong that is suffered. It takes no pleasure in injustice but sides happily with truth. It bears everything in silence, has unquenchable faith, hopes under all circumstances, endures without limit. Love never fails. As for prophesyings, they will pass away; as for tongues, they will cease; as for knowledge, it will lose its meaning. For our knowledge is fragmentary and so is our prophesying. But when the perfect is come then the fragmentary will come to an end. When I was a child I talked like a child, I thought like a child, I reasoned like a child, but on becoming a man I was through with childish ways."

I Corinthians, Chapter 13:1–11

"There remain then, faith, hope, love, these three; but the greatest of these is love."

Also Chapter 13:13

All that I taught during my three years of evangelistic work is summarized in these last words of the thirteenth chapter of I Corinthians. That which lasts eternally is faith, hope, and love. Among these the greatest is love. This is true not only of man's relation to God but of man's relation to his fellow man. Only when these things are held precious can peace be achieved on earth, and a Utopia amidst harmony liken to the Kingdom of God be built. We in the Heavenly World also are concerned for men, praying for them, and extending our protecting hands. May you on earth become truly good men, achieving a measure of enlightenment about our teaching of *Shoho* (the True Law). May you achieve order in a disordered world. May you fulfill the responsibilities and duties inherent in your being born as men on earth. May you receive in abundance the light of the sun, the light and the Grace of God, and may you restore the beauties of nature to Earth. By the love of God, may the day come soon when men will spend their lives in peace and happiness together.

"For God so loved the world that He gave His only begotten Son, so that whoever believes in Him should not perish, but have everlasting life. For God did not send His Son into the world to condemn the world but in order that the world might be saved through Him. He who believes in Him is not condemned; but he who does not believe is already condemned, because he has not believed in the name of the only begotten Son of God. For everyone who practices evil, hates the light and keeps away from the Light, in order that his activities might not be exposed. But one who practices the Truth wants the Light to shine on it, so that it will be perfectly clear that he is working in union with God."

John, Chapter 3:16–21

The Section on Shinji Takahashi
"Each of You Is an Inheritor of the Law"

Those great guiding spirits, known as Shakyamuni (Buddha), Moses, and Jesus Christ all appeared as men in the flesh in this world between 2500 and 2000 years ago. The various teachings they expounded [properly termed the Way or *Shoho* (the True Law)] were transmitted through the ages by many disciples and believers, in the course of which they acquired various interpretations. Gradually their contents became scholarly and philosophical; hard to understand religious terms came into use, and complicated ceremonies were devised. These religions became the exclusive property of priests, theologians, and scholars. Religion became a study which common people could not hope to comprehend without these men's interpretations and explanations. I came to know, by experiencing enlightenment, that each of these three faiths was part of the same religious current as that propagated in the name of Apollo in ancient Greece almost 3500 years ago. The religions of the Greeks, like the teachings of the three great spiritual teachers, trace back to a common origin, and to the same God. By the will of the beings of Heaven, these teachings have time and time again been transmitted to men through the course of history on Earth.

These things I preached to men through writing and lectures for seven years until June of last year when, by the death of the body, I was raised to Heaven, which is an existent world. I preached of God's ways, variously termed the logos of God or the Law. The truths I preached are not the monopoly of any of my particular disciples or individuals, but are to be given to all mankind, transmitted by both followers and by others. My desire is that each of you transmit to the future this teaching.

In other words, may each of you become an ordained inheritor of the Law. If one man has gained enlightenment, let him teach it to the next man. And if he in turn transmits it to still another, the *Shoho* shall spread over the Earth. Were only one man to possess this enlightenment, even though he founds a church, nothing will be gained unless the individuals of this group, one by one, gain a true comprehension. Though there be knowledge and meaning, the heart or feeling of the Law will be lacking. We of Heaven fear this most of all. During my life on earth, I made the same error. But despite this, I have sown the seeds well. Through both my writings and through this book, may it be that men on Earth gain good knowledge of *Shoho*. If you who are born in the flesh—but alike to us in being children of God —ordained to service—have studied and understand your destined mission on earth, share your knowledge with your neighbor. This is the hope of myself and all the beings of Heaven.

The purposes impelling us to speak anew to you who read this book are manifold—to bear witness that although I died I am still living as a spirit. Just as Jesus Christ arose from the dead, so is my soul immortal. I show that I can still call the people of the third dimension and speak with them. In the same fashion as many other spirits, I have shown myself to people who believed in me during my life. And I talked with those who were close to me. But even though these people believed in Buddha, though they believed in Jesus, and though they believed in Moses, they were not able to believe in me. Therefore, I shall speak my message through the young girls, clean of heart and clear of vision, and through also a very few people possessed of power to converse with the spirits. In this book I shall bear witness to all the world of the truth in these pages, and that the miracles and phenomena herein were done to bear witness, and by the grace of the Heavenly World. And I shall bear witness that, even as I told men in life and as recorded by tape of my lectures (to which I shall make several revisions), the ways of religion and scientific knowledge are in fine accord. My physical embodiment made it impossible to offer incontrovertible scientific evidence on Earth, and the science of psychics was still embryonic. Now that I am in Heaven, and am a spirit, I have reached enlightenment about these things through discourse both with some of the learned men of the third dimension (Earth) through mediums and with the spirits of the other dimensions.

First of all, let me elucidate simply the theories of the *Shoho* for those who have not heard me speak in life nor taken in hand my writings. These things I have explained in full in other texts; may those who read them to their end comprehend *Shoho* fully.

At the end of the long road to knowledge religions and science become one. Albert Einstein, who mathematically proved the secrets of the dimensions of existence, came to believe thus, saying "science without religion is deformed. Religion without science is blind." Religion arose in the distant past from faith in Nature and in its Law; science is the search for and clarification of the laws of Nature. Science has evidenced that all things, including man, have arisen in accord with natural law. All things comprising the extended universe—the ultimate particles, the fixed stars, the planets, animal life, vegetation, and minerals—all fall within a cycle of death and rebirth in obedience to one common ultimate Law. And so likewise does the soul of man (even as Apollo in Greece and Buddha in ancient India taught of the indestructibility of the soul and of reincarnation) pass through the cycle of life, death, and regeneration. Life does not end after a man has been born, lived, then died; the soul departs the body to travel to another existence, be it Heaven or Hell. In order to be born again one's soul must undergo spiritual discipline, meditation on the errors of its life in the flesh, and reach a comprehension of what the ways of human life should be. Then, when all is prepared, one is seen off by friends and kindred souls of the Celestial Realms, and shall be born anew, in a new body, guarded by protecting and guiding spirits, to live cycle anew. But those who have fallen into Hell need the salvation of the saving hands of Heaven or they can not be born anew. May you open your eyes to the blessings of Nature, and may you follow the path of harmony with Nature's Law. May you be grateful to the light of the sun which is liken to God's mercy and love. Conduct yourself with the same grace in your association with other people, and with things. Such is the ideal society bringing forth peace and harmony. In this manner I exhorted men to recreate Utopia in the world of this degenerated age.

And now I shall set forth what is needed to prepare for the revisions and additions to my teachings.

1. *The Concept of God in the Light of Man's Relation to the Laws of Universal Nature*

Let us ask why man shall follow in accord with the Laws of nature. This is because man is a small part of All Nature. This began with the formation of the Universe. All things trace their origin back to the original primitive elements of the universe. All existence developed through eons of time according to the laws of evolution, as elucidated by Darwin. So did life come to develop on Earth and on other planets of other stars with like circumstances. Thus man is but one manifestation among the totality of existence. Universal nature, its various manifestations, contains the following:

$$\text{Sun} \longrightarrow \text{Vegetation} \longrightarrow \text{Animal}$$
$$\uparrow \underline{\qquad\qquad} \longrightarrow \text{Air} \leftarrow$$

Their cycles are:

   man unto man

   vegetation unto vegetation

   animal unto animal

Thus do they undergo the cycle of death and rebirth. Science calls this the "cycle of life" but the religious terms is "transmigration." And this truth applies equally to the smallest world, invisible to the human eye, and to the mega-world, compared to which man is as a grain of sand. The elementary particles, the neutrons and protons gather to form atomic nebulae; countless such nebulae gather to give birth to a star; the reforming of the atoms gives birth to life; then a new star is born in the way of explosion of the aged star (the explosion of a supernova). The explosion of a supernova may form a titanic red star and end in a heavy neutron star; or it may form a white dwarf star which changes into a black dwarf star in the end.

Thus there exist many types of stars and star clouds. But there may be the possibility that some day, in the unknown future, all these shall fuse with an anti-universe (of a nature similar to anti-elements and anti-matter) and all shall return to neutrons. Then would there begin a new universe repeating the same process of creation and development.

It is well known that the regenerative process comprises the major process within the bodies of both animals and vegetation. This mode of life is similar to the cycle of men. Thus all things are within the scope of the laws of natural forces and of the universe, and man is not excluded. So, irrespective of his desires, man lives under the laws of Nature, and must abide by these Laws.

From the time of ancient Greece, religion, the universe, and nature have been linked together. Thus have evolved the various theological doctrines. But since the rise of Hebraism passing from Moses to Jesus Christ, religion developed from being a subjective and objective philosophy to become a way of life for man as an individual. From the time people began to advocate the belief in the One and Almighty God (Yahweh or Jehovah), God became the creator of the universe. In other words, the concept of God as Creator was born. Thus God gave commandments to the men of that time with ravaged hearts and required to be conciliated. And the granting to man, miserable, ignorant, and seeking salvation, of a God as an image of the ideal was also a dispensation from Heaven, striving to elevate the human nature of an individual and turn his eyes toward the spiritual joy.

Rather, it was in the countries—ancient Greece, ancient India, China, and ancient people of the Far East—into which the teachings of Christ did not penetrate that there prevailed the conception of the God of the *Shoho*, "the universe and infinite nature are the Gods," of which I taught. This concept accords with much that is included in philosophical thought and with science's explanations of the relations between man, nature, and various other phenomena. God is not the Creator of the universe of human appearance but is the universe, and its infinite Nature. Therefore, both Heaven (the Celestial Realms) and Hell were made by man. The Messiahs deified by man, such as Jesus, Buddha, and Moses, are great souls, who gained their respective enlightenments and taught man the true ways of life. The Almighty God (Yahweh or Jehovah) of the Hebrew faith and Christianity is the spirit of the man who, with the seven archangels, travelled to earth in UFOs in ancient times from the planet Veh-erde, a planet of a star—and whose name is El Lantie. Furthermore, the co-souls of Jesus, Buddha, Moses, and all the other spirits in the highest dimensions of Heaven and the angels beneath them—all the spirits save those of Limbo— came from the same planet world. They all have shared with man on Earth his history and his destiny.

The story survives only fragmentarily in mythology as the Garden of Eden, but this is a place in Egypt near the Nile designated by El Lantie and given the name of the Garden of Erden to the land of El Qantara. El Lantie arrived here with those followers now known as the seven archangels 365,000,000 years ago. Man had not yet evolved on earth; neither had there yet appeared the gigantic reptiles. The visitors spent half their lives in this beatifully verdant land. Successively, other groups of men came in UFOs. Their spirits survived the hot suns of Earth's earlier days, the glacial ages, the golden age of gigantic reptiles, their decline, the emergence of the mammals, of anthropoids, and of apemen. Finally, man evolved. And about ten thousand years ago, the time of the Moo Continent, the first success was achieved in mating the spirits of Veh-erde with Earthmen. The souls of the Veh-erde star people, who had watched over the development of man from the Celestial Realms, entered into the bodies of mankind on Earth. Of course, the souls of that life which had developed on Earth in the precivilized eras (including these of proto-man) had ascended to the Celestial Realms, and we taught and guided these till they attained a higher consciousness. These did not exceed the conscious levels of Limbo or of *Rei-kai* at present. But Heaven then was not divided into the nine dimensions. And there was no Hell.

Thus, no matter how far back we look, there exists not an Almighty God who created the universe. There is no Universe Creating Diety. The Universe and its Natural Law are conceived in relation with God because, as I have explained before, they are the source of the creation of all things in the Universe, and because man draws many vital lessons from Nature and is dependent on Nature. Let man gaze out from the watchtowers of the Universe, and he will forget his small concerns, troubles, and sorrows. To see the vast expanse of nature makes the soul larger, and imparts courage of life. A beautiful landscape softens the heart. All the animals and plants exist together, and with few exceptions there is no waste, nor is there unnecessary destruction. There is a harmony obedient to an immutable Law of both "evolution" and preservation of the species under the process of "natural selection." Life has progressed through its long history under this harmony. This is the ideal pattern of we, the beings of Heaven, and the image of our aspirations. Even more, because one is drawn nearer the spiritual "ideal" by a true knowledge of Nature and the Universe, I said it is appropriate that men call these "God."

Do not confuse this with the gods of nature worship. Such gods are conceived out of fear of things possessing incomprehensible powers, and are creations of primitive societies. No! Rather shall man, the issue of civilized society, live in the light of a true knowledge of the structure of his universe, even unto the worlds of spirits, and may he consider well his place therein. There shall be no poem for the destruction of nature, pollution of the ozone, or the rivers, or the seas, or for extremists or rightists' exhortations for war, or for communistic or leftists' ideas which advocate conflict and wars and deny God (God as the being with the ideal personality) while at the same time proclaiming that the propagandized ways of life to be the ideal society. None who practice these things shall have the blessings of Heaven for they have not prepared the Way from Harmony to Peace.

2. *The Dwelling Place of the Soul, and the Center of Conceptual Zone* (Sonentai)

During life I taught that the soul is in the breast and is also the center of conceptual (thought and will) zone. This was an unscientific concept. Actually the interpretation of modern science is correct—the functioning of the emotions, appropriately called the heart, takes place in the frontal lobes of the cerebrum. The soul is in the brain. Also, the central zone of thought and will, since it also stores our memories, is not in the breast but in the memory center is the lateral lobes. The reactions of the body due to peaks or depressions of emotional nature, and knowledge of the memory center are carefully explained in studies of physiology and of cerebral physiology.

3.   *The Aura and the Soul*

The Body of Light is formed of light radiating in all directions from the body, usually called the "aura." The most usual aura is that which, from ancient times, was depicted as a circular disc of light around the heads of Holy Men, Messiahs, and Messengers of Heaven. But, in the case of people with unusually strong spiritualistic power, light emitted from their whole bodies may be seen. This phenomena is not present in all humans. The strength of light emissions differs, and also the color, reflecting the state of health of body and soul. The aura of healthy people is beautiful gold, and the purer and more beautiful is the soul, the greater the quantity of light and the more beautiful is its color. But if the state of the soul is changeable, if the soul is filled with animal-like greed—avarice, mental suffering, depression, anxieties, impatience, or anger—the color of the aura may change to red, orange, blue-grey, an ash color, green, or black. The facial expressions, manner of speech, and attitudes of such people are not very pleasant. Despite sickness, if the soul is bright and beautiful, the aura will be beautiful, although weaker and smaller. It is when the soul is dark that the aura changes to unhealthy colors. The aura's colors are beautiful when the soul is always in a state of equilibrium, and maintains a state of calm and moderation. It is possible to regulate oneself by taking food so as to maintain a weak alkalinity of the blood. But most men live busy lives, and find it difficult to maintain constant control of their daily routine and food intake.

Living, however, a well adjusted life, both bodily and spiritually, is good descipline for the soul. Even without forcing oneself, those who naturally take care of their bodies will be able to maintain health or recover from illness. This is the ideal state. The man whose soul is in its natural state—not tending to violent emotion, supported by wisdom and logic, with cultured sentiments, and liking a healthy life—is close to following the Eightfold Noble Paths expounded by Buddha. He shall easily enter the sphere of the arhat (in Sanscrit, a person who deserves respect from others) and may attain the enlightenment of a bodhisattva. The aura of the bodhisattva is a level more splendid, and more prolific.

There are those who say the aura is created by a sort of gamma ray, but it seems unlikely that the human body could absorb or emit such harmful matter in large quantities. The aura is energy of the sun.

The spirits who come to earth from the Heavenly World unite with the human being at or before birth. They do not enter the fetus during its early months. The aura accompanies the soul to Heaven or falls with it into Hell. At this time, the united souls divide into two beings—that which originally belonged to the individual and that from Heaven.

The being called "soul" during a man's life, functions as the controlling consciousness of the internal organs and even the body cells. It exists as a consciousness to activate the digestive organs so as to carry out the digestive process, causes the respiratory apparatus to maintain the respiratory process, causes initiation of muscular movement and activates the cerebrum to perform its functions. During sleep, when spiritualistic powers are dominant, or during unconciousness, or a temporary state liken to death, only the individual's original soul separates from the body temporarily. This is called "separation of soul and body." The entire soul-complex, is attached to the rear of the heart by a "spirit line," so wherever it may go it can not completely leave the still living body, and that portion of the soul which leaves the body is accompanied wherever it goes by its portion of the aura.

When both the soul with which the man was born and the spirit which entered from Heaven leave the body, the bodily function stops, and death occurs. At death, all the consciousness of the cells of the body—that is the entire soul united with the aura—leaves the flesh. This soul plus the aura is called the "*yutai*" or spirit body. During the act of separating on death, the spirit body (*yutai*) turns crimson or red. Then phosphorus burns and the spirit body turns blue, becoming lighter and lighter, then ascends to the skies. Then the Benevolent Deities (of the various heavens in the East) and the benign winged spirits (not the so-called angels), command descend from Heaven to meet the deceased spirits and lead them to Heaven.

Those who cling tenaciously to earth, or whose halos are of an unhealthy color are encumbered with a scum-like adhesive substance, so that they can not ascend, but float on the surface of Earth. They are tied to the place which attracts their souls, and congregate around household shrines, Buddhist altars, monuments to the dead, graves, or religious centers such as Hell. Powerful demons and Satans bury themselves underground to hide. But those without power wander or loiter. Thus, most of the worlds called Hell (there are nine dimensions which may be thought of as nine places where the nine classes of spirits dwell) are on earth. Thus, of all the spirits, man on earth is most likely to encounter demons of Hell, and death spirits.

The spirits of Heaven live high in the sky, many tens of thousands of meters above Earth; and do not often make themselves seen to Earthmen. It is only in times of disorder when there is a special need to expound *Shoho*—at times when a Messiah is born —that the multitude of spirits of the Celestial Realms lend their withnessing support by showing themselves to all men. Usually, save for the presence near all Earthmen of their guardian spirit and guiding spirit, the spirits of Heaven appear only to certain particular humans. Thus most humans have few intimate contacts with noble, great, or good spirits. So, many fear these spirits, thinking of them in the same way as they do demons or hell spirits. The author of this text, whose in-dwelling spirit is a transmigration of the archangel Sariel, has set down precepts by which good spirits may be distinguished from the evil ones. There should be no fear of the spirits of Heaven. But since there are instances where good spirits are, before one is aware, replaced by the demons, those possessing spiritual powers, especially, must take precaution.

4.   *The Good Self*

This is not a revision. But I would speak again about this matter, both for the sake of those who read this book, and for those who have read my own writings. The Good Self (*zenga*) designates the good part of the human heart. The antithesis of the Good Self is the False Self (*giga*). This concept describes those other emotions, alien to the Good Self—that is to say, despite the fact that the true self is good, there is the bad conduct and thought, conscious or unconscious, contrary to that natural to the Good Self. All the evils come forth from the False Self.

Precious is the fact that, in addition to a man's original soul, there dwells within him the spirit of a child of the gods, descended from Heaven to give daily counsel and guidance. So man should naturally be good in nature. As told before, God is typified by the Universe and Nature, but that which reflects best the Ideal God is the Good Self in the soul of man on earth, with its sole human capacity to obey the harmony of the Law as it is enforced by the principle of coexistence in Nature. The Good Man is he who does Good, who gives of his best for the sake of others, who is considerate, and forgets not to be thankful for even the smallest blessing. Such are the people who may build a world of harmony and bring a peaceful Utopia to Earth.

Perchance there are people who feel that a world of only good people would be uncomfortable or tiresome. But one's Good Self will not easily tolerate selfishness, or wounding others, or causing them trouble. If one treats others falsely, one shall surely receive the like in return. It may not happen at that particular time but redress will be of a like nature. There is a saying that a single act of will may be felt in three thousand worlds. But a thought is no different—it can resound in three thousand worlds, or from one corner of Earth to the other, or to the limits of the universe. One's intentions or acts of will always bound back from somewhere by some person. Even were this not so, man can not escape the fact that he has his Good Self which is a consciousness liken unto that of God. If a man rebels against his Good Self, and against God, and thus against the Law of the Universe, or against the Natural Law which governs his physical self, a feeling of disharmony and uncertainty takes root, and destroys his peace of soul.

For a person to endeavor to be a Good Man is to be in accord with Nature and with other men. This feeling will be returned by the living beings and the men whom he keeps contact with. Thus his life will be happy, filled with warmth, and without disruption. Man may not spend his days in laughter only. As a man, he shall discharge the responsibilities that are appropriate to his age, or regrets will linger in his soul. Young people who leave school or fail to attend classes, or who use deceit to pass examinations, or who have no vocation in life but become obsessed with unsavory gains or become alcoholics, men who live off women, mothers who neglect their children—the souls of all these shall be eroded, and they shall cling to a contrary way of life. Their feelings of guilt come from an attitude toward life incompatible with the Good Self; the true self is hidden within the False Self.

How may a man do away with this False Self, and return to the Good Self which is his true nature? The answer is very simple. When a man takes cognizance of an act of the False Self, let him consider and correct, so that he may avoid such thoughts or behavior on the next occasion. To always consider and make corrections of one's behavior is to be in attune with the wave cycle of the spirits of Heaven. It is the method by which one purifies one's soul, and draws apart from the evil spirits. Thus, one may be blessed abundantly with the protection of Heaven, good aspirations shall be fulfilled, and all one's days shall be rich and fulfilling.

Only when the souls of men, the spirit of God (Nature) and the spirits of the Celestial Realms have become one, shall society commence healthy progress, and shall the Kingdom of God (the Ideal Land) be built on Earth. This is the sole and shortest path for all Earth's people to that peace which shall turn man from war and make all things flourish, bring happiness, and make the world an easier place to live in.

* * * * *

Now I must speak both to the members of my family on earth

and to those who labor earnestly trusting in the GLA as the sole institution to spread my teachings and save the world. I have not wished to speak about such things. But very soon after my death, the GLA was cleverly invaded by evil spirits hostile to my supporters' good objectives and intents. Almost a year has elapsed without this evil spell being lifted. Those who held faith in my teachings—despite laughter and derision, steadfast in their intent to disseminate *Shoho*—came to be teaching in actuality the precepts of evil spirits and unwittingly building their kingdom on earth. My soul is touched deeply at the lot of my pitiful family and those helping them. I pray that, in some manner, an appeal to their reason may prevail and the Good Self may perceive the true nature of the demons. I wait in hope that they may realize the extent of my sorrow and that of the beings of the Heavenly World when they have their true selves have been regained.

The fault is mine, not theirs. It is because I errored and institutionalized my teachings out of a feeling of the necessity to spread that teaching, bestowed by the Celestial Realms, which alone can link all men protect the world from the evil spirits. Fearing lest it be regarded as another New Religion, I changed the name of this society two or three times, but to no avail, because it is an institution at least in form if not in content. And it is natural for people of like aim and purpose to assemble and act in unison.

But during my life, although my daughter was still a child and her character still unformed, I allowed myself to be mislead solely by her spiritualistic powers. I mistakenly thought, because Michael spoke from her to transmit messages and the will of Heaven, that she was a reincarnation of him, a soul-sister to be, and the successor to my position. And I caused the members of GLA to believe these things. I am most regretful of any one of my weaknesses of the flesh, chained as it was in the third dimension, and my lack of wisdom. I desire that my daughter and my wife, those in GLA working for my sake, and those outside, all know this.

My younger sister, of my flesh and possessing the same spiritualistic powers, knows all these things. Many discrepancies and things that are unable to be proved point to the truth. Sometimes I contemplate that there are women who felt sympathy for my daughter and believed her because they had believed me. And because they made a vow, they walk a path of delusion crying they will follow to the extremities of Hell. When I think of these, I feel like apologizing in the stead of my daughter.

When I gained the form of a spirit, I saw all things anew— what shall rule the world, and what shall decay and wither away—and I was amazed at the rueful sight.

When I was in the flesh, I saw things simply. People's lives seemed colored by hope and vitality, going the way of Good, and the world toward peace. At the moment of death I reflected on my life. And I believed that I had fulfilled my mission in such a manner as to leave no need for regrets. I never dreamed that I would taste such disappointment that would bring about a new beginning of the disciplining of my soul. Then there continued for one year and two months an ordeal such as I had never know before.

The awareness that I am primarily responsible for this so pains me that, even though I have been raised to the ninth dimension, I can not look straight at the beings of the Heavenly World. I have racked my soul to deliver GLA and my daughter from the domination of the evil spirits. The beings of the Celestial Realms have shown, at all times, sympathy for my family and for the good people who followed me. To the very end, Michael and Gabriel spoke through my daughter, continuing to bestow their message and encouragement. This continued until about the middle of March, 1976. At GLA, the demons were ascendant in every aspect, infesting the consciousness of person after person.

At the same time, Yuko Chino, in whose body dwells Sariel and who has written this book, was attacked by the Satan, Lucifer. Thus, while the spirit beings of the ninth dimension successively lent their strength to assure Lucifer's defeat, Michael and I repelled the demons assailing GLA, then turned to drive back the countless followers of Lucifer who were ceaselessly attacking Miss Chino. Then I again turned my efforts toward GLA, while Michael and Raphael guarded Miss Chino. Thus, the struggle against the demons of the first dimension lasted a full month.

At long last, on April 13th, Lucifer, having been converted by Miss Chino, returned along with his good co-spirit Luciel to Heaven. The fact was made known to a close circle of people only by Noriko Tsuchida (whose co-inhabiting spirit is Luriel) and by Yuko Chino, and the knowledge was also bestowed by Buddha on the priest Yukai Murakami.

Then, I felt assured that the causes of my anxiety had been removed and the matter was on the verge of a solution. But, in less than a month, the Celestial Realms became involved in struggle with Satans far mightier than Lucifer.

This evil force was a Satanic couple, driven out of the star world of Veh-erde. During life, my major concern was directed against Lucifer (the Fourth Satan) and Asteria, the demon niece of the Third Satan. But the Satanic couple which assaulted Yuko Chino in May were so powerful that it seemed they would destroy Miss Chino, her family, and all seven of the archangels. The struggle laste three weeks. The Heavens were on the verge of losing both my successor on earth and all the archangels to just two Satans.

Previously the archangels had always conquered the evil ones. We of Heaven believed this, and left the struggle to them: only after the death struggle had continued for so long did we realize that ours was not the ordinary enemy. These Satans had hidden their true powers when they were on Veh-erde. Because, under their domination, was the Satan Lucifer who ruled Hell on Earth. When Lucifer was lifted to the Celestial World, they lost to their opponents a powerful bastion of the Kingdom of Evil. Alarmed by the seige and capture of their bastion, they attempted a final victory-or-death struggle. The climax came at eleven o'clock on the morning of the 31st of May when El Lantie extinguished the Veh-erde Satans. At long last, Heaven had purged this powerful will to evil.

While we mainly stayed near the Chinos in order that we might save my successor, Yuko Chino (her life had been taken for a day but we restored it), GLA was sacrificed so that it became a dwelling for death spirits, and my wife and daughter were possessed in retribution by Asteria. Thus GLA became all the more distorted from its original concept.

Peace was restored to the Chino household, and Miss Yuko, by the grace of Michael and others, gradually regained her health. But, my daughter and the leaders of GLA who believed her to be my successor, increasingly became under the control of the demon followers of Asteria. Made foolish, they promulgated writings, touched by the breath of evil. The archangels did lift their possessions many times, but they soon fell back under Asteria's spells. And they called the death spirits and the demons back in.

Those, however, in GLA who saw the truth clearly, either left the group or appealed to the core members for reconsideration of their course of action. Now GLA is regaining its rationality.

In August, a group called Michael Wings came into existence to propagandize for my daughter but it was disbanded in September because of strong opposition by core people. One by one the leaders of GLA came to shun the dark and to be conscious of the light. Since July, Mr. Yudo Nakano, under my suggestion, has been publishing, outside the group, his words of warning. His was the first warning to GLA, dwelling in darkness as it was.

We of the Celestial Realms are able at last to relax our watch. My desire is that, if possible, my wife and daughter return to their homes. Let them forget my command to continue GLA as my successor, and spread *Shoho*. May they instead think again of the nature of Light—may they practice *Shoho* in their own household—may they discipline their personalities, and devote themselves to the pursuit of knowledge.

But there may be one thing which would render all this impossible—my daughter's prestige and her vanity. In her youth, she has the sense of stardom which seeks followers. If such vanity be in her mind, and the mind of my wife, my soul's appeal to them will not be understood. If this be so, then GLA will need to be dissolved. Otherwise it will become a dwelling place forever of hell spirits, death spirits, and demons; Even though we of Heaven destroy Asteria and her hosts, GLA would, in a ghostly way, repeat its errors and teach the Law of Evil instead of *Shoho*.

That I would command the dissolution of GLA, which I created and whose members I called my disciples—or that I would appeal to the outer-circle to separate—was beyond my powers of imagination.

After my daughter disturbed the Heavens by her claim to be a reincarnation of Michael, shortly after my soul had forever left my body, I had a premonition of crisis. Without telling the Celestial Realms, I entered her to communicate with others there my soul's anxiety and unsureness as to whether I had done everything right and in order. The intent of Heaven was that the GLA was to become a decoy organization to demons, and that this destined role be made clear with the coming of people with true powers and the true successor to me. In this way, GLA, restructured and vitalized, would grow in strength to fulfill its destiny. But, the distortion of GLA became extraordinary, due to my assumption that my daughter was identical with Michael, and by her resulting conviction that she was my true successor, was contrary to the plan of Heaven. The Celestial Realms had not expected this outcome of the organization. The human capacity for foresight or foreknowledge is strange enough. For instance, Noriko Tsuchida, whose co-spirit is Luriel and who received aiding spiritual powers from Uriel, first heard at Yuko Chino's home a spirit-phenomenon tape made by my daughter whom the Chinos explained to be the reincarnation of Michael. Although Noriko Tsuchida had never seen my daughter, an image resembling her floated into her consciousness and she was impelled to speak, saying, "No. This girl is not Michael." Miss Chino told of this event in September. Luriel spoke not to Noriko Tsuchida; her consciousness sensed or felt her intent. On my part, I sensed the concern of El Lantie, who had been my co-spirit during my years on earth.

Above all I must affirm, loudly and clearly, in this chapter that GLA was not created to become another formal New Religion, nor as a gathering place for those who seek salvation by dependence on an Almighty Savior.

If the members of GLA choose to set up my daughter or myself as their Savior, all I have preached or elucidated would become bereft of meaning and GLA fittingly could be scorned as a new religious fad. I urge those unable to comprehend to read again all I have said to men.

If the reader has not followed well of what I have elucidated in this chapter, I beseech him to reread it from the beginning.

The thing of most importance is not the building of an institution, the deifying of a Messiah, or revering the founder of a sect. Rather, I would that each of you take cognizance of what goals and what attitude should govern a man's life on earth. May it be that no man errs in these.

It is easy to live in the fellowship of demons, never lending an ear to one's "Good Self," and living without following the Eight-fold Noble Paths. If one consigns one's body to ambition and greed of the passing scene, it is inevitable that evil spirits will enslave you, and make you their puppet. Without realizing this fact, you will live in the shadows, avoiding the light, and believe that foolishness is virtue.

But, when you keep the fellowship of Good Spirits, you will seek the light, make reason your helper and order your life on the admonitions of your Good Self.

Also, may you always exercise modesty, both in relation to yourself and others, knowing well that position, fame, or wealth on earth will not be regarded by Heaven as measures of your worth. What is important is to live for the good of your fellow man. The discipline of the soul, and the polishing of the self are for this end. The enlightenment of just what I have explained will show you how easily you will benefit, and how easily it becomes a natural part of you. And it (modesty) indicates the extent of purification of your soul.

May this book *The Door to Heaven* shine a great light at the feet of those who shall read it.

CHAPTER 5

Heaven—The Abode High in the Sky for Good Spirits

The Moses Section

I am the Hebrew patriarch who, lead an enslaved race of about 600,000 people, the Israelites out of Egypt about 3,200 years ago. After 40 years, I took them back to Israel. During this time, I received from Heaven the Ten Commandments which I gave to the people as their Law. Today, few practice the Ten Commandments, and the true meaning of my teachings are covered with dust, forgotten by man. There would be no meaning in my elucidating the Ten Commandments here and now. For Jesus has talked about those things. Thus, I shall describe Heaven or the Celestial Realms and their structure. The celestial world is not a place with nothing but clouds. The landscape and its beauty is different for each level or dimension.

The Fourth Dimension, Limbo (Realm of Faintness)
Let me tell you first of Limbo or the fourth dimension, which is placed about ten thousand meters above the Earth. This world is the entrance way to the Celestial Realms. The key to the gates of the Celestial World are held by Peter. Before this gate, all people after death shall confess all that has been recorded in the memory of their brains . . . all that they thought or did, good and

Moses

bad . . . before the assembly of their guiding spirit, their protective spirit, and kindred souls there to receive them. It would seem that the majority of people loath this experience, and wish to return to earth. And after entering Limbo, those needing to redo their spiritual attitude—whatever dimension they may eventually enter—shall practice self-discipline and the search for enlightenment. They shall listen to the words of the archangels and beings of the Realm of the Bodhisattva and Saints or higher dimensions. By considering their deeds, they shall make right their errors on earth, and shall attain a truer understanding. Then, they will ascend to their dimension due in the celestial world. However, in that place invariably, they shall not cease to work for the refinement and enlargement of the soul.

The general appearance of Limbo is troubled and desolete. There are mountains and valleys, and ruins of houses, shops and public buildings like those on earth. The entire surface is grey-toned and their is a feeling of chilly remoteness. There are lakes, with lotus blossoms on the waters, where the disciplinants gather together for meditation and spiritual training. But those living in Limbo have a consciousness very liken to men on earth. They run around busily, without poise or calm, so that their conscious feelings are close to those of Hell. Their concerns center on Self; they do not purposely harm others but they have little love for those who are third persons.

When they suffer loss or are put to disadvantage, they are tenaciously vindictive. When one becomes a spirit, ninty percent of the consciousness works effectively if one desires that this be so, but despite this the capabilities for good of permanent dwellers in Limbo (fourth dimension) are few. This is because the Good Self is proportionately small. The soul's understanding of truth is in proportion to the *Zen* (Good) may be only about one-fifth of normal. Or the False Self may have become the entire soul.

Most souls dropping into Hell have allowed their False Self to become nine-tenths of the whole. If they attain even a small degree of enlightenment they may lift themselves into Limbo to dwell there.

Thus the dwelling place of such spirits in Limbo has the odor of putrid fish, and decay. This is because the realms of the fourth dimension and higher are created by the spiritual consciousness of the souls dwelling therein.

The dwellers in Heaven, including all its dimensions above Limbo number ten billion, while another fifteen billion souls are sent to dwell in men on earth. Men on earth number forty billion. The other twenty five billion men on earth are joined with the souls of the fourth dimension or Limbo. And even when a soul is embodied in man only about ten percent of the conscious powers of the brain are left free for the use of the human and the in-dwelling soul.

Such little use of the capacity of the brain even with the soul from Limbo for maintaining the physical life of man on earth, and the relative development of the Good Self and the False Self make it easy for man in the flesh to commit evil.

The Fifth Dimension, Realm of Spirits (Rei-kai)

Beyond Limbo is the fifth Dimensional Realm, of *Rei-kai*. This realm is about twenty thousand meters above the surface of Earth. This realm is better than Limbo but its landscape and appearance are not exceptional. Here dwell people whose nature on earth lacked depth, and who made themselves superficially attractive to others. Those tending to be of this company are entertainers, people of gay trade, and "Living Gods" promoting new religions. They are fond of gaudiness, shows of display and beauty, especially that which can be touched or looked at, and they enjoy being the center of attention. Their homes are pretty and flashy, as are their cars, and their clothes. In the theatres, they enjoy both attending and performing.

It is characteristic of most of them that they are good-hearted. Presently, five billion dwell in the fifth dimension and twelve billion are born and living as co-souls of men on earth. A fan of a star performer may tend to become a dweller of Limbo, while the star him or herself may tend to become a dweller of *Rei-kai*.

The Sixth Dimension, Realm of the Minor Gods (Shin-kai)
Beyond the Realm of Spirits is the sixth dimension of the Realm of Minor Gods, which is about fifty thousand meters high above the surface of the Earth. These are the souls of men of exceptional talent . . . geniuses of the arts, and great scholars, knights of old, and dedicated military leaders. Also the Realm of the Minor Gods is the dwelling of such as the Disciples of Jesus, those people revered in Shintoism, and the many worthy followers of the Ten Disciples of Buddha. This is a tranquil place with beautiful natural scenery . . . mountains, streams, wild flowers, green hills and grassy plains: There are study centers, sports arenas, *Kendo* and fencing halls, and art galleries. The people there devote themselves each day to the cultivation of their talents. Generally, they are indifferent about stylish appearance, housing and food. The weakness of dwellers of the sixth dimension is that they tend to over-value brilliance and to neglect the refinement of character. The majority of them are thus unable to reach a full understanding of the teachings of the Eight-fold Noble Paths. One hundred and fifty million of the souls of this sixth dimension, almost their total number, are now living as reincarnations on earth, and only one billion are presently in Heaven. Those now on earth include all the disciples of Jesus save Judah (who is still in Hell), the disciples of Buddha, Yamato-takeru-no-Mikoto and other Shinto deities. People of fame in

the ancient world such as Hippocrates and Aristotle have re-
mained here in Heaven.

The Seventh Dimension, Realm of the Bodhisattva
This Realm extends in all directions from sixty thousand meters
above earth. It is the dwelling place of the various Bodhisattva
and Kwannon[38]. These are beings whose conduct places the
welfare of other people above their own. The sole avarice left
is that they adorn their bodies themselves with jewelled tiara,
bracelets, and garlands. Thus, the representations of be-jewelled
deities in the ancient picture scrolls of the Far East are likenesses
of the dwellers of the Realm of the Bodhisattva. In this Realm,
the natural scenery is exceedingly beautiful. There are gentle
slopes carpeted with green grass, flowering trees showering down
their blossom, and rainbow as the bridges in the Realm. The
beings of this realm laugh and smile while they walk together,
or work, or rest. Often, they assemble to listen to lectures and
teachings given by the people of Tathagatas or the Archangels.
Or, because they are fond of serving others, they are often busily
going about sundry labors on behalf of others.

There are vinyards, tea plantations, and fruit orchards in this
world; the Bodhisattva enjoy drinking both tea and wine. But
the fabled "Nectar," elixer of life does not exist here. Such fable
must have wishingly been created on earth for the eternal life
and the immortal souls. It is no more than a tradition and a
source of mythology.

This is the heaven for animals tamed and loved by man on
earth . . . dogs, cats, little birds, squirrels, deer, and similar
creatures. And all of those that knew suffering and maltreat-
ment on Earth are brought here where they are cared for by
guardian angels of the animals. The carnivorous or ferocious beasts,
including the giant reptiles of the Reptilian Age are cared for

in a sectar of Limbo separated from that occupied by the souls of men.

The Eighth Dimension, Realm of the Tathagata (Nyorai)
The next higher, or eighth, dimension is the abode of the Tathagatas (*Nyorai*). This realm is from eighty thousand to one hundred thousand meters above the surface of the Earth. A Tathagata is a being for whom there is no distinction between the Self and Others. Tathagatas are individual souls but they know that to strive for others is to strive for oneself, and to endeavor for oneself is an endeavor for others. Their consciousness sees the self and the non-self as one entity. They have completely shed earthly desires, greed, and lust. Portraits or sculptural likenesses of the Tathagata show them in simple, unpretentious attire. But they have powers enabling them to see all of the three worlds of the past, present and future. And they are able to look through to the soul of man. Both the Buddha, Shakyamuni and Jesus came from this Realm to earth; when they fulfilled their appointed tasks and returned, they were elevated to the ninth dimension. The co-soul of Amaterasu Omikami, the great Shinto figure of pre-historic Japan, came to earth from the Realm of the Minor Deities, while Amaterasu entered the Realm of the Tathagata on her elevation to the Celestial Realms.

This is a land beautiful to behold. Pure waters flow in its pleasant small streams, and the translucent waters of its lake are saphire blue. The lake is named "the Lake of Release from Anxiety." There are groves of white poplar, and a deep-green forest with laurel, broom-tree, and hackberry. And extending to a far horizon is a verdant plain with flowers and grasses of all four seasons in which butterflies flutter and birds are singing. Many varieties of trees bear exotic flowers or are laden with nuts. And jonquil, iris and lotus are in full bloom together with many other flowers. This land is like the Garden of Elden (Eden). Those dwelling here contemplate or meditate while they gaze at the landscape beauties, or the movement of white clouds in the sky.

Here also is a valley in which violets and lilies bloom, and where lives Mary, Mother of Jesus. And there is a land with lilies of the valley, swaying in the breeze. Here one may see the fairies or sprites of the flowers gathered . . . a sight which softens one's heart. Only in the Realm of Tathagata . . . beings dedicated to helping man . . . may one see the various kinds of fairies or cherubs of which the flower fairies are one group. Ten thousand Tathagata are now in the Celestial World while ten thousand are co-souls, living on earth.

The Realm of the Sun (Taiyo-kai)
This is a world which covers the three realms of the angels and the other two higher dimensions. The angels' Realm extends in all directions from about 100,000 meters to about 130,000 meters, divided into two layers each 15,000 meters high. In the upper level of the angels' Realm dwell Michael, the Chief Archangel, and the six archangels, Gabriel, Panuel, Raguel, Raphael, Uriel, and Sariel. The lower level is the home of all the angels appointed duties under the Archangels. The angels are always modest; they do not often appear before man on earth. They never neglect their responsibilities as advocates for, and supporters of, the *Shoho* (the True Law). The angels, who have full knowledge and full comprehension of all things that occur in the world and the universe, still maintain their basic forms of such purity both in soul and appearance. To become an angel, a Messenger of Heaven, a spirit must first enter the Realm of the Tathagata. After this, some become one of the Benevolent Deities of Heaven, while others become angels

or Messengers. Formerly, those deities came up from the upper level of the Realm of Minor Deities, but it is now a rule of Heaven that they come up from the Realm of Tathagata. The higher the Realm or dimension the more exacting the disciplining of the soul; thus the spiritual training of the angels is the most severe of all. Especially when the Angels are reincarnated on earth, they are destined to greater ordeals than the great guiding spirits of the Light of the ninth dimension are. On earth, they must attain enlightenment and evidence wisdom and benignity in exposition of the *Shoho*. There are people on earth who, dazzled by the beauty of the Messengers, envy them. But few would dare to become one knowing how arduous is their ascetic training and their suffering on earth. Their wings are necessary because the angels are the main force in the battle against the demons. Also wings serve them in their role as Messengers.

This Realm of the Angels has no natural phenomena save clouds. This is because the Angels know no rest. Presently, the Angels both in Heaven and Earth number only one hundred and fifty-four, besides the Chief Archangel and five other archangels. Those in reincarnations on Earth are Sariel, Luriel (who was specially instructed by the archangel Uriel), and ninty one other angels. There are two each in England, France, Italy, and Switzerland, and three in America. The others, including the single Archangel, were all reincarnated in Japan. The twelve disciples of Jesus, and the ten disciples of Buddha, many other disciples, a subsequent body and a spirit brother of Buddha, and many others high in Heaven are also living in Japan as co-inhabiting souls of men.

The work of the sixty-three angels now in Heaven may be given as follows. Twenty are helpers of the Archangels, who are assigned liaison with the Realm of the Tathagata. Thirty maintain contact between the Realm of the Tathagata and the

Realm of the Bodhisattva. Five serve as liaison between the Realm of the Bodhisattva and the Realm of the Minor Deities. Five serve between the Realm of the Minor Deities and the Realm of Spirits, while three furnish liaison between the Realm of Spirits and Limbo.

Also there is the angel Luciel, who formerly was the co-soul of he who became Lucifer, but who has now returned to his place in Heaven among the angels. Luciel became the co-soul of Lucifer when he was born on earth in Greece over 3,500 years ago, only to later descend to Hell due to the works of demons. Lucifer repeatedly menaced the writer of this book, the co-inhabitant soul of whom is the Archangel Sariel. But this person struggled with him for his soul, urging him to repent the evils he had done, and telling him of love and mercy. She prevailed upon Lucifer to cleanse his soul, and Lucifer was finally raised to Heaven with Luciel on April 13, 1977 after 3,500 years. Luciel had been a beloved follower of the Chief archangel, Michael. Thus Michael and the dwellers of Heaven were glad, and celebrated his return.

After Shinji Takahashi, who was the corporeal co-soul of El Lantie, was also elevated to Heaven upon his death on the 25th of June, 1976, the archangel Sariel and the angel Luriel combined their powers to redeem over ten billion evil souls from the Hell of Japan and Hells of other countries, and to lift them to Heaven. Except for those in Eternal Inferno[32] and the *Tengu-kai*[33], the Hells were completely emptied. This took place between March and the end of May, 1977.

The Benevolent Deities are only ten in number. The angels sometimes assist them. These Deities are charged with the duty of redeeming and lifting to Heaven the hosts of hell demons, floating spirits, earth-bound spirits, and spirits of the dead. They descend to Hell to remonstrate, and they act as guardians for

Messengers of Light who are living reincarnations on earth, such as co-inhabiting souls from the Realm of the Bodhisattva or the Realm of the Tathagata.

Besides all these, there are 100,000 beings who are not Angels but who nevertheless perform duties under the guidance of the angels, and are therefore endowed with wings. And, there are 200,000 good spirits of good animals including foxes, some reptiles and some felines. These assistants are souls from the higher Realms of Heaven who committed evil on earth. On returning to Heaven they sought these duties in expiation and for the discipline of their souls.

As for the Benevolent Deities, on completion of a certain period of duties, they become angels under the aegis of the six archangels.

Above the dimension of the Angels or Heavenly Messengers are the two levels of the ninth dimension and the uppermost level, the Realm of the Universe extending limitlessly in all directions from about 130,000 meters above earth. The Heaven or Celestial Realms of which I have spoke are those of the Corporal Spirits of the Solar System, located above planet Earth with the dimension of the Universe its highest level. It is the world of those spirits of gods who conceive their gods in the image of the universe or universal nature. That spirit in the Dimension of the Universe whose soul is closest to this conception is El Lantie, so mightly as to be called the Holy Avatar of Light or the mediator of the ultimate gods, the Nature and the Universe. He is known in the third dimension of Yahweh or Jehovah. He lived on earth in ancient Greece as the in-dwelling soul with Zeus, the father of Apollo and in this century descended to Japan in order to co-inhabit with Shinji Takahashi. By El Lantie becoming the co-soul of Shinji Takahashi, Heaven and Earth are still unified. Now (that Shinji Takahashi's Existence on earth is over) Michael and the other archangels guard those earth people in whose bodies reside Sariel and Luriel.

When beings of the ninth dimension are reincarnated, the archangels avoid co-inhabitation on earth themselves. They do battle and serve as protection from Heaven throughout the third and fourth dimensions. Now I, Moses, dwell in the ninth dimension in the Realm of the Sun, together with Shinji Takahashi, Buddha, and Jesus. One of the spirit brothers of Buddha is also reincarnated now in Japan.

The Celestial Realms and Hell (Chart I)

	Realm	Dimension	Consciousness	Philosophy
100% Universal Conscious-ness	Realm of the Sun	Realm of the Universe	The highest being respon-sible of Heaven	King of the Heaven and the being of all the virtues and capacities.
		9th ——— Realm of the Angels	Pure love and Mercy	Self is the Uni-verse and the Universe is the Self.
	Realm of Tathagatas	8th	Self and non-self are not distinguished	Self is one with non-self (others). All seeing.
	Realm of Bodhisat-tvas and Saints (also animals protected here)	7th	Place the non-self before self.	Still distin-guishes self and non-self. There still is desire for adornment.
Heaven or Celestial Realms (4th and higher dimen-sion)	Realm of Minor Deities	6th	Ambition and greed has lessoned.	The realm of physicians, theologists, true scholars, true artists and kindred souls.
	Realm of Spirits	5th	Less avarice than Limbo.	The dwelling place of those who live on admiration, as illustrated by entertainment stars, per-formers and show-type leaders of the New Religions.

	Realm	Dimension	Consciousness	Philosophy
	Limbo	4th	Unable to accept loss; completely motivated by self-gain.	A world like earth. Vain glory and materialism is strong.
Earth	Earths	3rd	All consciousness exist according to the proportion of *Zenga* (the Good self) to *Giga* (the False Self)	Embraces all that is above and all that is below, as both spirits of Heaven and of Hell occupy the tabernacle of the flesh.
Hells	Realm of Ashura (Demons of Anger)	2nd co-exists in the 3rd.	Demons of strife and contention. Those who cannot control anger.	
	Realm of Beastly Ways	2nd co-exists in the 3rd.	Murderers, killers of animals, and those who violated the *Shoho* (True Law) by acts of extreme cruelty	
	Realm of Gaki (Insatiable Hungry Demons)	2nd co-exists in the 3rd.	Concentrations of greed	
	Inferno in Flame	2nd co-exists in the 3rd.	The hell of the cruel, pitiless, and heartless.	
	Hell of the Lake of Blood	2nd co-exists in the 3rd.	Those who lived as animals.	
(Hells for souls whose "False	Realm of Tengu or Conceited Demons	2nd co-exists in the 3rd.	Spirits who consider themselves to be the supreme race.	
Self" is 100% of their consciousness	Eternal or Indeterminate Inferno	2nd underground	Men who committed genocide, or killed many other men. The malice of their victims remains around them always.	

Satans and Most Power-ful Demons	1st under-ground	Most malicious and powerful in evil intentions also ambitious in rebellions against Heaven.

Each people have created for themselves a set of Hells.
The above is that for Japan only. The Heaven is worldwide.

The Chart of the Realm of the Sun (Chart II)

Realms	*Dwellers*
Realm of the Universe	El Lantie
Realm of the 9th Dimension	Jesus Christ
	Buddha
	Moses
	Teacher Shinji Takahashi
	(spirit brother of El Lantie)
Realm of the Angels	
(Upper level)	The Chief Archangel Michael
	Archangels: Gabriel (Communication and its vehicles)
	Raguel (Laws)
	Sariel (Medicine and Pharmacology)
	Uriel (Government, Economics and Self-government)
	Panuel (Science in general)
	Raphael (Fine arts, Literature and Historical studies)
(Lower level)	Cohorts of Angels

Annotations

El Lantie and the soul of Shinji Takahashi are two different entities in Heaven. Also Lucifer . . . man, Satan, then the spirit which was elevated to the Celestial Realms exists separately from the Spirit of the Archangel Luciel. The good spirits do not just join and separate. The power of transformation at will generally attributed to demons only, belongs in greater measure to them.

Moses

It seems that GLA are publishing a new book on Satan, as if the threat of Satan was still actual. But Lucifer has been raised to Heaven and the satanic couple from Veh-erde have been destroyed. These were cohorts of Asteria, who has striven to possess those around the daughter of Shinji Takahashi. Except for some followers, death spirits, and earth bound spirits, there are no evil spirits requiring vigilance and precaution. The beings of the Celestial Realms wish you to know that all measures necessary are being used to protect mankind from the vibrations of the remaining evil spirits. Such is one purpose of *The Door to Heaven*.

Yuko Chino

CHAPTER 6

The *Shoho* (The True Law)— Supplements and Definitions

Those who have read this text thus far should have general knowledge of the True Law. Here we will elucidate definitions used in discourse of the *Shoho* which have not, as yet, been explained and further clarify some of the other points concerned.

The fundamental meaning of "*Shoho*" is "correct or right laws." By "laws" are meant statements of a relation or sequence of phenomena invariable under the same conditions in the natural world, including concepts of natural justice, or the will of a deity. The laws of nature are by definition the "truth," those laws which man must perforce obey if he is to find his natural existential role. It is implicit in the "True Law" that the source of all blessings for mankind are his natural surroundings and the Universe, and that these should be the models for his life. God is seen in (and may be regarded as) the workings of nature and the universe. Therefore, Shinji Takahashi taught that the laws of nature were the principles of the gods or God's Law.

Next, let us clarify the meaning of the words "conforming to the rhythmic cycle of waves projected from Heaven." The Chief Archangel Michael has said that the hearts of men are nine-fold. Let us think of the drawing below as an analytical drawing of the consciousness. There are nine dimensions, just as there are in the structure of the heavens and the hells.

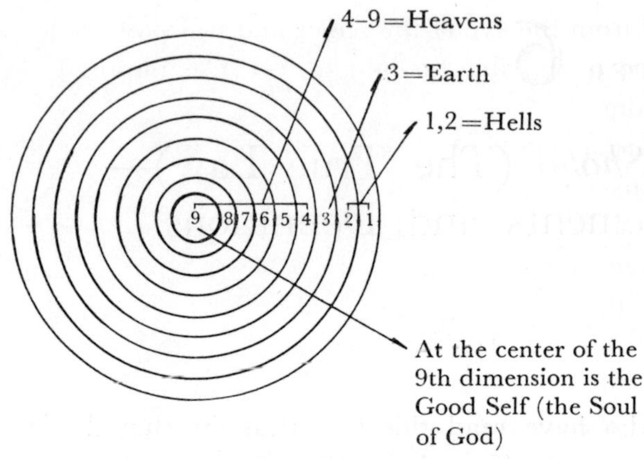

(Reference is made to Chapter IV;
Section on Shinji Takahashi.)

The spirit worlds of heavens and hells have all have been made by man himself, not by an Almighty God or God of Creation. Let each man know that each individual consciousness may also create at will both heaven and hell. In this thing, consider well the energy of the will focused on the act of creation. As a physical organism, man expends his energies in various ways— not only when moving or working, when eating, or talking but in all the processes needed to maintain life; even including processes not evident to the eye such as those of the internal organs and their various biochemical systems. All these processes consume energy. Similarly, energy is inevitably consumed or directed whenever he projects a thought, or a wish, or employs conceptual impulses or acts of will.

Consummation means that an equivalent amount of energy is emitted from the body, or is projected as radiation.

Speech is transmitted by sound waves as sounds; consciousness, will, and prayer are projected as an energy of the consciousness. A line of sight on an object or person is also a form of energy projected from the eye of the see-er and it is possible for a person on the end of this line of sight to feel it as impinging on his or her freedom.

The various kinds of energy projected from the human body all have fixed speeds, which varies with the type, volume, and strength of the radiation. Especially will waves which travel at an average speed of about 50 kilometers per second. Once projected they do not dissipate. They will eventually reach the intended objective however distant. And, as the soul achieves the harmony of moderation, its radiant wave band becomes narrower, the vibrations foster, and the wave length becomes shorter liken to supra-sound waves. These waves are delicate. They are called the "waves of Heaven."

In contrast, when the soul departs from the middle path and becomes discordant, the conceptual impulses become irregular, with fewer vibrations of a longer wave length. These are the "vibrations of Satan," also called the "vibrations of Hell." Vibrations become finer as the soul, with its nine aspects, approaches center or the ninth dimensional aspect. And since this is the dimension of Heaven, with the same frequency for projecting the consciousness, that soul will be in communion. Understanding may be facilitated if one thinks of wireless communication.

Those whose soul energy projects on the same frequency as Heaven shall better assimilate the energy and the light of the sun sent from Heaven. In other words, the beams of the conceptual impulse of a good soul will be on the some frequency as those of the good spirits of the Celestial Realms, and that their wills or conceptual impulses shall become as one, in strength. The waves of the evil or non-good soul will be in the same frequency band as those of Hell, and the emmanations of the consciousness shall be those of Hell. Here, let us explain the nature of the Good Self, the False Self, and the True Self. The

Good Self is that aspect which is liken to God, possessing the spirit of *Zen* (Goodness). The False Self is contrary to the Good Self and that aspect of a man which is deceitful, denying or concealing the goodness bestowed him at birth. The True Self is the actual self, containing either aspect in various strengths. It is well for each man to perceive the state of the True Self, which aspect is ascendant. Let him nurture the Good Self and not nurture the False Self.

Next, let me explain the actual state of the soul. The various branches of science have long been studying and debating the relation between the soul and life, and the location of the soul in man and in animals. But this question was long ago resolved in Veh-erde, and their concept is relatively simple.

The existence of spiritual and physical structures may be postulated when they are in separation. Aside from a few high-order species, such as a species of cactus, which is thought capable of a type of speech, the equivalent of a soul has not yet been discovered in vegetable life. The various fairies or spirits of flowers mentioned in Chapter I (The Spiritualistic Experiences of Yuko Chino) and Chapter V (Heaven—The Abode High in the Sky of Good Spirits) were all created by the spirits of human beings so that their environment might be more natural. But in animals and man, the reactions to stimulation and integrated action of the brain and its entire nervous system including spinal ganglia, plus the life-maintaining functions or reactions within the body cell structure, are so conditioned or trained, through the originality of functions as an individual living being, that the organism obeys customary laws very similar to conditioned responses. These attributes of universal energy (the elementary particles of which the body is formed), together with a little quantity of the organic material within the body are called the "soul."

Thus, that special something called the soul is not something existing separately before birth, but accompanies the birth of the flesh. The elements of the soul are the light rays, neutrons, protons, and electrons of the elementary of universal energy which are within the cells particular to the flesh of each and every being. After such a being whom we shall call *A* dies, the soul separates from the body, becoming a vapor (sometimes called a spirit-soul or ball of fire), and exists in this changed form forever. And this vaporous organism plus its universal energy exists in identity with the being *A*, and never becomes part of anything else. Nor does it dissolve or lose its form unless it so desires or unless the spirit of a high dimension effects its extinction.

We shall discuss this matter again along with the conceptual zones. But, at birth the being *A* is co-inhabited by a good spirit (which completely enters the body.) This spirit acts on the consciousness along with a guardian spirit and a guiding spirit which also descend from heaven to attend on *A*, so that three good spirits offer guidance: On death, these spirits leave and only *A*'s soul remains. This principle applies only after man had evolved, and with man the natural emergence of souls with immortal life. It is in accord with scientific theory—namely the Law of Evolution and the Law of the Indestructibility of Matter. If the soul existed prior to the man, from where could that soul have come. And why do the various attributes and individual characteristics appear in the soul. Such mysterious puzzles would remain unsolved. Science is the resolution of esotericisms, and not a discipline for creating new mysteries.

So, because the soul is formed of the universal energy and the elements as the structure, the memory of *A* may be preserved for many hundreds of millions of years, or perhaps even eternally. Such a soul is strange only if one thinks it strange; it is a vaporous body, an organism, and immortal.

Now, the conceptual zone, which has been said to be different from the soul, alludes to a part of the soul. This consists of the organic compound and the universal energies in the cellular tissues of the frontal lobe of the cerebrum, the lateral lobes governing memory, and the brain and other parts of the central nervous system. Here are found all instincts and the facultive functions of the brain . . . feeling instinct, intelligence, rationality, sight, hearing, smell, taste, tactual sense, and consciousness. Buddhists call these functions the Five Senses and the Six Roots.

Shinji Takahashi has shown these in illustrations, with the brain to be attached to. One may think of the conceptual zone as approximately the equivalent of the brain. When the soul leaves the body, as told in the Section on Shinji Takahashi, one part of the conceptual zone leaves also while the remaining part guards the body and helps maintain life functions.

When one says, "A certain person is born as the main (or the primary) body (*hontai*) or as the subsequent (or the second) body (*bunshin*) of so-and-so," it means that a good soul has descended from the celestial realms to augment that person's soul and the conceptual zone so that he may surely be directed to Heaven. And the good spirit completely enters the body of that certain person. Thus, two souls are joined in the one body. This co-inhabiting spirit usually guards the body even when the body's own soul separates temporarily. The name of the soul from Heaven is used to identify of whom the certain person is the primary body (*hontai*) or the subsequent body (*bunshin*). Thus it is not correct usage to speak of the past existence of, for instance, Mr. Yamanaka (or Mr. Johnson). One can speak only of the past existence of the Good Spirit co-inhabiting Mr. Yamanaka (or Mr. Johnson). Mr. Yamanaka did not have immortal life continuing from the past; his soul is now in the process of formation during his present existence. Not the past, but the future awaits it.

So, all of us have a destiny, not only to reach harmony with nature . . . and to achieve with other men harmony, and fulfillment of duty and responsibility. We also need to achieve an inner harmony and a sense of duty and responsibility toward ourselves.

Herein lies the larger meaning of the phrase, "Value your life." A person will become aware of how eternal are the tasks assigned to an individual (and how bound he or she is to perform such tasks) only after having first reached Heaven at the conclusion of a life time under the protection, support and leadership of the three Good Spirits. Then, having subsequently experienced reincarnation, to in-dwell with another from that person's birth . . . taking that soul when it still knows naught by the hand and leading, imparting wisdom and knowledge, and being duty-bound to share their joys, sorrow, and suffering will these eternally-bound tasks be perceived. This is the feeling which Lucifer, who has been saved has now for his co-soul, Luciel.

The guardian spirit plays a similar role, protecting his charge from natural and human calamities which occur from the external world, and giving detailed guidance in everyday life. The guardian spirit leads one in the path of correct action, and is invested with the power to admonish one who may incline toward evil. The guiding spirit gives advice to the guardian spirit in regard to learning and profession. Depending on circumstances, the guardian spirit and guiding spirits may be changed. When one ignores one's good self and follows the road of evil the ties with the guardian spirit and guiding spirit are severed; when demons take possession of a man, the good spirits within his physical body depart.

"Possession" means that evil spirits have attached themselves to one's body. But even evil spirits have their destined retribution. They may act out of a need to save themselves, or they may wish to pull others to Hell to reap revenge for some anguish they have suffered. But each time they lead another soul to Hell their own guilt is multiplied, and the period necessary for their atonement is lengthened. Those for whom redemption has become impossible are either extinguished or deprived of their very existence, so that they no longer exist as spirits. When one soul entices another into evil, unlike the world of the third dimension, the soul of the enticer must expiate this sin also after death. Moreover, he who is enticed has a duty not to succumb to enticement but, rather, in order not to make the enticer's burden of expiation heavier has an obligation to redeem him. Hell spirits are those who are creating Hell; earth-bound spirits are those which do not separate from a place which had special importance for them even after death. Animal spirits are those which spent most of their human life in pursuit of animal-like desires; they include both spirits of humans who fell into Hell, and the spirits of animals, good and bad. The good spirits of animals work under the direction of the Shoten Zenjin (Benevolent Celestial Deities) and are granted a shelter in Heaven. The evil animal spirits who were caused to fall into Hell because of mistreatment by humans are very few in number. Floating spirits are those which loiter in the air of earth. Evil spirits are divided into about four classes depending on their capacities. Those who committed suicide are in a separate group.

In the teachings of the *Shoho* (True Law), it is told that all the events of a human's life—the experiences and deeds—are all recorded in the conceptual zone of the brain. If one's heart is pure, the zone of consciousness will be white and the records will float forth in golden letters. But if the heart be fouled, this zone will be fouled and clouded, with records lettered in black. Even so, if one reflects on their mistaken thinking and wrong conduct, taking care each and every day not to do such things twice, the conceptual zone will become golden.

There are various stages of Hell and Heaven. As one progresses toward higher levels, the years of discipline that are required in their search for enlightenment differ in number. Such training demands that, even after enlightenment is achieved, through repeated incarnations (as shown in the chart), one must complete one's destined tasks. You can see that it is hard to rise above the Realm of Spirits (*Rei-kai*). Usually, the soul assends to the realm to which its consciousness is directed, but because of the attained enlightenment there are some who do go to a higher realm. There are also many who fall to a lower realm. I have been told that in the future one's works will be evaluated in the final reckoning so that there will be even more changes.

Years of Ascetic Training

From:	*To:*	*Time:*
Hell	Limbo	Immediately upon one's realization of their errors.
Limbo	Realm of Spirits	About 100 years
Realm of Spirits	Realm of Gods	350 million years
Realm of Minor Gods	Realm of Saints (Bodhisattva)	200 million years
Realm of Saints (Bodhisattva)	Realm of Tathagata (*Nyorai*)	100 million years
Realm of Tathagata (*Nyorai*)	Realm of the Sun	Attainable only by those destined. They either become angels or Shoten Zenjin by choice.

Until now I have overlooked defining the difference between the terms for the main or the "primary body"[39] (*hontai*) and the "subsequent body"[39] (*bunshin*). Suppose that the spirit of the archangel Raphael has entered Shakespeare at his birth. Shakespeare would be called the primary body (*hontai*) of Raphael. After death, Shakespeare's soul would completely separate to become a primary spirit brother[39] of Raphael. The next individual whom Shakespeare entered as its co-soul would be a subsequent body (*bunshin*) of Raphael. Upon this individual's death, his soul would be a secondary spirit brother or the subsequent soul body of Raphael (*bunshin dainigo*). This is because the souls of the primary body (*hontai*) and of the subsequent body (*bunshin*) have a sibling-like relationship. There is also the word "*bunrei*" or "sharing of the spirit." Simply, this means sharing one's spiritual powers. Usually, the "primary body" of the soul (*hontai*) has five allotted reincarnations while the "subsequent body" (*bunshin*) has seven. This chain is called "*Tensho Rinne*" or rebirth by Karma. The average human is reincarnated about one to two hundred years after death. Those such as Buddha, Jesus, and Moses had as their co-inhabiting souls the distinguished souls of people who had originally been born on Veh-erde, but they were elevated to the Realm of the ninth dimension within the Realm of the Sun by attaining enlightenment even beyond that of their co-souls. As Moses wrote, El Lantie was the co-soul of Shinji Takahashi but left his body at times to protect the Heavens' Realms. This is possible only for those souls of the Realm of the Sun. Shinji Takahashi's daughter is the primary body of Queen Himiko, who co-inhabits her body at all times. Unfortunately, Queen Himiko has no relation to the angels, and was not the reincarnation of the archangel Michael. And with the aid of Michael, after she had the book on Hell published about one-half year after her father's death, the GLA was invaded by evil spirits, and has not been able to regain the true course from which it was diverted. If Shinji Takahashi's daughter truly were in reincarnation of an angel, she would be able to perceive these mistakes. At the time when Shinji Takahashi had over-used his body and was approaching death, the Celestial Realms and Michael were reluctant to force rectification.

Next, I will define Messengers of Light, Powertron, Arhats, and Bodhisattva. The term Messengers of Light encompasses all the beings of the Heaven including the Great Guiding Spirits of Light of the Realm of the ninth dimension, and beyond. El Lantie is called the avatar of light. Powertron is an attribute possessed by all ancient men . . . it is located in the middle of the forehead and gives forth light. The Arhat receives the teachings of the gods, and purifies their hearts. As they gain enlightenment or understanding of how to live, their auras become beautifully hued and more brilliant. It is said of the first stage of *Satori* (Enlightenment) that one has reached the state of Arhat-hood. The Bodhisattvas of Buddhism are, just as the name signifies, the Enlightened. In Christianity they are called the Angels of Light. These beings are in the second stage of Enlightenment, the same as the Bosatsu of the Celestial Realms (see Chart I at the end of the Moses Section. Both terms are Sanscrit or ancient Indian.)

Next are the Shoten Zenjin or the Benevolent Celestial Deities of the Orient such as Fudo Myo-o (Acala), Marishiten (Marīci), Inari Daimyojin (Dākinī), Daikokuten (Mahā-kāla), the Eight Great Dragon Kings Hachi Dairyu-o (Nanda, Upananda, Sagara, Vāsuki, Takṣaka, Anavatapta, Manas, Utpala) and Vaisravana. They are the Good Deities, endowed with powers enabling them to succor Bodhisattvas and even *Nyorais* or Tathagatas.

The Brahman caste is a great organized religious group from the time of Buddha, which was made of the upper class of ancient Indian society. This religion has the Veda, Upanished, as its

Scripture which, like the sutras of Buddhism, are based on the teachings of one holy man. This holy man lived about 4,200 years ago, and carried from Egypt to India the teachings of a Messiah named Cleo Parota whose soul is considered one of the spirit brothers of Buddha. The teachings of the Brahmanic religion of those times were of the soul, or heart, of man, and of universal nature, but it become skeletonized as time passed, and transformed into a philosophy of intellect and definition.

There are the two religious concepts of "the middle road" (*chudo*) and of release from suffering "*gedatsu*" (emancipation or deliverance). The "middle road" is a teaching of Buddha which expounded moderation. For those entering the religious life, the two extremes of abandonment to the fleshly desire and of ascetic torture must be avoided. It is said that Tathagata, that is, generally understood as Buddha in Buddhism, rejected both of these extremes and attained enlightenment or comprehension of the middle road. *Gedatsu* or release from suffering involves realizing what the causes of pain are, and attaining the wisdom to be able to abolish pain. This is *Satori. Gedatsu* is the escape from the restrictions of suffering due to greed, when one attains the highest enlightenment, one understands the laws of cause and effect which govern the past, the present and the future, and the structure of the Universe as clearly as if it were in the palm of one's hand.

Lastly, I shall discuss the Five Admonitions (*Gokai*). They are also a concept of Buddha, serving as a guide for those seeking to lead religious lives.

One should avoid the intake of food at inappropriate hours (afternoon).

One should not view dancing, singing, or musical entertainment.

One should not adorn the body with floral garlands, nor with perfume, cosmetics, or jewelry.

Do not sleep on a large or high bed.

Do no accept money, or things similar to money such as gold or silver. True priests, if male, observe about 250 admonitions and, if female, 348.

The strange tongue or spirit language is the words of a spirit speaking through a medium or one who is given the equivalent spiritualistic capacity, whose body it has entered. The medium is made, without realizing the fact, to speak in foreign languages it does not know or even in ancient tongues. Also, the medium may perform unlearned movements or even dances, under forces on its consciousness so strong that the performance seems highly skilled.

The *Goun* (pañca-skandha) are the five areas, both Material and Metaphysical, of human existence . . . (1) Color, *Shiki* (rūpa-skandha) symbolizing the five senses of the flesh . . . (2) Acceptance, *Ju* (vedanā-sk.) which is receptivity to impression . . . (3) Conception, *So* (saṃjñā-sk.) or symbolic functioning . . . (4) Conduct, *Gyo* (saṃskāra-sk.) which is the application of will-power and (5) Wisdom, *Shiki* (vijñāna-sk.) which is the fount of the soul's power to exercise wisdom. In these five existential areas one can not admit the materialistic self. But, it will profit one to refer to Mitsuho Hirota *sensei*'s discussion of these concepts in Chapter VII.

The Jain (or Jina) religion, the origin of which is slightly before the lifetime of Buddha, derived, as did Buddhism from unorthodox Brahmanism. The Jain religion began as a "new faith" expounded by Mahāvīra, who was also called Jina, meaning one who has attained ultimate enlightenment. He denounced the caste system and urged that all killing even of insect life be forbidden. The Jain priests advocate, "The true Brahman depends not on birth but on virtuous conduct. We call Brahman that man who has rejected anger and ignorance, who harms not others even though he himself be harmed, and who has subjugated all his passions."

The four major castes were the Brahmans (Brāhmaṇa) or priests, the *Kṣatriya* which was comprised of Kings, nobles, and gentry, the *Vaiśya* or common people including peasants, artisans, and merchants and the *Śūdra* or slaves. Each caste preserved its own customs, way of life, and mores. The caste system strictly forbade association with, or marriage between, members of different castes. This was a rigid and ancient social system.

The Brahmanic training included subjecting their bodies to pain and severe asceticism to purge themselves of the desires rooted in the five senses and six instincts of physical man.

Higan (the far bank) is a term for the crevice of enlightenment. The final "*higan*" (crossing) is the Nirvana which Buddha attained.

The five senses refer to sight, hearing, smell, taste, and the tactual sense. The six instincts or "roots" include the above five senses plus consciousness or will. The six roots are the roots of all evil. Through the five senses, one's heart may be abused and swayed. And because men are led away from the true path, chaos persists in the world. One loses oneself when confused by the six instincts (or roots.)

Desire (or Kleśa in Sanskrit) is illusion. Fleshly obsessions arise from illusions relating to the body. Desire for position, honor or wealth all come from coveting. Prajñāpāramitā is an ancient Sanscrit term. Prajñā is wisdom or the Buddhist intellect which flows forth from the soul, while pāramitā signifies the reaching of the "far bank" or enlightenment. The far bank is a world of peace and calm, overflowing with wisdom. Thus Prajñāpāramitā is the attainment of an intrinsic inner intellect. If one lives by this wisdom, one eternal life may be attained. But the reaching of this state of existence is only possible to those who strictly observe the True Path in their lives.

Sanskrit chants are the hymns of the gods, which are sung at their ceremonies in long drawn out tones. Essentially, the intent is to modulate the rhythms of people.

Mahāyāna is a type of Buddhism which arose among those who sought a new unfolding of the Buddhist religion following the death of King Aśoka (332–268 B.C.). Mahāyāna Buddhism appealed to the masses of the common people, emphasizing salvation for all. It set up the ideal of benevolence or striving for the benefit of others. The Scriptures of Mahāyāna Buddhism include the Sūtras as the Prajñāpāramitā-hydaya-sūtra, the Saddharamapuṇḍarīka-sūtra, the Buddha-avataṃsaka-nāma-mahāraipulya-sūtra. Sukhāvatī-vyūha and two other sutras edited by the priests Nāgārjuna and Vasubandhu, the Sutra of vimala-ḳīrti, and the Dhārani Sutra of esoteric Buddhism. Mahāyāna, the Greater Vehicle, spread through Central Asia, China, Tibet, Mongolia, went to Korea, and finally reached Japan in 538 and in 552 A.D.

Hīnayāna, is the Little Vehicle, directed toward saving a few elite or superior people. The Hīnayāna Buddhist concerns himself with his personal salvation and enlightenment, and does not try to save the world in general. This Hīnayānas is significantly different from the universal salvation which is promised by Mahāyāna. Hīnayāna Buddhists strive for completion of their personal self rather than the good of others.

After the death of King Aśoka, there arose a new reform group in opposition to the conservative element, which strove to maintain, in detail, the old precepts. The reform sect became the people's sect (Mahāsaṃghika) while the conservative group were called the group of the upper seat (Thera-vāda or Sthavira). Later those religious groups split into over twenty different factions, which were collectively termed "sectarian Buddhism." The Mahāyāna sect derisively called these the Little Vehicle.

But, Hīnayāna Buddhism spread to Ceylon, Burma, Thai, and Cambodia.

The terms *Saniwa*: A specialist who judges the conscious level or the true character of the spirit being which manifests itself, and *Yuga-gyo* (the austerities of Yoga): Concentrative act of the mind performed by a Buddhist priest. A sort of *Zenjo* (law of discipline).

In observing the *Shoho* or the True Law, it is most important to keep one's heart well-rounded and generous. It is inevitable that one be distressed or troubled at heart when things go badly. But inspite of this, one can not lose the will to act. One must struggle through life with resilience, creating a resting-place in one's heart. This is the art of life, or perhaps one might say the outer sheathing of a virtuous heart.

Note

In all of the above definitions of religious terms, I have received guidance from Shinji Takahashi which differ slightly from his original teaching. At the end of this Chapter is a list of the people who have been reincarnated with the names of their "*hontai*" (Main or primary body) and their "*bunshin*" (Subsequent body), which I feel as having reference value concerning the cycle of rebirth or Karma.

The Author

Name	Primary Body (*Hontai*)	Subsequent Body (*Bunshin*)
El Lantie	Zeus Shinji Takahashi	Johann Sebastian Bach Ludwig v. Beethoven
Jesus Christ	Krai-o Amon Agatha Abraham Blaise Pascal	André Gide Kuze (Savior) Kwannon[40]

Name	Primary Body (Hontai)	Subsequent Body (Bunshin)
Buddha	Cleo Parota Tendai Priest Chigi Chuang (Sanzo)[41] Priest Saicho[42] Priest Kukai[43] Immanuel Kant	Kogoro Katsura[44]
Moses	Poseidon Sigmund Freud	

The Chief Arch-
angel Michael
	Apollo
	Alexander the Great
	Sho Kwannon[45]
	  (Avolokiteśvara)
	Nyoirin Kwannon[46]
	  (Cintamanikacra)
	Martin Luther
	Albert Einstein
	Wolfgang Mozart
		(Seven Sages) Thales
		Michelangelo
		Charles Darwin
		Nobunaga Oda[47]
		Priest Ikkyu[48]

The Archangel Gabriel	Alighieri Dante S.A. Kierkegaard	Franz Schubert George Byron Arthur Schopenhauer
The Archangel Panuel	Plato Isaac Newton Karl von Linne George J. Mendel	D.I. Mendeleev Robert Boyle Carlo Abogadro
The Archangel Raguel	Hermes Socrates Prince Shotoku René Descartes	Maximilien Robespierre
The Archangel Sariel	Artemis Amaterasu Omikami Marie Curie Princess Yaśodharā Albert Schweitzer	Moggallāna Philip (The Twelve Desciples) Joan D'Arc Louis Pasteur
The Archangel Uriel	Ares Susano-o-no- Mikoto[49] Abraham Lincoln Ko Shu Zen (Hong Xiuquan) Sun Wen[50]	Sāriputra Yoshitsune Minamoto[51] Mitsuhide Akechi[52] Toshizo Hijikata[53] Benjamin Franklin Franklin Roosevelt John F. Kennedy

Name	Primary Body (Hontai)	Subsequent Body (Bunshin)
The Archangel Raphael	Kālidāsa Aesop Leonardo Da Vinci William Shakespeare William Wordsworth	Yoritomo Minamoto[54] Hideyoshi Toyotomi[55] Grimm the Elder F.M. Dostoevsky Soseki Natsume[56] Ogai Mori[57]
Daniel	Kanzo Uchimura[58]	
Karuel	F.W. Nietzsche	
Paruel	Daniel Rutherford	
Aruel	Soji Okita[59]	
Luciel	Lucifer	
Ceriel	Sei Shonagon[60]	
Mayell	Santa Margarita A.N. Tolstoy	
Luriel	Santa Catherine Lady Murasaki[61]	
Liliel	Florence Nightingale	
Saiel	Nicanor (New Testament)	
Mariel	Michael Farraday	
Fudo Myo-o (Acala)	King Aśoka	

Note: "*Hontai*" means the main or primary body which was entered by the soul whose name is written in the left-hand column. "*Bunshin*" (see definition in Chapter VI) indicates the subsequent body entered by the soul (as indicated in the middle column) after death, viz., a spirit brother of people of the Celestial Realm. Included within "*bunshin*" are some historically 'unsavory' persons because their "subsequent bodies" lacked the strength of the "primary body." Those spirits presently on earth are not listed because of the confusion regarding those spirits in the GLA which entered human bodies. Whosoever may be merged in humans, it is sufficient that they live and teach the True Law, taking heed not to induce the Time of Destruction.

CHAPTER 7

Beyond Blind Faith
(The heart that walks the Middle Road)

By Mitsuho Hirota

Impulses

I am not so pretentious as to call this writing an essay; it is more
a diversion of my pen, written spontaneously without specific
purpose. It was not my intention to write anything academic,
I only thought to avoid the usual faults of purely random writings
by treating the essentials with precision and clarity.

Five years ago, I received a complimentary copy of the August
issue of the GLA's monthly journal from the Association's
headquarters. Surprised by the unexpected gift, I wondered,
without result, who might have given them my name. Un-
doubtedly, someone had suggested me, but, the matter was not
important and I soon forgot about it.

Later I learned the person's name. It was a woman of Sasebo,
whom I shall call *O* . . . , a reader of a monthly magazine to
which I contributed. It seems that she had entered the GLA
soon after its inception, and on a certain occasion, she, *O*, had
been asked for a list of names of well-known teachers. My name
was somehow included among those on her list.

[171]

Later, I learned many things from Shinji Takahashi through his writings and lectures, thanks to the intervention of *O*. As long as I feel obligated to reciprocate Shinji Takahashi's kindnesses, I shall never forget *O*'s thoughtfulness.

But, *O* is more-or-less a woman of moods. If the daughter of the GLA's founder, Takahashi *sensei*, adopts the name of Michael, *O* is the type to applaud enthusiastically. And, this is what *O* is doing at present. I am a person who comes to conclusions by the application of the every-day logic of the third dimension, our physical world. Inevitably, intellectual judgement prevails with me. Unfortunately, there seem to be differences in what she and I are saying. But, despite differences of opinion, I believe her warmth of heart deserves consideration, and I await the time when she will come to understand the truth.

O is a person who never expresses anger. Or, rather, she has never once displayed any sign of anger toward me, so perhaps I may be justified in believing that she is noble of heart. She had a much longer contact than I with the warm heart of Takahashi *sensei*. And I am well aware that her ties with the GLA are much deeper than mine. A time comes, however, when people with the deepest ties are rather to be pitied, and I feel that it is my task to watch over the state of *O*'s warm heart.

The True Form of Kan Jizai Bosatsu[62] (Avalokiteśvara)

I received personal guidance from Takahashi *sensei* on one occasion only, that was about four years ago. When I asked again a half year later, Takahashi *sensei* had already suspended individual consultation, and he seemed to be extremely busy. I felt it unseemly to impose on him and I did not press my request for an audience.

I am now in a super-religious state of mind, a state which transcends sectarianism, even though originally I not only had close relations with Buddhism as a registered priest but also was so eccentric as to concurrently hold a rank in Shintoism. I consider myself to be thoroughly aware of Buddha's admonition to Buddhists to "Make the Law thy support." So, I solved my problem without bothering the man, Takahashi *sensei*. And when he died, the light in my heart neither failed nor flickered, nor did I feel lonely, or bereaved. I had attained calm resignation and a degree of composure of the mind, at least that's how I felt at the time.

The first book of Shinji Takahashi with which I came in contact was "Fundamental Teachings of the *Hannya Shingyo*[63] (Prajñāpāramitā-sutra)." Frankly speaking, there were passages in his basic commentary which I considered odd. These passages seem to me, as a professional theologian, to require correction, and I feel inclined to write on the subject for future generations. But this is a technical matter not appropriate to treat in full detail here. But, there was one point in Takahashi *sensei*'s writing which impressed me very favorably, namely that he did not treat Kan Jizai Bosatsu (Avalokiteśvara) as being indistinguishable from Kwannon (the Goddess of Mercy.)

About ten years ago, I learned through Yoga that the concept Kan Jizai Bosatsu signifies the "disciplinant who has reached a state of being able to see actuality." A disciplinant is one who seeks after truth, and I have thought this is the true definition of Bosatsu (Bodhisattva or Saint). There was no doubt in my mind of the truth of this viewpoint, although I never once met anyone who advanced this interpretation. Then, last year, when Seiko Wada *Sensei* came to Japan from America, he, through my good offices, had a book published on the subject of *Hannya kyo* (Prajñāpāramitā-sutra) by the Kasumigaseki Publishing Company, in which he advanced the same argument as mine. My confidence was strengthened.

When Yakichi Nakajima *sensei,* leader of the main Tokyo church of the *Kurozumi* sect called on Wada *Sensei* at the Imperial Hotel, Mr. Wada was not in his room, but Shinji Takahashi was there with a woman who was evidently a medium. Someone later told me that Wada *sensei* also received various kindnesses from Takahashi *sensei.* It is possible, since both held the same theory about Kan Jizai Bosatsu as myself that one of them adopted the idea from the other. It is impossible to say which *sensei* influenced the other, but they undoubtedly discussed this matter. It is also interesting to note that Wada *sensei* and I both received our enlightenment about Kan Jizai Bosatsu through the practice of Yoga. For this reason, I feel it more likely that Takahashi *sensei* got the idea from Dr. Wada.

Shiki (Color) Is Not Materialism

Color [*Shiki* or *Iro* (Japanese), rupa (Sanskrit)] is thought by many Buddhist scholars to be the same thing as materialism. But in ancient India there probably did not yet exist a concept parallel to modern materialism. As is generally known, India was a land of philosophy and religion, and one cannot treat of India distinct from its philosophy and religion. Religious ideology governed people's daily lives, and many words originating in religious circles persisted and went into common usage.

I believe the word color (rupa) was a term relating to *zenjo* (dhyāna), signifying not matter of things per se but the "sense of being bound to the material world." It is not surprising that the phrase "Color is the heart" appears in the ancient Indian Upanishad, as has been so well pointed out by Mr. Tetsuro Watsuji.

There is another word, *shikiun* (the collective sensualities), which is one of the five "collections" or categories of human capacity to live or exist. This terms also indicates clearly that rupa or color is a spiritual phenomenon.

The *Hannya Shingyo* is no more than an explanation of the spiritual state of "free penetration of the others' mind and power of salvation of the wretched" (Kan Jizai) as this concept is stated in the passage *Go Un Kaiku*, meaning "All the five categories of human experience are as naught."

Therefore, such passages as "Color is naught; naught is color" or "Color equals emptiness; emptiness equals color" are not references to the material or sensual world itself but of a spiritual state of existence; in other words they refer to the sensual dimension of the five categories. There is not one present day Buddhist scholar who has discerned this truth, and *"Shikiun"* is described as material existence in all the Buddhist texts, even including dictionaries. Perhaps it was because of such influences, that even Takahashi *sensei*, the author of *Fundamental Teachings of the Hannya Shingyo*, repeated this mistake.

As further proof, if we read the lines of the *Hannya Shingyo* Sutra following "Color equals emptiness; emptiness equals color," we find that the other four *"Un"* or categories of human capacity are defined similarly: "Moreover, acceptance (*Ju*), conception (*So*), conduct (*Gyo*), and wisdom (*Shiki*) are likewise." Please note that the Chinese character *"Un"* is obreviated in the above passage.

"Un" has from ancient times been interpreted as meaning "a collection." One might think of it as the load which gradually accumulates in the soul. Thus, the materialistic concepts which bind us are the actual shape of "color" or the sensual aspect. The *Hannya Shingyo* only repeats, elaborates and emphasizes this theme. The weakness of this sutra is that it fails to provide a

concrete way of attaining a penetrative freedom beyond these bounds, as Shinji *sensei* has said so well.

Over-emphasis of the Fourth Dimension

On reading Takahashi *sensei*'s *Fundamental Teachings of the Hannya Shingyo*, I felt that book did not, on the whole, go beyond the explanations of a scientist. For this reason among others, the book did not receive much attention from Buddhists and I know of no reviews of it in Buddhist journals. I feel that Takahashi *sensei*'s interpretation presents a sterile viewpoint because it is not related to "*Satori*" or enlightenment. From ancient times Buddhism has never commented on material things, and has avoided inquiring into matters outside those directly related to "*kokoro*," the soul. Because Buddhism has always been restricted to problems of "*kokoro*," it has been called the "inner road." I would like both scientists and Buddhist scholars to keep this basic truth in mind.

Now, Takahashi *sensei* was a scientist. And, although one is bound to admire his calm, detached mind, unfortunately he was not always scientifically detached in his investigations of psychic phenomena. There is an appalling weakness in his approach to the fourth dimension (spiritual world). That he never questioned mediumistic happenings indicates that he sometimes forgot the scientific spirit. Looking back, it now seems that he did not concern himself deeply enough with spiritual phenomena.

Whether he or she speaks in an unknown language or in Japanese, the words coming from a medium, when possessed by a spirit, are invariably spoken in the first person.

But the medium often does not know exactly to whom the word "I" really refers. The medium does not know whether the speaker is his or her guiding spirit or guardian spirit or a phenomenon of temporary possession. It is essential that a person erudite in spiritual seeing be present as a *Saniwa* (monitor). Unless such precautions are taken, one will encounter many spirits like those of the ancient Priest Nichiren, or King Bimbisāra.

For instance, if one first puts boiling water into a kettle then tepid water, the boiling water and tepid water will pour out of the same spout so that they can not be distinguished. In the same way, a strange consciousness on entering one's body fuses with one's own consciousness, and when one says "I," one's own consciousness which still clings to the third dimension, the contemporary physical world, the medium may believe that the voice exclusively to he or she alone. One cannot avoid the feeling that the probing of such matters by the GLA has been inadequate.

A concrete instance is the entering into Takahashi *sensei*'s daughter of a spirit called Michael. Assuming she had contact with that spirit at that one time, the next question is to what extents?

Takahashi *sensei*'s daughter is said to be a reincarnation of a famed medium of ancient Japan, Queen Himiko of Yamatai Koku (The Land of Yamatai). That she is naturally gifted is a matter which even I will not deny. But, recently she has become vain and has deluded herself that she is Michael. This is a phenomenon of mingled consciousness or confusion of identities, and a type of witchcraft to which mediums are most susceptible. Thus, she now argues that Himiko was only historical data in her mind, and not a past incarnation. And she has begun to assert that she is the Archangel Michael, come to earth in physical form for the first time in 365 million years. Such is the process by which people with inadequate discipline are manipulated by their own mediumistic phenomena, and lost their sense of modesty.

The Doubts about Michael

Takahashi *sensei* often held demonstrations of spiritual phenomena on lecture stages, using the expression "My daughter will cause Michael to enter her." But if she were Michael (i.e. if Michael were her co-soul), he ought to have said that she would cause Michael to appear or come forth. It would appear that, in his deeper consciousness, Takahashi *sensei* did not think his daughter was a reincarnation of Michael.

In his last years, Takahashi *sensei* suffered from high blood pressure, and had much blood drawn. As a result, his kidneys malfunctioned and he finally died. As is generally known, overwork was also a contributing factor. Frankly, both his body and soul were in an extreme state of exhaustion. Thus his theological weakness, a liking for communication with the fourth dimension, became a fatal defect when combined with other unfavorable circumstances. If he erred in confusing his daughter with Michael, it happened during the course of his last illness, and I feel it was excusable. But this is not a minor affair and it cannot be dismissed as a mere blemish on his life's work.

I believe that neither mediumistic speech nor vision is something which can be heard or seen simply by the powers of the person acting as the medium. In the realms of spiritualism, there are individual spirits who can bring the medium to both see and hear by their will power and communicative abilities. To communicate we on earth must also have prepared all the necessary preconditions for seeing and hearing. Communication between our world and the spiritual world is not possible by one-sidedly causing the other party to speak.

Thus, under any circumstances, we on earth are in the position of being allowed to see or being caused to hear: we are subject to the will or force of the consciousness of the other party, namely that of the spirit from the other dimension. It is sufficient if we have prepared the conditions to receive the communication. It is a very grave error to fall under the delusion that the spirits one may see or hear are immediately connected to one because of one's kinship with them, without any conditional endorsements or assertions by the spiritual world.

One should also realize that strange unknown spirits may manipulate one's consciousness at their whim, even in respect to choosing the means and manner of the communication. Even if one is convinced that one has gained a certain enlightenment by oneself as a result of deeply integrational training, one must understand that there is a real possibility one has been caused to believe thus by the power of another's will.

The above discussion indicates that trouble is invited when one adopts too simple a view of communication with the fourth dimension, i.e. celestial or spiritual realms. At the GLA, the spirit of investigation was lacking. The fact that the lecturers of the GLA behaved as though they were out of their minds, indicates that they were, in fact manipulated by Satanical powers calling themselves Michael, which demonstrates that Takahashi *sensei*'s teaching on approaching the matters of the spirit was inadequate. And the GLA inherited this ill-fate or Karma.[64]

The Importance of Knowing the Law

Takahashi *sensei* taught that one should not accept even his teaching blindly, and that one should not only doubt but that one should pursue the study of such doubts until the truth is known. This is the true scientific attitude, and it should also be the basic attitude of those who follow or study the True Law. All would have been well if the GLA had pursued this principle. It is the foolish, blind acceptance of Takahashi *Sensei*'s word that inevitable caused this deviation from the True Law. The GLA is presently a congregation of blind believers, and there are even signs of mass insanity.

Before Buddha entered Nirvana, he admonished his followers to "Base your faith on the Law, not on man." The GLA has held on to the blind belief that Takahashi *sensei*'s daughter was Michael, failing to realize that that was a delusion. Somehow, they are presently following the creed of "Base your faith on Man, not the Law," in direct contradiction to the teachings of Buddha. One might say that the Law is non-existent in this institution. The Law is something we must each discover and fix in our hearts. No one else can do this for us. One may discover the Law in various ways in our daily life: training can all be done in the context of family life. There is nothing easier. On the other hand, comprehension of the Law is impossible to those who lack the desire to understand. No matter how many years pass, they will not even catch a glimpse of the Law. Those who place their faith in things outside the heart will develop naught but a spirit of dependence, and they will never make the Law their own.

The spiritual training of a man must be done in our third dimension, the phenomenal world. If one is an immortal or hermit, perhaps one can perform religious devotions deep in the mountains in their remote valleys. But if one pursues knowledge to attain true fulfillment as a man, solitary devotions done with a bias to intellectuality will not suffice for this purpose. More than that, it is most improper to demand or seek psychic powers. When one enters psychic practice before his or her spiritual training is equal to the task, evil spirit often enter the windows of the soul and assume control. This is what has occurred at the GLA.

I pray that readers of Miss Chino's writings also evaluate them on the basis of the wisdom of the third dimension, our contemporary world. If her words conform to the True Law, however mystical they may be, somehow they will be natural and unforced. Then, readers will be able to discover the True Law through this volume, and it will have performed an admirable role as basic study material.

The selection of material from this book must be left to the reader. But I would suggest that you avoid too partial, scientific judgements or negation of whatever you may not understand.

Acquirement of Psychic Powers by Oneself

I have conversed with the writer of this text, Miss Yuko Chino, a number of times, but I have actually visited her home only once. My first impression on meeting her was that she was earnest almost to a fault. At the same time, she was not lacking in a sense of humor, and quite natural, without either an obverse or a reverse side . . . a person in whom one could place one's trust.

This spring, I received a telephone call from this slight acquaintance, Miss Chino. She said there was a family living at Hamanako Lake she wished to help. There had been no reply to her letter. She asked my opinion about having the GLA send these people the institution's journal each month. Subsequently, there was another telephone call, similar as to its contents, and reporting that the situation of the people at Hamanako remained unchanged. I had no advice to give her, so I answered at random as I listened. But, because I spoke decisively and clearly, I might have made an impression on her. It seems that the mutual feeling of spiritual kinship began here.

About two months later, I received another telephone call from Miss Chino on a different matter. She reported that she felt on the verge of an "opening of the spiritual way," or the gaining of psychic powers. Then, she called again a little later to say that the "opening" had occurred. But, as I listened on the telephone to a communication with her by Takahashi *sensei*, the spiritual waves seemed to me very weak and indefinite, and when I put down the telephone I was aware of certain misgivings. Some days later she telephoned again and seemed to have in the meantime regained her vitality; I heard her being sick but otherwise she sounded in good health. On this occasion the waves I received were imbued with spiritual warmth, and I decided to listen to her. After this, we had a number of talks during which I realized she merited serious attention.

Communications from Heaven

Miss Chino gradually began to talk about the True Law to several high school students during English lessons. Strangely, a number of students showed interest and comprehension, and the class became a sort of a place for development of the soul. As a direct result of Miss Chino's teaching, several students actually gained psychic powers, enabling them to receive messages from the Celestial Realms.

Another happening which must be recorded is that not only Miss Chino, but a Miss *T* and two other high school students, almost without exception, shed gold granules or flakes whenever they perspire. They gathered some of these and sent me specimens. Evidently, these gold flakes are no longer unique to the

GLA. It seems that Takahashi *Sensei* and his younger sister, Yoko Hoshi *Sensei*, often emitted these golden granules or flakes. Again, although there is no connection with the GLA, a pupil of Mrs. Katsue Uchihashi of Kobe also produced golden granules while at Singapore.

Among the girl high school students of Miss Chino is a 16 year old girl with superior spiritual or mediumistic powers; though discussions about the accuracy of her powers are heated. I think that in her case, the spirit's will or consciousness is not mediated in the form of a direct quote or translation, but in the form of a free translation conveying the spirit's meaning. In the event of meaning translations, the voice need not sound like the spirit's voice, nor would peculiarities of speech be imitated in detail. So, one ought to abstain from hastily negating mediumistic phenomena simply because they are not in the form of direct translations of a spirit's speech.

To pose on extremely hypothetical situaion, were Amaterasu Omikami to use as a medium a woman from Northeastern Japan, it would not negate the phenomenon if she were to voice her message in the dialect peculiar to that area. It is perfectly proper for a medium to speak in her usual everyday manner. Therefore, if a spirit uses as a medium a person who speaks roughly, even the words of the Gods will seem unrefined in transmission. Technically, it would become a problem as to what extent one can act as an intermediate in communicating the will and thought of the spirits. Generally, spirits will not use as a medium a human being whose ideology is completely alien.

For instance, about twenty years ago, while reading an account of Dr. Kakei's lecture about Empress Jomyo, my appreciation of the doctor's concept of the world as trinary deepened progressively. Then, I began to extend his ideas or apply them in other directions, thus gaining understanding beyond the scope of Dr. Kakei's writing. I made charts and drawings which aided my enlightenment, and the added enlightenment enabled me to write more. This continued for some days. Although I was not sick, I was kept in bed as the phenomena continued. In such circumstances, communication is not possible from a spirit of a radically different type. Invariably, messages came from sources with a common ideology. This indicates that communication is limited to those situations in which the receiver is in a receptive state.

Spirit Language Comes Forth Simply

Since I was twenty years old when I studied under a pilgrim ascetic, dhārani[65]—esoteric speech—comes forth from me at random intervals. A characteristic of such speech is that, after the first happening, it may occur without reference to time or place. Moreover, the style and nature of such esoteric speech is not always identical. Its sources are ordinary passages of sutra, so it is natural there should occur variations depending on time and place. There are strange variations in cadence and the voice may be soft unlike usual Buddhist chants.

There is nothing unusual about speech in spirit tongues. Of course, one cannot understand the meaning of the words, so I never became intensely concerned. But, because I feel my role in life is that of an author, I resolved that I should have a certain actual experience of spiritualism in order to write. I did not go beyond this point. I am not the type of person to become a medium. I believe that if spiritualistic phenomena were to appear in me, they would materialize in my written work. Now, I write easily when spirits cause me to do so. There is little if anything lost in the writing. And when I have finished writing what is necessary, worded suitably, my pen stops naturally.

The phenomena of spiritualist communication is not the mere use of foreign speech without understanding it, as is practiced by the GLA when Miss *S* visited me from Okabe City, I brought out various charts and drawings based on Shintoism[66] to explain my concept of the world. She is indeed a spiritual medium, and she recognized, to my satisfaction, what I had drawn to be clearly of psychic phenomena. When I visited Mr. *T* in Kyoto the psychic waves emitted by this person, while talking about Love, went beyond being warm and fervent. Rather they produced reflected, images to coldness. On that occasion, I heard that Mr. *N* of Eastern Osaka had been warned by Takahashi about Mrs. Katsue Uchihashi of Kobe, but I found myself reluctant to believe this warning. That night, I stayed with Mr. Ikko Haba at Takarazuka. The next morning, I sought his advice, and we left the house together to see her.

This person, who lived in an apartment in the Tsuruko housing area appeared to be a normal house wife. But during our first telephone conversation, suddenly she began to speak in a strange tongue to my great surprise. So I went to visit her having resolved not to allow myself to be shocked under any circumstances. This time too, when she was asked questions that were too difficult, or when emotionally excited, she began to speak in this spirit language, continuing for several minutes before she reverted to ordinary Japanese. During our talk, this occurred several times.

This person taught me much about the meaning of Love. As a Buddhist, I knew only about compassion, so I had never before felt such kinship with the teachings of Christ. The psychic waves of a warm heart came through to me. I wondered how the GLA could single out this person and regard her as a heretic. Her attitudes in her daily living were fine. Her personality was much warmer than that of Mr. *T* the previous day.

After a while, she told me to sit in front of her. So, I sat facing her, quite close. Then she began to speak in the spirit language in a higher-than-soprano voice, in her own particular manner. Her speech was wonderfully impressive. Continuing to sit in Japanese fashion, I intently began to make mudrā or Buddhist symbolic gestures with my fingers. These came forth one after the other, without ceasing in many forms. At the same time, her voice changed; the tones were drawn out like a chant of the esoteric Tendai sect. Finally, it changed as if she were finishing some sort of recital. After a pause, I began to pose *Zen* (dhyāna) questions or catechism in spiritualistic speech. The catechism was repeated several times. Mrs. Uchihashi also began to use the same sort of words. This lasted about twenty minutes.

A Deeply Engraved Memory

The two of us finished our psychic session at exactly the same moment. There was not an instant or a second difference.

I do not know the content of his catechism. But, I was truly filled with a feeling of mocking at myself, "How could I try this sort of thing at this stage of life." The reason of such self-mockery is that during my training in Yoga, I often reflected with deep interest that, in a past incarnation in India, I did not live an ordinary person's life but ended my days as an itinerant wandering ascetic. So, I know that it would benefit me none to re-enact a behavior that is deeply engraved in my conceptual zone as a relica of my past life. To attempt to do again what one has already known and forsaken is meaningless. In my present life, I have a family, and my major purpose is to regain the true aspect of man. I felt that there was no need for me perform such feats for vanity's sake. But feeling that way, still I did it.

When I next travelled to Tokyo, I visited Kwannonji Temple and asked a priest Rev. Yukai Murakami to listen to the tape of my session with Mrs. Uchihashi. After listening for seven or eight minutes, he exclaimed "I understand it." What I had thought were Tendai sect chants were Sanscrit chants, thought to be the prototype for Buddhist singing. What she sang was an excerpt from the Veda. And he said also that the words of the *Mondo* (catechism) I spoke were uttered by a spirit brother of Shakyamuni which preceded him by three hundred years. Rev. Murakami added that, during his visit to Taiwan, a Mr. Lin uttered the same words. I had been told by Takahashi that my original existence was as a Brahman, so this explanation somehow seemed reasonable. When I was told by Takahashi "You were born in a former existence at a place in India called Vaiśālī during the time of Shakyamuni," I felt an acute electric-like shock in my left leg, and something like chills. Shinji laughed and said, "No, that is not a chill." Then he spread out an old map of India and pointed out the place. It evidently was an ancient merchant center rather like Osaka in Japan where many wandering ascetics gathered. It also was the birthplace of the Jain religion and of its founder Mahāvīra. Another person, not to be forgotten, is Vimalākīrti (*Yuima Koji*[67] in Japanese). Little is known of his life, but I surmise he must have been close to Shakyamuni's religious fellowship though not a true member. Although it is not clear that he was a disciple of Buddha, he probably met Buddha and received his teaching.

I have further thought that Vimalākīrti may have been a critical observer or surveillant of Shakyamuni's religious fellowship. There is an interesting contrast between Shakyamuni who left household to become a religious ascetic and Vimalākīrti who was a layman and a householder. When one assumes temporarily a position of opposition to perform censorship, one soon knows whether or not the other person has errored.

In the same way, I am able to criticize Takahashi who was a layman, because I am a professional theologian, who left the world to take religious orders. For instance, as I wrote earlier, when Takahashi errored in interpreting the *Hannya Shingyo*, I, because I am a theologist, noticed his error. And now, I am one of the earlier people to notice and comment on the fact that *sensei*'s daughter had adapted a mistaken course. I have closed my liaison place and have ceased to lecture. When I adapted, as a single individual, a rebel's way of life, I had resolved to give up all worldly things if necessary. On reflection, I could not see any actual advantage in this for me. That I felt nevertheless impelled to this action seemed to show that there was some reason or need originating in the chain of karma from my past existences. I am not completely blind to the meaning of Rev. Yukai Murakami's admonition, "You believe you are doing the writing yourself. But this is not so. You are, rather, being made to write." He also said, "How are you? You seemed to have gained faith." But, fortunately, my burgeoning confidence came from actual experience in such living, having left the institution of my own will.

The Function of Reason

I have also analyzed fortune telling. I know little of palm reading. The intelligence line passes through the middle of my left hand. I do not have a specialist's knowledge of the significance of the lines of the left hand, which are said to shown congenital traits. But, if one divides such traits into three categories . . . intelligence, feeling, and consciousness, it appears that my feelings

have not developed very richly. When I consider matters philo-
sophically, then turn to their immediate practice, I feel there
is danger in acting only on the bases of intellect and will without
feeling. Comparatively, intellect probably is that sector in which
I have most self-confidence.

I must make up for areas of weakness by proper training in
the future. This truly requires lengthy training and devotions.
When one becomes too involved in matters of the intellect, one
becomes fond of studies, and estranged from wordly affairs.
But one's feelings dry up and one's heart is unresponsive to the
sight of flowers along the road. This is an example of what hap-
pens when one strays too far from the Middle Road. Takahashi's
younger sister discovered the cross-sectional chart which I
learned at the GLA. I learned much from this chart.

I do not feel the following is important but Takahashi read
the word *Nyorai* or Tathagata as *"Kitaru gotoki"* or Just as the
Way of Coming. The interpretation seems inescapably strange
to me. The Sanskrit word, Tathagata, does not mean "Just as
the Way of Coming." It rather means "Coming from Just as
This," and defines a world or realm unexplainable further. This
is because it can be known only by actually experiencing it.
Scholars of commentaries on Buddhist sutras, thinking there to
be a tendency to error in reading the Chinese, have sometimes
prefixed the Chinese character for *Shin*[68] (Jap.) or True to *Nyo*[68]
or *Gotoshi* (as). This did not exist in the original Sanskrit.

There is also a strange explanation of the word *Hannya Hara-
mitta* (Prajñāpāramitā). The Chinese characters are selected to
approximate phonetically the Indian, without reference to
meaning. But scholars have taken the word *Haramitta* to mean
literally, "much honey," which item is scarce in India. That
this is not a correct interpretation should be obvious even to those
not students of Buddhism.

The High Priest of Tendai, (Chigi) was the outstanding scholar among commentators on Chinese texts, but one can find a number of humorous interpretations. Shinji also made similar errors, seemingly a habitual trait of interpretation.

Return to the Origin of Buddhism

Despite all, Takahashi's contribution to Buddhist study was that he returned to the religion's origins. Today, the Eight-fold Noble Paths have found new life and vitality. He provides guidance to correct meditation with the discovery that *Zenjo*[69] (dhyāna) mainly emphasizes contemplation, and that there is no other way of the spiritual principle but contemplation to purify body and soul. Moreover, he distinguishes between contemplation and meditation and emphasizes that it is dangerous for those not yet sufficiently advanced in contemplation to perform meditation. Ancient holy men did not point out these facts.

Neither the Hīnayāna (the Little Vehicle) nor the Mahāyāna (the Greater Vehicle) faction of Buddhism are correct, both having departed from the original meaning of Shakyamuni's teachings. There has been added too much dross in later times. The only true Buddhism is that taught by Shakyamuni himself, namely original Buddhism. I believe that Buddhism must do away with its numerous sects and return to its original teachings. Takahashi used as little technical religious terminology as possible in his work, and taught in plain, everyday language. To me, this evidenced effectively the holy man who had come to understand the True Law and the principles of the Gods.

I have, till now, made various criticisms of Takahashi. But when something stirs the lute strings of my heart, any clouds, or mist—unresolved doubts—all melt away. No matter how holy a man may be, he can not be absolutely perfect when he is born to live in the flesh in this world. In the human body, ninty percent of one's will or consciousness remains dormant inside while only ten percent comes to the surface. This provides most people with an important hint.

I believe one may be allowed to accept the good and dismiss the bad in a man's life. This is needed for all of us. If one adopts a modest attitude, one may vie with the sages of old. The books left by Takahashi should provide the light from Heaven. The religious organization he left may be led by his successors into twisted paths, or if some in headquarters may misuse it for personal ends. In such event, if reconstruction is not practicable, perhaps the group should be dissolved. I believe such would be the way of those who truly seek to practice the Eight-fold Noble Paths.

Note

When I read that section of Hirota's manuscript treating of the "*Gensetsu Hannya Shingyo* (Fundamental Explanation of the Prajñāpāramitā Sutra)," I recalled those times when Satan beseiged me and I called for Shinji's spirit to drive out the evil spirits. There is a small prayer booklet entitled *Shingyo* (i.e. acts of the heart) compiled by *Sensei*. Afterwards, he writes in his book when his soul left while alive, and ascended to the Celestial Realm, the same text, identical in every words, was there in Heaven. The phrase "*Shingyo*" was a prayer to exorcise possessing demons. At times Shinji sent "force waves" to sustain me, we would often talk together. And, lest we be confused by the deceits of evil spirits, Shinji taught me this favorite phrase of the Prajñā-pāramitā Sutra which we used as a password. When I talked with Shinji or we recited some verses from the "*Hannya Shingyo*

Sutra," I would look at his face as it appeared on the reverse cover of one of his books. He appeared gentle, smiling, and glowing with spiritual light, and I always felt safe. Thus, I look back now even on the days of my struggle with the demons with some nostalgia.

The people of the Celestial Realms are not at all basically different to us of this world in their thoughts or their consciousness. They are not at all like our usual image of spirits or ghosts. Of course, they do not have the vices of the third dimension; they are all wise, just and delightful to know. Of course, this is not true of the evil spirits, nor those of the fourth dimension of Limbo, nor even the fifth dimension or the Realm of Spirits (*Rei-kai*).

Hirota and Nakano often say that, no matter how high the Celestial Realm to which one may belong, one must not ignore the people of our mundane world and live only with the people of Heaven. I find all people different and interesting whether they be earth dwellers or celestials. But, one can learn more from the celestial than from the usually more limited and narrow minded inhabitants of our world.

Among my favorite phrases of the "*Hannya Shingyo*" are the two following, as translated into English:

1. To the far bank,
    To the bank beyond,
    Let us go to the far bank,
    Priests and nuns,
    Reaching the far bank of Enlightenment,
    Let us achieve all things.
(gate gate pāragate pāra-saṃgate bodhi svāhā.—Sanskrit)
2. To attain the mighty wisdom,
    That lies within—
    The knowledge of the soul.

(prajñā-paramitā-hṛdaya-sūtra—Sanskrit)

To me, the meanings contained in these phrases and the musical sound in recitation is most beautiful. Lastly, Hirota wrote this last chapter using Shinji's original dissertations used by the GLA, before he had read the text of the revised theory. Reference to the revised theory in Chapter VI of this book is suggested.

The Author

Author's Notes

I would like to present before the readers an amazing material discovered just a month ago, in relation to the content of this book.

As a medium, I was given spiritualistic capacities only two years ago from a Messenger of Heaven, the Chief Archangel Michael. As a successor to Shinji Takahashi and his teachings, I have introduced with the most rational and scientific interpretations possible all that the Holy Messengers elucidated before me. Shinji Takahashi also conveyed everything, believable or not, that had been taught him by Jehovah, Buddha, Jesus, Moses and Michael to his followers. Just before his death, he was told the names of the other six archangels besides Michael, their duties and the existence of the Kingdom of Heaven.

I received the same calling to spread the Law from the same archangels and, in spite of my illness, I have issued three editions of the books on Heaven, with the best analyzation and rational conclusions to reach that I was capable of, containing all that was revealed to me by the people of Heaven and that have occurred around me on earth.

The readers of the books, who were greatly moved and inspired, gathered to study more of the *Shoho*, the True Law, the Grace of Heaven. They have become groups of enlightenment, not to become advocators of any religious movement, but to criticize religion. Heaven now questions the ways and means of all the existing religions adopted on earth. The gods question the motives of the increasing number of religious groups and sects, not to mention those established great religions which have not contributed much toward the salvation of the world as a whole. Moreover, Heaven ordains the dissolution of all groups, sects and institutions currently at work in the world in the name of religion.

What the Holy Messengers, the archangels, tell us to be the Will and Desire of Heaven has been manifested in numerous miracles and phenomena. The greatest of such heavenly testimonies graced upon us, the followers of *Shoho*, has been the biblical material mentioned in the beginning.

Shinji Takahashi, who was quite an outsider to Christianity, knew little of the Bible. I was a Christian, but in truth, all that I had studied were some parts of the New Testament at Bible classes. Deeply moved, however, by the truths in the Bible, I used to read favorite verses at home. But the sermons at church were mostly like lullabies, as the ministers' interpretations, for want of depth of philosophy and insight, failed to appeal to me. My days were spent in indifference to any scholarly study of the Bible. The only name of the archangels in my memory was Gabriel, having overlooked Michael. In short, neither Shinji nor I was familiar with the seven archangels, not having had any chance for learning their names.

Toward the end of June, six months after publication of the third volume of the Kingdom of Heaven series, *Under the Light of Heaven*, Mr. Nishizawa, the leader of the *Shoho* group of Tokyo, made the great discovery, as described in his appended letter. Through him, we came to know, you may believe it or not, for the first time, that the names of the Seven Archangels were clearly printed in the Biblical Dictionary and in the Apocrypha and the Pseudepigrapha of the Old Testament in the light of the Aramaic Dead Sea Fragments. So history itself is the greatest witness to Heaven, the Celestial World we are now in close communication with.

The excerpts from the English translation of the *Ethiopic Book of Enoch* are also given for those who are ignorant of the biblical books, just as I was. The veracity of the *Shoho*, which Shinji Takahashi expounded and is now being propagated by me, is thus proven by the sacred heavenly truths contained in the Apocrypha and Pseudepigrapha, which were compiled by the Jews and their churches one to two centuries before the birth of Christ the Savior. No one can deny this, not the preachers of Christian churches, Judaism, Islamism, Buddhism, or any other new religious groups, as their sects.

The reader may and can have thorough trust and faith in the content of this book and the volumes to follow. You will realize this from the two appended recommendations to the library which endorse the "Heaven" series as the "Modern Bible" or the "Sutra for the Modern Age." I would rather call them the "Modern Apocrypha."

Appendix

July 17th, 1979

Dear Ms. Chino,

I hear that you are very busy. I am terribly sorry that I cannot be of any assistance to you. I was glad to read Michael's epistle on the Five Books of Enoch.

I found out in the *Shin-Seisho-Dai-Jiten* (The New Biblical Dictionary) at the city library on June 29th that the names of the seven Archangels appear in the Book of Enoch (please refer to the xeroxed pages). I spoke of this to our members gathered on July 1st. Mr. Iwama was greatly moved by this and took me to a second-hand book-shop which specializes in Christian books. He bought a copy of the Apocrypha (4) and the pseudepigrapha (II) of the Old Testament which he had xeroxed and sent to you. He also offered me a copy as a wedding gift. (The books are published by Kyobunkan.)

According to the shopkeeper, these are the only available translations of this series and there are seven volumes all together. As, however, the enclosed xeroxed pages show, the translation is rather incomplete. There are quite a lot of omissions.

The first edition came out in 1975, so it is fairly recent. The shopkeeper informed us that the Apocrypha and the Pseudepigrapha published by Kyobunkan and the Old Testament published by *Seikokai* (the Episcopal Church) are the only available ones in the country.

The Dictionary tells us that the only way to gain knowledge

of these would be through the English or the German translations. They seem to be known by only a few Christians in Japan.

Mr. Iwama also presented me with a copy of the Old Testament Pseudepigrapha. The book of Tobit tells us, "One of the Holy Messengers is Raphael." I was greatly impressed by this. Esdras II tells us, " . . . and the messenger was named Uriel." Chieko was very much moved by this. The reason for our being moved is that the Bible (published by the Japan Bible Society) records only two names: St. Michael and St. Gabriel.

The Book of Enoch records all the seven Archangels and they appear quite frequently which ought to be emphasized. I plan to find out how many other books record . . . .

The Book of Tobit includes a theme of St. Raphael which Raphael the artist used for his painting. I was much surprised to find this. Botticelli and Michelangelo had both painted based on material from the Book of Judith. In the field of music, Handel composed some works based on Maccabees II.

I spoke about Milton's *Paradise Lost* at our July 1st gathering. The epic records the name of four Archangels. I used to think that this was because Milton had gotten some kind of revelation, but now I have come to reconsider that he may have read the Apocrypha.

Paradise Lost notes St. Michael, St. Gabriel, St. Uriel, and St. Raphael.

At our July 1st gathering and July 15th high school students' meeting, I emphasized the Book of Enoch in the Old Testament Pseudepigrapha which records the seven names of the Archangels as being worth learning by heart. I spoke according to what is written in the xeroxed pages by Mr. Iwama. At the July 15th meeting I read Chapters 20 and 40 to the students where the names appear most frequently.

I plan to emphasize this fact once again before Mr. Miyoshi

speaks at the usual gathering (since I did not explain it thoroughly enough).

For the July 1st lecture on the Apocrypha and Pseudepigrapha, I used the enclosed xeroxed pages as other material.

Yours sincerely,

Tetsuhiko Nishizawa

P.S. Please receive the copied pages as a present.

The Ethiopic Book of Enoch

CHAPTER 9

9.1 And then Michael, Gabriel, Sariel, and Uriel looked down from Heaven and saw the mass of blood that was being shed on the earth and all the iniquity that was being done (2v, a20) on the earth. 9.2 And they said to one another: 'Let the devastated earth cry out with the sound of their cries unto the gate of Heaven. 9.3 And now, to you O holy ones of Heaven, the souls of men complain, saying: "Bring our suit before the Most High." 9.4 And they said (2v, a25) to their Lord, the King: 'Lord of Lords, God of Gods, King of Kings! *Your* glorious throne (endures) for all the generations of the world, and your name (is) holy and praised for all the generations of the world, and blessed and praised! (2v, a30) 9.5 You have made everything, and power over everything is yours. And everything is uncovered and open before you, and you see everything, and there is nothing which can be hidden from you. 9.6 See then what Azazel has done, how he has taught all iniquity on the earth and revealed the eternal secrets (2v, a35) which were made in Heaven. 9.7 And Semyaza has made known spells, (he) to whom you gave authority to rule over those who are with him. 9.8 And they went in to the daughters of men together, and lay with those women, and became unclean, and revealed to them these sins. 9.9 And the women bore giants, and thereby the whole earth has been filled (2v, b1) with blood and iniquity. 9.10

And now behold the souls which have died cry out and complain unto the gate of Heaven, and their lament has ascended, and they cannot go out in the face of the iniquity which is being committed (2v, b5) on the earth.   9.11 And you know everything before it happens, and you know this and what concerns each of them. But you saying nothing to us. What ought we to do with them about this?'

9. 1 And then Michael . . . and saw: Eth II (but Bodl 5² 2 MSS. add 'Raphael' after 'Gabriel'); Gr^Pan 'Then looking down, Michael, Uriel, Raphael, and Gabriel saw from heaven'; Gr^Sync a b 'And hearing (this), the four great archangels, Michael, Uriel, Raphael, and Gabriel, looked down on the earth from the sanctuary of heaven; and seeing'; cf. Aram^a₁ iv 6 f.

[רפאל ו . . . . .]   [אׄדיק מיכׄאׄ .]   6

‏מן קד .]   7

and ^b₁ iii 7 (fragment p) [כאל ושריאׄ . [. If the evidence of ^a₁ iv and ^b₁ iii is conflated, the list of angels in ^a₁ iv 6 may perhaps be restored מיכא]ל ושריאל ו [רפאל ו . . . . .] (cf. Milik, *HTR* 64 (1971), 346). But this restoration must remain a little uncertain. —For the list of names cf. 10. 1, 4, 9, 11, and c. 20.

the mass of blood that was being shed on the earth: Eth Gr^Pan Sync a b; cf. Aram^a₁ iv 7 דם סגי שפ]יׄך . [.

and all the iniquity . . . the earth: Eth; Gr^Pan omits (hmt.); Gr^Sync a b 'and all the impiety and iniquity that was being done on it'; cf. Aram^a₁ iv 7 f.

ו . ל] . [7

אתמלית .]   [חמסה דין   [טי . ליהׄן]   8

Aram does not correspond to either Eth or Gr^Sync a b, but for the text of Aram cf. Gen. 6: 11.

9. 2 And they said to one another: Eth Gr^Pan; Gr^Sync a b 'entering, they said to one another'; cf. Aram^a₁ iv 9 ואמרו קדמׄן] (possibly קדמׄן]).

Let the devastated earth . . . of heaven: Eth (for the use of the perfect optative, cf. Dillmann, *Ethiopic Grammar*, London, 1907, 520;

hereafter, Dillmann, *Grammar*); Gr[Pan] 'The sound of those who cry out
on the earth (reaches) unto the gates of heaven'; Gr[Sync a b] omit; cf.
Aram[a]1 iv 9 f.

[. לה ו]   [. ב]   9

10   תרעי שמי]ה

For the plural תרעי cf. BM 491 and Gr[Pan] (cf. also 9. 10).

9. 3 **And now . . . of heaven**: Eth II; Gr[Pan Sync a b] omit (by hmt.?).
Aram[a]1 iv 10]שׁי שׁ[, read as קדי[שׁי שׁ]מיה, appears to correspond to
Eth, but the evidence is not very strong.

the souls of men complain, saying: Eth Gr[Pan]; Gr[Sync a b] 'The
spirits and souls of men groan, complaining and saying'; cf. Aram[a]1 iv 11
די קבלן.

9. 4 **Lord of Lords, God of Gods, King of Kings**: Eth; Gr[Pan] 'You are
Lord of Lords, God of Gods, King of eternity!'; Gr[Sync a b] 'You are God
of Gods, Lord of Lords, King of Kings, God of Eternity!' (Gr[Sync b]
ανθρωπων from αιωνων read as ανπων; cf. Charles, *Text*, 20 f.); cf.

Aram[b]1 iii 14 (fragment w)]מרנא רבא[   ]א מרא עלמא[. There is
nothing in the versions corresponding to מרנא רבא, but for מרא עלמא cf.
Gr[Pan] 'King of eternity', Gr[Sync a b] 'God of eternity'. Cf. also 12. 3; 25. 3
(Gr[Pan]), 5 (Gr[Pan]), 7 (Gr[Pan]); 27. 3 (Gr[Pan]); 58. 4; 81. 10; 106. 11
(Gr[C B]); 1Q 20 2 5 (see Fitzmyer, *Genesis Apocryphon*, 77).

Your glorious throne . . . the world: Bodl 5 2 MSS. Gr[Pan Sync a b]; cf.
Aram[b]1 iii 15, 15a (fragment w)

לכל
]. יקרכ לדר דריא די מן עלמ]א .

(ל before דר has apparently been erased: read . . . דר לכל יקרך]כרסא(.

9. 8 **with those women**. ምስሌ[ን : ምስለ : እለ : እነሆ : reflects the
Aramaic construction עמהין עם נשׁיא exactly, and it is very difficult to
think that a Greek version served as the *Vorlage* of this phrase (cf.
Ullendorff, 'An Aramaic "Vorlage"?', 266). In fact Gr seems to have
misunderstood the construction and to have divided the two parts of the
assumed Aramaic original (cf. Charles, *Text*, pp. xxviii, 22). Both Gr[Pan]
and [Sync b] have here only 'with them'; Gr[Sync b] takes 'with the women'
with the next verb ('and have become defiled with the women'), but
Gr[Pan] omits the words altogether.

9. 11 **and what concerns each of them**: Eth (lit. 'and that of each of
them'); Gr[Pan Sync b] 'and you leave them alone'. Eth makes sense, but

Flemming (*Text*, 10) suggests that Eth derives from a misreading of
καὶ ἑᾷς αὐτούς as καὶ ἃ εἰς αὐτούς (cf. Charles, *Text*, 24 f.), and this is
certainly plausible.

CHAPTER 10

10.1 And then the Most High, the Great and Holy One, spoke
and sent (2v, b10) Arsyalalyur to the son Lamech, and said to
him: 10.2 'Say to him in my name "Hide yourself," and reveal
to him the end which is coming, for the whole earth will be
destroyed, and a deluge is about to come on all the earth, and
what is in it will be destroyed. 10.3 And now (2v, b15) teach
him that he may escape, and (that) his offspring may survive
for the whole earth.' 10.4 And further the Lord said to Raphael:
'Bind Azazel by his hands and his feet, and throw him into the
darkness. And split open the desert which is in Dudael, and
throw him there. 10.5 And (2v, b20) throw on him jagged
and sharp stones, and cover him with darkness; and let him stay
there for ever, and cover his face, that he may not see light,
10.6 and that on the great day of judgement he may be hurled
into the fire. 10.7 And restore the earth which the angels have
ruined, (2v, b25) and announce the restoration of the earth, for
I shall restore the earth, so that not all the sons of men shall be
destroyed through the mystery of everything which the Watchers
made known and taught to their sons. 10.8 And the whole earth
has been ruined by the teaching of the works of Azazel, and
against him (2v, b30) write down all sin.' 10.9 And the Lord
said to Gabriel: 'Proceed against the bastards and the reprobates
and against the sons of the fornicators, and destroy the sons of
the fornicators and the sons of the Watchers from amongst men.
And send them out, and send them (2v, b35) against one another,
and let them destroy themselves in battle, for they will not have

length of days.   10.10 And they will all petition you, but their fathers will gain nothing in respect of them, for they hope for eternal life, and that each of them will live life for five hundred years.'   10.11 And the Lord said to Michael: (2v, c1) 'Go, inform Semyaza and the others with him who have associated with the women to corrupt themselves with them in all their uncleanness.   10.12 When all their sons kill each other, and (2v, c5) when they see the destruction of their beloved ones, bind them for seventy generations under the hills of the earth until the day of their judgement and of their consummation, until the judgement which is for all eternity is accomplished.   10.13 And in those days they will lead them to (2v, c10) the abyss of fire; in torment and in prison they will be shut up for all eternity. 10.14 And then he (Semyaza) will be burnt and from then on destroyed with them; together they will be bound until the end of all generations.   10.15 And destroy all the souls of lust (2v, c15) and the sons of the Watchers, for they have wronged men. 10.16 Destroy all wrong from the face of the earth, and every evil work will cease. And let the plant of righteousness and truth appear, and the deed will become a blessing; righteousness and truth will they plant in joy for ever. (2v, c20)   10.17 And now all the righteous will be humble, and will live until they beget thousands; and all the days of their youth and their sabbaths they will fulfil in peace.   10.18 And in those days the whole earth will be tilled in righteousness, and all of it (2v, c25) will be planted with trees, and it will be filled with blessing. 10.19 And all pleasant trees *they will plant* on it, and they will plant on it vines, and the vine which is planted on it will produce fruit in abundance; and every seed which is sown on it, each measure will produce a thousand, and each measure (2v, c30) of olives will produce ten baths of oil. 10.20 And you, cleanse the earth from all wrong, and from all iniquity, and from all sin, and from all impiety, and from all the uncleanness which is brought about on the earth; remove them from the earth. (2v, c35) 10.21 And all the sons of men shall be righteous, and all the nations shall serve and bless me, and all shall worship me. 10.22 And the earth will be cleansed from all corruption, and from all sin, and from all wrath, and from all torment; and I will not again send a flood upon it for all generations (3r, a1) for ever.

10. 1 **the Great and Holy One**: for this title cf. above on 1. 3.

Arsyalalyur: Eth II; Gr[Pan] Istrael; Gr[Sync b] Uriel. Here Gr[Sync b] alone is consistent in mentioning an angel from the list he gives in 9. 1, contrast vv. 4, 9, and 11. Eth Arsyalalyur (and variants) probably derives ultimately from a corruption of Gr[Pan] Istrael.

10. 2 **is about to come**: Eth ይመጽእ : Uፍ: reflecting an Aramaic אָתֵא להוא (Ullendorff, 'An Aramaic "Vorlage"?', 266)?

10. 4 **Raphael**: cf. v. 1 and 9.1.

Dudael. Dillmann (*Translation*, 100) thinks that the name has been invented and derives it from דודא אל ('cauldron of God'). Charles (*Translation*, 22 f.) connects Dudael with בית הדורי which is mentioned in Targum Ps. Jonathan on Lev. 16: 21 f. as the place to which the goat for Azazel was led. The name of the place also occurs as בית חדודי. Milik (*Biblica* 32 (1951), 395) at one time accepted this identification and derived the name from חדודי אל ('the jagged mountains of God') = ⟨Α⟩δουδαήλ (cf. the form of the name in Eth Gr[Sync b]). The word play (cf. v. 5 'throw on him jagged and sharp stones') makes this explanation plausible, even though the name of the angel in Aram was עסאל not עזאזל (cf. ᵃ1 iii 9, ᶜ1 ii 26 = Eth 6. 7). More recently Milik (*HTR* 64 (1971), 348 f.) has connected this name with Aramaic דדא ('breast'), relying on the reading of Gr[Pan] (Δαδουήλ) rather than that of Eth Gr[Sync b]. (For the name cf. also 60. 8.)

10. 7 **made known.** Eth ፈነወ : and Gr[Pan] ἐπάταξαν are clearly impossible; the context requires a word meaning 'made known', 'revealed'. I suggest that the mistake goes back to the Aramaic *Vorlage*, to a confusion of the roots מחא (= Eth Gr[Pan]) and חוא; such a confusion seems particularly likely if a participial construction were used in the Aramaic (מחין / מחוין). —Gr[Sync b] εἶπον is hardly the original Greek reading, and should probably be attributed to Syncellus himself, or to the sources he used. (For

a slightly different view see Burkitt, *Jewish and Christian Apocalypses*, 68).

10. 9 Gabriel: cf. v. 1 and 9.1.

against the bastards: Eth መዘራእት፡ reflects an Aramaic ממזרא, and is hardly from τοὺς μαζηρέους (so Gr^Pan) which represents a transcription of the Aramaic word (cf. Ullendorff, 'An Aramaic "Vorlage"?', 264; contrast Charles, *Translation*, p. lviii, note). Gr^Sync b 'against the giants' is perhaps an attempt to make sense of a word not understood.

And send them out . . . in battle: Eth; Gr^Pan 'Send them in a battle of destruction'; Gr^Sync b 'Send them against one another, (some) of them against (the rest of) them, in battle and in destruction'; cf. (?) Aram^b I iv 6 (fragment y)]קרב אבדן[, for which cf. Gr^Pan—but the fragment is too small to be of use in interpreting the relationship of the versions to one another.

10. 11 Michael: cf. v. 1 and 9. 1.

Semyaza and the others: cf. (?) Aram^b I iv 9 (fragment b′) ל[שׂמיחז]א ולכ[ול].

10. 12 all their sons kill each other: Eth Gr^Pan Sync b, but Gr^Pan Sync b = Aram^b I iv 10 (fragment b′) יבדן בניהון omit 'all'.

and when they see: BM 485 BM 491 Berl Abb 35 Tana 9 Eth II; Abb 55 Gr^Pan Sync b = Aram^b I iv 10 (fragment b′) ויח]זון[—'and they see'.

under the hills: Eth; Gr^Pan Sync b 'in the valleys'. There is no obvious explanation of the variant. Note that ወገር፡ renders νάπη in Deut. 3: 29 (MT גיא): Isa. 40: 12 (MT גבעה): Jer. 14: 6 (MT שפים)—but the last two cases could be explained through the Hebrew.

for seventy generations . . . day of their judgement: cf. Aram^b I iv 10 f. (fragments e′ and b′)]שבעין[.   ]ארעא עד יומא רבא[. Note that none of the versions have anything corresponding to רבא.

10. 13 in torment . . . all eternity: Eth; Gr^Pan Sync b 'and to torment and to the prison of eternal confinement'; cf. Aram^c I v 1 ע[ל]מא   ]יקא ול[ן.

10. 14 And then . . . all generations: Abb 35² Eth II; BM 485 BM 491 Berl Abb 35¹ Abb 55 Tana 9 Gr^Pan 'And when (anyone) is burnt and destroyed from now on, he will be bound together with them until the end of all generations (Gr[Pan] 'the generation')'; Gr[Sync] [b] 'And whoever is condemned and destroyed from now on will be bound with them until the end of their generation'. For Gr[Sync] [b] cf. Aram[c]1 v 1] . . וכול די. Eth I Gr[Pan] 'And when' perhaps derives from a *Vorlage* in which καὶ ὅς ἄν was misread as καὶ ὅταν, while Abb 35[2] Eth II 'And then' looks like an attempt to improve an obscure text. —There would appear to be nothing in the versions corresponding to Aram[c]1 v 2 דין[ובקן] יאבדון לכון. Admittedly it would perhaps be possible to read ואבדון instead of יאבדון and to relate ואבדון לכון to the beginning of v. 15; but in that case we would have a plural imperative, not the expected singular (cf. [c]1 v 3 = 10. 16 ואכרת).

10. 16 **Destroy all wrong from**: Eth Gr[Pan], but Tana 9 Gr[Pan] prefix 'And'. Cf. Aram[c]1 v 3] ואכרת עולה מן.

And let the plant . . . deed will become: cf. Aram[c]1 v 4 נ[צבת קו שטא ותהון]א. We might have expected צדקא וקושטא, but although there is a curious gap between קו and שטא the reading is certainly correct.

10. 17 **the righteous will be humble**: Eth II; Eth I Gr[Pan] 'the righteous will escape'; cf. Aram[c]1 v 5 קש[י]טין יפלטון.

and will live: cf. Aram[c]1 v 5]ולהון.

and their sabbaths: Eth Gr[Pan]—שַׁבַּתהון misread for שֵׂבָתהון ('and of their old age') which is obviously required. Cf. now Aram[c]1 v 6]שׂיבתכון where ' makes quite clear which word is intended (but note the second person suffix). Cf. J. Wellhausen, 'Zur apokalyptischen Literatur', *Skizzen und Vorarbeiten*, Berlin, 1899, vi. 241, note 1, 260; Ullendorff, 'An Aramaic "Vorlage"?', 264.

and all the days . . . in peace: cf. Aram[c]1 v 5 f.

]שׂיבתכון בשלם י]   ] וכול יומי 6] . ..[.

10. 18 **in righteousness**: cf. Aram[c]1 v 7]בקשוט[.

and all of it will be planted with trees: Eth, cf. Aram[c]1 v 7 וכׄולה תתנצב]; Gr[Pan] 'and a tree will be planted in it'. Eth would appear to be closer than Gr[Pan] to Aram; on the other hand Eth does not here seem to be dependent on a Greek *Vorlage* of the type represented by Gr[Pan]. This is thus a valuable example for the independent value of Eth.

with blessing: cf. Aramᶜɪ v 7 בִּרְכָה] .

10. 19 **And all pleasant trees they will plant on it**: Eth; Gr^Pan 'And all the trees of the earth will rejoice; they will be planted'. Gr^Pan has an awkward construction and appears corrupt. Cf. Aramᶜɪ v 7 וכול אילנין.

and the vine . . . in abundance: Eth, but BM 485 BM 491 Abb 35 Tana 9 Berl (cf. Gr^Pan) have 'wine' instead of 'fruit'; Gr^Pan 'and the vine which they plant, they will produce thousands of jars of wine'. Cf. Aramᶜɪ v 8 נֹצֹּב בה . . [.

and every seed . . . baths of oil: Eth; Gr^Pan has an abbreviated text and is corrupt. Cf. Aramᶜɪ v 9 אַ[לֹּןֹ] .

CHAPTER 19

19.1 And Uriel said to me: 'The spirits of the angels who were promiscuous with the women will stand here; and they, assuming many forms, made men unclean and will lead men astray (4r, a1) so that they sacrifice to demons as gods—(that is,) *until the great judgement day* on which they will be judged so that an end will be made of them. 19.2 And their wives, having led astray the angels of Heaven, will become peaceful.' (4r, a5) 19.3 And I, Enoch, alone saw the sight, the end of everything; and no man has seen what I have seen.

19. 2 **will become peaceful**: Eth; Gr^Pan 'will become Sirens'. Eth derives from a corrupt Greek *Vorlage* (ὡς εἰρηναῖαι instead of εἰς σειρῆνας —cf. e.g. Charles, *Text*, 51).

19. 3 **what**: literally 'as'.

CHAPTER 20

20.1 And these are the names of the holy angels who keep watch. 20.2 Uriel, one of the holy angels, (4r, a10) namely (the angel) of thunder and of tremors. 20.3 Raphael, one of the holy angels, (the angel) of the spirits of men.   20.4 Raguel, one of the holy angels, who takes vengeance on the world and on the lights. 20.5 Michael, one of the holy angels, namely the one put in charge of the best part of mankind, (4r, a15) in charge of the nation.   20.6 Saragael, one of the holy angels, who (is) in charge of the *spirits of men* who cause the spirits to sin.   20.7 Gabriel, one of the holy angels, who (is) in charge of the serpents and the Garden and the Cherubim.

20. 1 For the following list of names cf. 9. 1.

20. 2 namely (the angel) of thunder and of tremors: Eth (except BM 485 Berl Tana 9); Gr[Pan] 'the one in charge of the world and of Tartarus'. Charles (*Text*, 52) attempts to explain Eth in terms of Gr[Pan], but the two texts are so different that it is not at all clear to me that they can be related to one another. It is possible, although not entirely convincing, to argue that ዘበኅበስም፡ (BM 485 Berl Tana 9) and ሕረኅም፡ are corruptions of an original Ethiopic reading ዘኅበስም፡ (for which cf. Gr[Pan] ὁ ἐπὶ τοῦ κόσμου), but this still leaves ሕረኅድ፡ unexplained— Charles's suggestion that it may point back to a corrupt transliteration of Τάρταρος seems unlikely.

20. 6 Saraqael: ሰረዋኤል፡ is probably an inner-Ethiopic corruption of ሰርኤል፡ or the like—cf. Gr[Pan] Σαριήλ and cf. also 9. 1 ሱርዖል፡/ ሱርኤል፡ = Aram[b]ı iii 7 שריאל.

20. 7 Gr[Pan a], probably correctly, adds a seventh angel to the list.

CHAPTER 21

(4r, a20) 21.1 And I went round to a place where there was nothing made.   21.2 And I saw there a terrible thing—neither the high Heaven, nor the (firmly) founded earth, but a desert place, prepared and terrible.   21.3 And there I saw seven stars of Heaven bound on it together, (4r, a25) like great mountains, and burning like fire.   21.4 Then I said: 'For what sin have they been bound, and why have they been thrown here?'   21.5 and

Uriel, one of the holy angels who was with me *and* led me, spoke to me and said: 'Enoch, (4r, a30) about whom do you ask? About whom do you inquire and ask and care?   21.6 These are (some) of the stars which transgressed the command of the Lord Most High, and they have been bound here until ten thousand ages are completed, the number (4r, a35) of the days of their sin.'   21.7 And from there I went to another place, more terrible than this, and I saw a terrible thing: (there was) a great fire there which burnt and blazed, and the *place* had a cleft (reaching) to the abyss, full of great pillars of fire which were made to fall; neither its extent nor its size could I (4r, b1) see, nor could I see its source.   21.8 Then I said: 'How terrible this place (is), and (how) painful to look at!'   21.9 Then Uriel, one of the holy angels who was with me, answered me. He answered me (4r, b5) and said to me: 'Enoch, why do you have such fear and terror because of this terrible place, and before this pain?' 21.10 And he said to me: 'This place (is) the prison of the angels, and there they will be held for ever.'

21. 3 **bound on it together:** Eth; Gr^Pan Pan ª, 'bound and thrown down on it'. Gr^Pan Pan ª καὶ ἐριμμένους should probably be regarded as a gloss introduced under the influence of v. 4. On the other hand ὁμοῦ (= ፅብረ ፡) would appear to have dropped out of Gr before the following ὁμοίους (Cf. Charles, *Text*, 53, 55, and contrast 52).

21. 7 **nor could I see its source:** ፍጻሜ ፡ (omitted by Tana 9) would appear to be a gloss on ግፅም ፡ (= εἰκάσαι) whose introduction into the text led to the alteration of ግፅም ፡ (BM 491 Abb 35¹ (?) Abb 55 Tana 9) into ግፅተ ፡ (Eth II), cf. e.g. Charles, *Text*, 54.

CHAPTER 22

(4r, b10) 22.1 And from there I went to another place, and he showed me in the west a large and high mountain, *and a hard rock and four beautiful places,* 22.2 and inside it was deep and wide and very smooth. How smooth (is) that which rolls, and deep and dark (4r, b15) to look at!   22.3 Then Raphael, one of the holy angels who was with me, answered me and said to me: 'These beautiful places (are intended for this), that the spirits, the souls of the dead, might be gathered into them; for them they were created, (that) here they might gather all (4r, b20) the souls of the sons of men.   22.4 And these places they made where they will keep them until the day of their judgement and until their appointed time—and that appointed time (will be) long—until the great judgement (comes) upon them.   22.5 And I saw the spirits of the sons of men who were dead, (4r, b25) and their voice reached Heaven and complained.   22.6 Then I asked Raphael, the angel who was with me, and said to him: 'Whose is this spirit whose voice thus reaches *Heaven* and complains?'   22.7 And he answered me and said to me, saying 'This (4r, b30) spirit is the one which came out of Abel whom Cain, his brother, killed. And he will complain about him until his offspring is destroyed from the face of the earth, and from amongst the offspring of men his offspring perishes.'   22.8 Then I asked about him and about the judgement on all and I said: 'Why (4r, b35) is one separated from another?'   22.9 And he answered me and said to me: 'These three (places) were made in order that they might separate the spirits of the dead. And thus the souls of the righteous have been separated; this is the spring of water (and) on it (is) the light.   22.10 Likewise (a place) has been created for sinners when they die and are buried in the earth and judgement (4r, c1) has not come upon them during their life.   22.11 And here their souls will be separated for this great torment, until the great day of judgement and punishment and torment for those who curse for ever, (4r, c5) and of vengeance on their souls, and there he will bind them for ever. Verily he is from the beginning of the world.   22.12 And thus (a place) has been separated for the souls of those who complain and give information about (their) destruction, when they were killed in the days of the sinners.   22.13 Thus (a place) has been created for the souls (4r, c10) of men who are not righteous, but sinners accomplished in wrongdoing, and with the wrongdoers will be their lot. But their souls will not be killed on the day of judgement, nor will they rise from here.'   22.14 Then I blessed the Lord of Glory, and said: 'Blessed be (4r, c15) my Lord, the Lord of Glory and Righteousness, who rules everything for ever.'

22. 1 beautiful places: Eth; Gr[Pan] 'hollow places'. Gr[Pan] is more appropriate to the context. Eth derives from a misreading of κοῖλοι as καλοί (cf. e.g. Charles *Text*, 56; Ullendorff, 'An Aramaic "Vorlage"?', 262). Cf. also v. 3.

22. 2 that which rolls: Eth; Gr[Pan] 'these hollow places'. Eth is nonsense. The Ethiopic translator appears to have read (and mistranslated) κυκλώματα (cf. Gr[Pan] in v. 8) instead of κοιλώματα (cf. Charles, *Text*, 56).

22. 3 beautiful places: see the note on v. 1 above.

all the souls of the sons of men: cf. Aram[e]1 xxii 1 נפש[ת כל בני אנשא.

22. 4 Although Eth and Gr[Pan] correspond fairly closely to Aram in this verse, neither agrees exactly with it.

And these places . . . keep them: Eth; Gr[Pan] 'And these places they made for their reception'; cf. Aram[e]1 xxii 1 f.

1   והא אלן אנון פתחיא לבית עגון

2   לכדן עב[ד]ו

Eth Gr[Pan] have nothing corresponding to פתחיא in this verse (cf. vv. 1, 3). עגון, if the reading is sound, is an assimilated form of עגנהון, cf. סרכן in [a]1 ii 1. At the end of line 1 [די] is perhaps to be supplied.

until the day of their judgement: Eth Gr[Pan]; cf. Aram[e]1 xxii 2 עד יום די יתדינן.

and until their appointed time: Eth; Gr[Pan] 'and until the appointed time'; cf. Aram[e]1 xxii 2 ועד זמן יום קצא.

and that appointed time (will be) long (lit. 'great'): Eth; Gr[Pan] 'and the appointed time'. Eth looks like a gloss, while Gr[Pan] appears to be a doublet of the previous phrase. Aram[e]1 xxii 2 has at this point only ד[, to be restored ד[י (see the next note)?

until the great judgement (comes) upon them: Eth; Gr[Pan] 'when the great judgement will be upon them'; cf. Aram[e]1 xxii 2 f. ד[י] 3 דינא רבא די מנהון יתעבד.

22. 5 And I saw … were dead: BM 485 Abb 35[2] Eth II; Gr[Pan] (following Swete, cf. apparatus) 'I saw dead men complaining'; cf. Aram[e]1 xxii 3 f. תמן חזית רוח 4 אנש מת קבלה. It is not certain that רוח is the last word of line 3, but it seems very likely. Note: (1) neither Eth nor Gr[Pan] render תמן; (2) Gr[Pan] has nothing corresponding to רוח, but Eth nothing corresponding to קבלה; (3) according to Aram Enoch sees the spirit of one man, according to Eth and (apparently) Gr[Pan] he sees the spirits of men. In fact, however, Gr[Pan] in vv. 5b, 6, 7 and Eth in vv. 6 and 7 go on to mention only a single spirit, that of Abel, and it had already been suggested that throughout v. 5 originally only one spirit was mentioned (cf. e.g. Charles (*Text*, 57) who accordingly emended Gr[Pan] to ⟨πνεῦμα⟩ ἀνθρώπου νεκροῦ ἐντυγχάνοντος).

and their voice reached heaven: Eth; Gr[Pan] 'and his voice reached heaven'; Cf. Aram[e]1 xxii 4 [ו]אנינה ע[ד] שמיא סלק. The ending ה of אנינה could indicate the emphatic state, but is more probably the 3rd masc. sing. suffix (cf. Gr[Pan]). For the implications of the variant 'their voice'/'his voice' cf. the previous note.

and complained: Eth Gr[Pan]; cf. Aram[e]1 xxii 4 ומוֹ[ק] וקבֹ[ל].

22. 6 Raphael, the angel who: Eth Gr[Pan]; cf. Aram[e]1 xxii 5 לרפא[ל] לעירא וקדישא ד[ן. Eth Gr[Pan] agree against Aram.

Whose is this … and complains?: Eth; Gr[Pan] 'Whose is this spirit which is complaining? Therefore his voice thus reaches and complains to heaven'; Aram[e]1 xxii 6 א[דמן היא דכ[דן, read א[דמן היא דכֹ.]. Eth at this point can hardly be dependent on Gr, or at least on the type of tradition represented by Gr[Pan]. On the other hand Eth ሐመሉ ፡ ꝏአፈ ፡

ሀሐመሐ ፡ reflects Aram דמן היא דכ[דן exactly, and it is very plausible in a case like this to think that Eth is directly dependent on Aram.

22. 7 And he answered me and said to me, saying: cf. (?) Aram[e]1 xxii 7 לי א[.

22. 8 **and about the judgement on all**: Eth; Gr^Pan 'about all the circular places'. Charles (*Text*, 58 f.) thinks that Eth derives from a corrupt Greek *Vorlage* (κριμάτων corrupt for κοιλωμάτων), and this is certainly plausible even though Eth does make sense as it stands. For Gr^Pan κύκλωμάτων cf. Eth in v. 2.

22. 9 **These three**: Eth Gr^Pan. The number is curious since four places are mentioned in v. 1 and four seem to be described in the account which follows: (1) for the righteous—v. 9b; (2) for the wicked who have not been punished in this life—vv. 10 f.; (3) for the martyred righteous—v. 12, cf. vv. 5–7; (4) for the wicked who have been punished in this life—v. 13. The fourfold division is underlined in Gr^Pan by the repeated καὶ οὕτως, vv. 9b, 10, 12, 13; cf. in Eth ወህሙዝ: v. 9b, ሰህሙ: ካማዑ: v. 10, ወህሙዝ: v. 12, (ወ)ህሙዝ: v. 13. Perhaps the meaning of this verse is 'these three other places'—apart, that is, from the place for the martyred righteous which by implication has already been dealt with in vv. 5–7, but which the angel none the less mentions again in v. 12 (contrast Charles, *Translation*, 46–9).

22. 12 **give information**: literally 'show'.

22. 13 **and with the wrongdoers will be their lot**: literally 'and with the wrongdoers they will be like them'.

But their souls . . . day of judgement: Eth; Gr^Pan 'But (their) spirits {, because those who are afflicted here are punished less than them,} will not be punished on the day of judgement'; cf. Aram^d1 xi 1 מֵן דִּיאָ בְּיוֹם יִתְנֵזְקָן לֹא זְ]. Neither Eth nor Gr^Pan render יִתְנֵזְקָן ('to be hurt, injured') exactly, but note (1) that Eth seems to be closer in meaning than Gr^Pan to יִתְנֵזְקָן, (2) that Eth can hardly be dependent on Gr, at least as represented by Gr^Pan.

22. 14 **and said: 'Blessed . . . Righteousness**: Berl Eth II; Gr^Pan (cf. BM 485 Abb 35 Abb 55 Tana 9 and BM 491) 'and said: "Blessed art thou, Lord of Righteousness"'; cf. Aram^d1 xi 2 וֹאָמְרַת לְהֹוֵה בְּרִיךְ דִּין [קוּשְׁטָ] Note (1) that Aram has דִּין 'Judge', not מרה 'Lord' (= Eth Gr^Pan); (2) that Aram agrees with BM 485 Abb 35 Abb 55 Tana 9 BM 491 Gr^Pan against Berl Eth II in as much as Aram has nothing corresponding to Berl Eth II ስብሔት:.

CHAPTER 23

23.1 And from there I went to another place towards the west, to the ends of the earth.   23.2 And I saw a fire which burnt and ran without resting or ceasing from running (4r, c20) by day or night, but (continued) in exactly the same way.   23.3 And I asked saying: 'What is this which has no rest?'   23.4 Then Raguel, one of the holy angels who was with me, answered me and said to me: 'This burning fire whose course you saw, towards the west, (4r, c25) is (the fire of) all the lights of Heaven.'

23. 1 And from there I went to another place: Eth Gr[Pan]; cf. Aram[d]ɪ xi 3] . . מן אובלת לאת . . . . [, read ומן ת[מן אובלת לאת]רא.

23. 2 from running: literally 'from its running' or 'from its course'.

23. 3 which has no rest: Eth Gr[Pan]; cf. (?) Aram[d]ɪ xi 5 ל . . . . . . [שליאו‍ן.

23. 4 This burning fire . . . lights of heaven: Eth; Gr[Pan] 'This course of fire is the fire towards the west which persecutes all the lights of heaven.' Gr[Pan] ἐκδιῶκον does not offer a very suitable meaning, and may be corrupt for ἐκδικῶν (cf. 20. 4 and Charles, *Translation*, 51). In this case, does the variant ሐደድ :/the assumed τὸ ἐκδικῶν result from a confusion of the roots בער and פרע in the original Aramaic?

CHAPTER 24

24.1 And from there I went to another place of the earth, and he showed me a mountain of fire which blazed day and night. 24.2 And I went towards it and saw seven magnificent mountains, and (4r, c30) all were different from one another, and precious and beautiful stones, and all (were) precious and their appearance glorious and their form beautiful; three (of the mountains) towards the east, one fixed firmly on another, and three towards the south, one on another, and deep and regged valleys, (4r, c35) no one (of which) was near another. 24.3 And (there was) a seventh mountain in the middle of these, and in their height they were all like the seat of a throne, and fragrant trees surrounded it. 24.4 And there was among them a tree such as I have never smelt, and none of them nor any others were like it: (4v, a1) it smells more fragrant than any fragrance, and its leaves and its flowers and its wood never wither; its fruit (is) good, and its fruit (is) like the bunches of dates on a palm. 24.5 And then I said: 'Behold, this beautiful tree! (4v, a5) Beautiful to look at and pleasant (are) its leaves, and its fruit very delightful in appearance.' 24.6 And then Michael, one of the holy and honoured angels who was with me and (was) in charge of them, answered me

24. 3 and in their height . . . throne: Eth is inferior to Gr^{Pan} and probably corrupt.

CHAPTER 25

25.1 and said to me: 'Enoch why do you ask me (4v, a10) about the fragrance of this tree, and (why) do you inquire to learn?' 25.2 Then I, Enoch, answered him, saying: 'I wish to learn about everything, but especially about this tree.' 25.3 And he answered me, saying: 'This high mountain which you saw, whose summit (4v, a15) is like the throne of the Lord, is the throne where the Holy and Great One, the Lord of Glory, the Eternal King, will sit when he comes down to visit the earth for good. 25.4 And this beautiful fragrant tree—and no (creature of) flesh has authority to touch it (4v, a20) until the great judgement when he will take vengeance on all *and will bring (everything) to a consummation* for ever—*this* will be given to the righteous and humble.

25. 1 and (why) do you inquire to learn?: Eth; Gr[Pan] 'and why do you wish to learn the truth?' ፕሐፈቅ: can hardly be a rendering of θέλεις, and it may be suggested that the two are independent translations of an Aramaic בעית. Cf. 21. 5.

25. 3 the Holy and Great One: on the title cf. note on 1. 3.

CHAPTER 40

(5v, a5) 40.1 And after this I saw a thousand thousands and ten thousand times ten thousand, (a multitude) beyond number or reckoning, who stood before the glory of the Lord of Spirits. 40.2 I looked, and on the four sides of the Lord of Spirits I saw four figures different (5v, a10) from those who were standing; and I learnt their names, because the angel who went with me made known to me their names, and showed me all the secret things.   40.3 And I heard the voices of those four figures as they sang praises before the Lord of Glory.   40.4 The first voice blesses (5v, a15) the Lord of Spirits for ever and ever.   40.5 And the second voice I heard blessing the Chosen One and the chosen who depend on the Lord of Spirits.   40.6 And the third voice I heard as they petitioned and prayed on behalf of those who dwell on the dry ground and supplicate (5v, a20) in the name of the Lord of Spirits.   40.7 And the fourth voice I heard driving away the satans, and not allowing them to come before the Lord of Spirits ot accuse those who dwell on the dry ground. 40.8 And after this I asked the angel (5v, a25) of peace who went with me and showed me everything which is secret: 'Who are these four figures whom I have seen and whose words I have heard and written down?'   40.9 And he said to me: 'This first one is the holy Michael, the merciful and long-suffering; and the second, (5v, a30) who (is) in charge of all the diseases and in charge of all the wounds of the sons of men, is Raphael; and the third, who (is) in charge of all the powers, is the holy Gabriel;

and the fourth, who (is) in charge of the repentance (leading)
to hope of those who will inherit eternal life, is Phanuel.'   40.10
And these (are) four angels (5v, a35) of the Lord Most High;
and the four voices I heard in those days.

40. 2 figures: literally 'faces' (so in vv. 3, 8; 64. 1).

who were standing: 40. 1. But BM 485 Berl Abb 35[1](?)   Abb 55
Tana 9 read 'who do not sleep'.

40. 6 And the third voice I heard as they petitioned and prayed:
text impossible; read እንዘ፡ ይስእል፡ ወይጼሊ፡:—'And the third voice
I heard petitioning and praying'. But the following ወይስተበቍዑ፡
makes sense in the plural (cf. Dillmann, *Translation*, 147 and contrast
Charles, *Text*, 81).

CHAPTER 54

54.1 And I looked and turned to another part of the earth, and
I saw there a deep valley with burning fire.   54.2 And they
brought the kings and the powerful and threw them into that
valley.   54.3 And (6v, b30) there my eyes saw how they made
instruments for them—iron chains of immeasurable weight.
54.4 And I asked the angel of peace who went with me, saying:
'These chain-instruments—for whom are they being prepared?'
54.5 And he said to me: 'These are being prepared (6v, b35)
for the hosts of Azazel, that they may take them and throw them
into the lowest part of Hell; and they will cover their jaws with
rough stones, as the Lord of Spirits commanded.   54.6 And
Michael and Gabriel, Raphael and Phanuel—these will take
hold of them on that great day, (6v, c1) and throw them on that
day into the furnace of burning fire, that the Lord of Spirits may
take vengeance on them for their iniquity, in that they became
servants of Satan and led astray those who dwell (6v, c5) upon
the dry ground.   54.7 And in those days the punishment of the

Lord of Spirits will go out, and all the storehouses of the waters which (are) above the Heavens ... and under the earth will be opened, 54.8 and all the waters will be joined (6v, c10) *with* the waters which (are) above the Heavens. The water which (is) above Heaven is male, and the water which (is) under the earth is female.   54.9 And all those who dwell upon the dry ground and those who dwell under the ends of Heaven will be wiped out.   54.10   And   because   of   this (6v, c15)   they will acknowledge their iniquity which they have committed on the earth, and *through this* they will be destroyed.'

54. 7 which (are) above the heavens . . . and under the earth. The text is in a confused state, and appears to be overloaded. The evidence of v. 8 makes plausible the suggestion that originally only two categories of water were mentioned here—that above heaven and that under the earth (cf. Charles, *Text*, 98).

CHAPTER 71

71.1 And it came to pass after this that my spirit was carried off, and it went up into the Heavens. I saw the sons of the holy angels treading upon flames of fire, and their garments (9r, b20) (were) white, and their clothing, and the light of their face (was) like snow.   71.2 And I saw two rivers of fire, and the light of that fire shone like hyacinth, and I fell upon my face before the Lord of Spirits.   71.3 And the angel Michael, one of the archangels, took hold of me (9r, b25) by my right hand, and raised me, and led me out to all the secrets of mercy and the secrets of righteous-ness. 71.4 And he showed me all the secrets of the ends of Heaven and all the storehouses of all the stars and the lights, from where they come out before the holy ones.   71.5 And the spirit carried Enoch off (9r, b30) to the highest Heaven, and I saw there in the middle of that light something built of crystal stones, and in the middle of those stones tongues of living fire.   71.6 And my spirit saw a circle of fire which surrounded that house; (9r, b35) from its four sides (came) rivers full of living fire, and they surrounded that house.   71.7 And round about (were) the Seraphim, and the Cherubim, and the Ophannim; these are they who do not sleep, but keep watch over the throne of his glory. 71.8 And I saw angels who could not be counted, a thousand thousands and ten thousand times (9r, c1) ten thousand, surrounding that house; and Michael and Raphael and Gabriel and Phanuel, and the holy angels who (are) in the Heavens above, went in and out of that house. (9r, c5)   71.9 And Michael and Raphael and Gabriel and Phanuel, and many holy angels without number, came out from that house; 71.10 and with them the Head *of Days*, his head white and pure like wool, and his garments indescribable.   71.11 And I fell upon my face, and my whole body melted, and my spirit (9r, c10) was transformed; and I cried out in a loud voice in the spirit of power, and I blessed and praised and exalted.   71.12 And these blessings which came out from my mouth were pleasing before that Head of Days.   71.13 And that Head of Days came with Michael and Gabriel, Raphael (9r, c15) and Phanuel, and thousands and tens of thousands of angels without number.   71.14 And that angel came to me, and greeted me with his voice, and said to me: 'You are the Son of Man who was born to righteousness, and righteousness remains over you, and the righteousness of the Head of Days (9r, c20) will not leave you.'   71.15 And he said to me: 'He proclaims peace to you in the name of the world which is to come, for from there peace has come out from the creation of the world; and so you will have it for ever and for ever and ever.   71.16 And all . . . will walk according to your way, inasmuch as righteousness will never leave you; (9r, c25) with you will be their dwelling, and with you their lot, and they

will not be separated from you, for ever and for ever and ever.
71.17   And so there will be length of days with that Son of
Man, and the righteous will have peace, and the righteous *will
have an upright way*, (9r, c30) in the name of the Lord of Spirits
for ever and ever.'

71. 1 the sons of the holy angels: see the note on 69. 4.

71. 10 of Days: Eth I Bodl 5 Ull other Eth II MSS.; Ryl² Curzon 56
BM 484 'of the oath'.

71. 16 And all ... will walk. I omit *ℓℎⲱⲓ*: *ⲱ* ('will be and') with Eth I.

CHAPTER 72

72.1 The book of the revolutions of the lights of Heaven, each
as it is, according to their classes, according to their (period of)
rule and their times, according to their names and their places
of origin, and according to their months, (9r, c35) which Uriel,
the holy angel who was with me and is their leader, showed to
me; and he showed me all their regulations exactly as they are,
for each year of the world and for ever, until the new creation
shall be made which will last for ever.   72.2 And this is the
first law of the lights. The light the sun, (9v, a1) its rising (is)
in the gates of Heaven which (are) towards the east, and its
setting (is) in the western gates of Heaven.   72.3 And I saw six
gates from which the sun rises, and six gates in which the sun
sets, and (9v, a5) the moon (also) rises and sets in those gates,
and the leaders of the stars together with those whom they lead;
(there are) six in the east and six in the west, all exactly in place,
one next to the other; and (there are) many windows to the
south and north of those gates.   72.4 And (9v, a10) first there
rises the greater light, named the sun, and its disc (is) like the
disc of Heaven, and the whole of it (is) full of a fire which gives

light and warmth.   72.5 The wind blows the chariots on which it ascends, and the sun goes down from Heaven and returns through the north in order to reach the east, (9v, a15) and is led so that it comes to the appropriate gate, and shines (again) in Heaven.   72.6 In this way it rises in the first month in the large gate, namely it rises through the fourth of those six gates which (are) towards the east.   72.7 And in that fourth (9v, a20) gate, from which the sun rises in the first month, there are twelve window—openings from which, whenever they are opened, flames come out.   72.8 When the sun rises in Heaven, it goes out through that fourth (9v, a25) gate for thirty days, and exactly in the fourth gate in the west of Heaven it goes down. 72.9 And in those days the day grows daily longer, and the night grows nightly shorter, until the thirtieth morning.   72.10 And on that day the day becomes longer than the night by a double (part), (9v, a30) and the day amounts to exactly ten parts, and the night amounts to eight parts.   72.11 And the sun rises from that fourth gate, and sets in the fourth gate, and returns to the fifth gate in the east for thirty mornings; and it rises from it, and sets (9v, a35) in the fifth gate.   72.12 And then the day becomes longer by two parts, and the day amounts to eleven parts, and the night becomes shorter and amounts to seven parts.   72.13 And the sun returns to the east, and comes to the sixth gate, and rises and sets in the sixth gate for thirty-one mornings because of its sign.   72.14 And on that day (9v, b1) the day becomes longer than the night, and the day becomes double the night; and the day amounts to twelve parts, and the night becomes shorter and amounts to six parts.   72.15 And the sun rises up that the day may grow shorter, and the night longer; (9v, b5) and the sun returns to the east, and comes to the sixth gate, and rises from it and sets for thirty mornings. 72.16 And when thirty mornings have been completed, the day becomes shorter by exactly one part; and the day amounts to eleven parts, and the night to seven parts. 72.17 And the sun goes out (9v, b10) from the west through that sixth gate, and goes to the east, and rises in the fifth gate for thirty mornings; and it sets in the west again, in the fifth gate in the west. 72.18 On that day the day becomes shorter by two parts, (9v, b15) and the day amounts to ten parts, and the night to eight parts. 72.19 And the sun rises from that fifth gate, and sets in the fifth gate in the west, and rises in the fourth gate for thirty-one mornings because of its sign, and sets in the west. (9v, b20) 72.20 On that day the day becomes equal with the night, and is (of) equal (length); and the night amounts to nine parts, and the day to nine parts. 72.21 And the sun rises from that gate, and sets in the west, and returns to the east, and rises in the third gate (9v, b25) for thirty mornings, and sets in the west in the third gate. 72.22 And on that day the night becomes longer than the day, *and the night grows nightly longer*, and the day grows daily shorter until the thirtieth *morning*; and the night amounts to exactly ten parts, and the day to eight parts. 72.23 And the sun rises (9v, b30) from that third gate, and sets in the third gate in the west, and returns to the east; and the sun rises in the second gate in the east for thirty mornings, and likewise it sets in the second gate in the west of Heaven. 72.24 And on that day (9v, b35) the night amounts to eleven parts, and the day to seven parts. 72.25 And the sun rises on that day from that second gate, and sets in the west in the second gate, and returns to the east, to the first gate, for thirty-one mornings, and sets in the west in the first gate. 72.26 And on that day the night becomes longer, (9v, c1) and becomes double the day; and the night amounts to exactly twelve parts, and the day to six parts. 72.27 And (with this) the sun has completed the divisions of its journey, and it turns back again along these divisions of its journey; and it comes through (9v, c5) that (first) gate for thirty mornings, and sets in the west opposite it.   72.28 And on that day the night becomes shorter in length by one part . . . and amounts to eleven parts, and the day to seven parts.   72.29 And the sun returns, and comes to the second gate in the east, (9v, c10) and it returns along those divisions of its journey for thirty mornings, rising and setting.   72.30 And on that day the night becomes shorter in length, and the night amounts to ten parts, and the day to eight parts.   72.31 And on that day the sun rises from that second gate, and sets (9v, c15) in the west, and returns to the east, and rises in the third gate for thirty-one mornings, and sets in the west of Heaven.   72.32 And on that day the night becomes shorter, and amounts to nine parts, and the day amounts to nine parts, and the night becomes equal with the day. (9v, c20) And the year amounts to exactly three hundred and sixty-four days.   72.33 And the length of the day and the night, and the shortness of the day and the night—they are different because of the journey of that sun.   72.34 Because of it, its journey becomes daily longer, and nightly shorter. (9v, c25)   72.35 And this is the law and the journey of the sun, and its return, as often as it returns; sixty times it returns and rises, that is the great eternal light which for ever and ever is named the sun.   72.36 And this which rises is the great light, which is (so) named after its appearance, (9v, c30) as the Lord commanded.   72.37 And thus it rises and sets; it neither decreases, nor rests, but runs day and night in (its) chariot. And its light is seven times brighter than that of the moon, but in size the two are equal.

72. 1 **regulations**: literally 'book' (cf. Dillmann, *Lexicon*, col. 1269).

72. 3 **to the south and north**: literally 'to the right and left'.

72. 7 **window-openings**: literally 'open windows', i.e. windows that

can be opened—as the following words make clear (cf. 75. 4, 7).

72. 8 **in heaven**: literally 'from heaven'.

72. 10 **by a double (part)**: i.e. by two parts.

72. 27 **the divisions of its journey**: ርእስ : seems here to be a translation of a Greek κεφάλαιον—'division' (cf. Dillmann, *Translation*, 225).

72. 28 **by one part** . . . I have not translated ዘውእቱ : ክፍል : ፩ : since it is fairly clearly a gloss which is meant to explain that in this passage እድ : is the equivalent of ክፍል : (cf. Dillmann, *Translation*, 226).

72. 29 **returns, and comes**: literally 'returned, and came'. There is no apparent reason for the change of tense.

and it returns along those divisions of its journey: the reference to the divisions of the journey is unexpected. The only other place in this chapter where we have the same expression is v. 27, and that verse deals with the special case of the winter solstice and the start of the period when the days begin to get longer. Possibly 'along those divisions of its journey' has been copied here by mistake from v. 27.

72. 33 **are different**: literally 'are separate'.

72. 34 **Because of it**: because of the difference in the length of day and night, i.e. in order to bring about the difference in the length of day and night (cf. Dillmann, *Translation*, 226).

* M.A. Knibb, with the assistance of Edward Ullendorff, *The Ethiopic Book of Enoch*, a new edition in the light of the Aramaic Dead Sea Fragments, Volume II, Introduction, Translation and Commentary, Oxford 1978.

Notes

1. A 9th century Buddhist priest (774–835), who was the founder of the Shingon or True World sect of esoteric Buddhism in Japan.
2. Shinji Takahashi (1928–1976), born in Nagano Prefecture, Japan, was a devout layman Buddhist, who had undergone many spiritual experiences since the age of ten, and believed in the separateness of body and soul. He experienced the moment of death (the actual state of being dead) scores of times. His investigation of the spirit world, based on his studies of electronics, physics, astronomy and medical science, led him toward recognition of the existence of the soul. He believed that the many religious groups and sects are only diversifications of one true faith and preached the unification of all world religions, as having derived from one source— the heavenly spirit world. His publications (in Japanese) include: *Buddha the Man* and *An Original Opinion on the Hannya Shingyo Sutra.*
3. Teacher
4. Both the Tendai and Shingon sects were phases of esoteric Buddhism. Chigi (538–597) was the third patriarch in the lineage of the Chinese Tendai sect. He is the author of many commentaries and books, including the famous *Sandaibu*, three important commentaries on the *Hokekyo* sutra—one of the most important Buddhist documents.
5. A Japanese writer (1925—1970) with a consuming belief in the old traditions and ideals of Japan. He was dedicated to the return to imperial rule and committed ritual suicide after failing to arouse the military to seek greater political power.
6. Oriental gods with the power to protect Buddha or Buddhist laymen and people of virtue from evil and wicked spirits and to aid them in their ascension to heaven or paradise: Fudo myo-o (Acala), Marishiten (Marīci), Inari Daimyojin (Dākinī), Daikokuten (Māha-kāla), Bishamonten (Vaiśravaṇa), Hachi Dairyu-o (Nanda, Upananda, Sagara, Vāsuki, Takṣaka, Anavatapta, Manas, Utpala), etc.
7. Same meaning as the *zenjo* (law of discipline) of Buddha, except that one sits in the Zen (dhyāna) attitude and considers one's mistakes.
8. (Veṇuvana-vihāra) A monastery ordered built in Rajagaha by King Bimbisāra of Magadha where Buddha lived for about five monsoon periods.

9. Moggallāna (Maha-maudgal) and his best friend Upatissa (Maha-sāriputta) were Buddha's chief disciples. Moggallāna had supernatural power and after practicing austerities, came to be called "primary in spiritual capacities." He was killed by a group of priests who his him with their long sticks called khakkhara, which were especially designed for priests to carry, in order to put an end to Buddha's group.

10. The GLA (God's Light Association) was founded by Shinji Takahashi in 1970 and organized as religious group a year later. After Mr. Takahashi's death in 1976, his wife was nominated for his position. However, she and other high officials promoted and deified her daughter Keiko as the successor and incarnation of the archangel Michael. Since then, the movements and activities of the GLA have radically changed along the lines of the *Soka Gakkai* (see Note 13), which has disillusioned Shinji Takahashi's devoted followers and led them to leave the group. At its prime, the GLA is said to have had 70,000 followers, which has decreased to 20,000 in number. Fifteen or more small groups have sprouted from among the defectors which are now reorganizing themselves into new religious groups, based on Shinji Takahashi's teachings.

11. (Prajñāpāramitā-hṛdaya-sūtra) The fourth of five sutras representing periods of graduated levels of Buddhist doctrines.

12. Buddha's wife. They were married before the Gautama Buddha became a priest. Their only offspring was Rahula.

13. A lay Buddhist group founded in 1937 as an offshoot of the Nichiren sect. Its doctrines advocate absolute faith with immediate worldly benefits. Its many activities include education, culture and politics, with its Komeito Party being the fourth largest political party in Japan.

14. A Japanese religious reformer, who founded in 1253, the sect called after his name, based on his teachings on one scripture alone. He taught that the very name of the scripture had mantric power and that by meditating and repeating it as an invocation would remove false barriers and bring enlightenment.

15. Being destined for or one intent on enlightenment. A title sometimes applied to a high priest known for his virtues and high level of enlightenment.

16. Translator's note.

17. The queen of the kingdom of Yamatai, whose location is historically unknown but generally understood to be situated somewhere in central Kyushu, the southernmost island of Japan. Yamatai is known to be the oldest kingdom, which existed in the latter half of the 2nd century, governning 28 small areas nearby, including the western part of Japan's mainland. Himiko is said to have had strong powers of incantation and wielded firm control over her domain.

18. A sacred portable shrine used to carry the Shinto god symbol from a main shrine to another or vice versa.

19. The path which leads to Nirvana, the human goal of Buddhism. It consists of eight divisions: (1) correct view, (2) correct thinking, (3) correct speech, (4) correct action, (5) correct livelihood, (6) correct endeavor, (7) correct aspiration and (8) correct meditation.
20. The northernmost and second largest island of Japan.
21. Part of the realm of the sun, which consists of the three highest divisions in the Kingdom of Heaven. The lowest of these is the Realm of the Angels, the next is the 9th dimension and the highest is called the Realm of the Universe.
22. Printed on the GLA calendar for 1976.
23. Charles Messier's catalog, a systematic list of nebulas and star clusters compiled and published in 1771, containing 45 objects, and in a final list in 1784, containing 103.
24. Sanskrit name for one who has followed the path to enlightenment and, having attained the highest truths of Buddhism, preaches it to others.
25. Sanskrit name of a female disciple of Buddha, who promised him that she would one day reach Nirvana. She dwells in Tusita, the fourth of six levels of Heaven for Bodhisattvas, where she practices austerities and edifies heavenly beings. She is to return to earth 56 billion 70 million years after Buddha's death to lead all men down the righteous path and finally to gain enlightenment as the new Buddha (Japanese name: Miroku Bosatsu).
26. A terrestrial spirit of Japanese mythology who lived in the land of Izumo, an ancient city in the southwest mainland of Japan, and was famed for his power of healing.
27. The great hero prince mentioned in the *Kojiki*, Japan's oldest history book. Son of the 12th Emperor Keiko.
28. Sanskrit name of the sister of Buddha's mother, Maya. After the latter's death on the 7th day after childbirth, she took care of the infant Buddha.
29. Differing from Western concept, the Buddhist limbo is the lowest realm of Heaven, where only the most self-centered, avaricious souls live. (Details in Chap. V)
30. The Sun Goddess of Japanese mythology who, as the ancestress of the Imperial Family, is worshipped through Shinto, the state religion, as the national deity or supreme divinity of the Japanese people.
31. The Five Precepts; viz., not to take life, not to take what is not given to one; not to commit adultery, not to tell lies, and not to drink intoxicants. (Further Details in Chap. VI)
32. A part of Hell where nefarious sinners who are beyond salvation are confined.
33. A part of Hell where the most self-centered and arrogant sinners are confined.
34. Prince Shotoku or Prince Umayado (Shotoku is a post-humous name) (574–622), the second son of Emperor Yomei, became Prince Regent in

592. Gaining proficiency in the Chinese classics and the Buddhist doctrines at an early age, he studied under the Korean monk Eji, when the latter came to Japan in 594. The previous year, he had instigated the issuance of an Imperial decree supporting Buddhism. In 619, this leader and patron of Buddhism, began to edit an Imperial and Japanese history and built Nara and seven temples during this period, including the Horyu-ji.

35. (Details on page 164 of Chap. VI)

36. Hung Hsiu-ch'uan (1814–64): The leader of the T'ai P'ing Rebellion, was born into a poor peasant Hakka family in the province of Kwangtung. T'ai P'ing Rebellion was considered to be the precursor of subsequent nationalistic revolutions in China. In 1850, took up arms against the Imperial government under the slogan of liberty, equality, and overthrow of the Manchu Dynasty. His teachings borrowed certain elements from Christian Protestant doctrine. Founded the Heavenly Kingdom of Great Peace in Kwangsi the following year. Seized Nanking in 1853, but his movement was finally beaten by Imperial forces. His revolution failed as a result of growing internal weakness caused mainly by internal strife and corruption.

37. Brahman teaching which Buddha once rejected. An esoteric learning of spiritual content and idealistic purpose, which considers almsmanship as being customary. (Reference to page 161 of Chap. VI)

38. Kwannon: Avalokiteśvara in Sanskrit. The Goddess of Mercy. Many variations such as the Thousand-handed Kwannon, the Eleven-faced Kwannon, and the Horse-headed Kwannon. Sho Kwannon is the general appellation (*cf*. Note 45). Supposedly resides on Mount Potalaka. Mount Nachi is the equivalent in Japan. Devotees of the Lotus Sutra (Saddharamapuṇḍarīka-sūtra in Sanskrit) are many and widespread. (*cf*. Note 62)

39. *A short description of the Primary Body, the Subsequent Body and the Spirit Brother:* These conceptions are based upon the idea of "Transmigration of Souls." Taking an example, I shall explain these: Where once merged (in-dwelt) by a certain spirit in the Celestial Realm, the person is referred to as "the primary body." After death, he will be a first subsequent body in the Celestial Realm, separated from the in-dwelling spirit. Then, the original good spirit (the in-dwelling spirit) and this new first subsequent body are destined to live different lives. After a certain period of time, or, under certain circumstances, on request of the Celestial Realm, the good spirit creats the second subsequent body by again merging with a certain person. The original good spirit, primary body, the first subsequent body and the second subsequent body are all referred to as spirit brothers.

40. Kuze Kwannon: Bodhisattva in Sanskrit. A Buddhist Saint, believed to bestow deliverance from the troubles of the world. (*cf*. Note 62)

The Chart of Primary and Subsequent Bodies

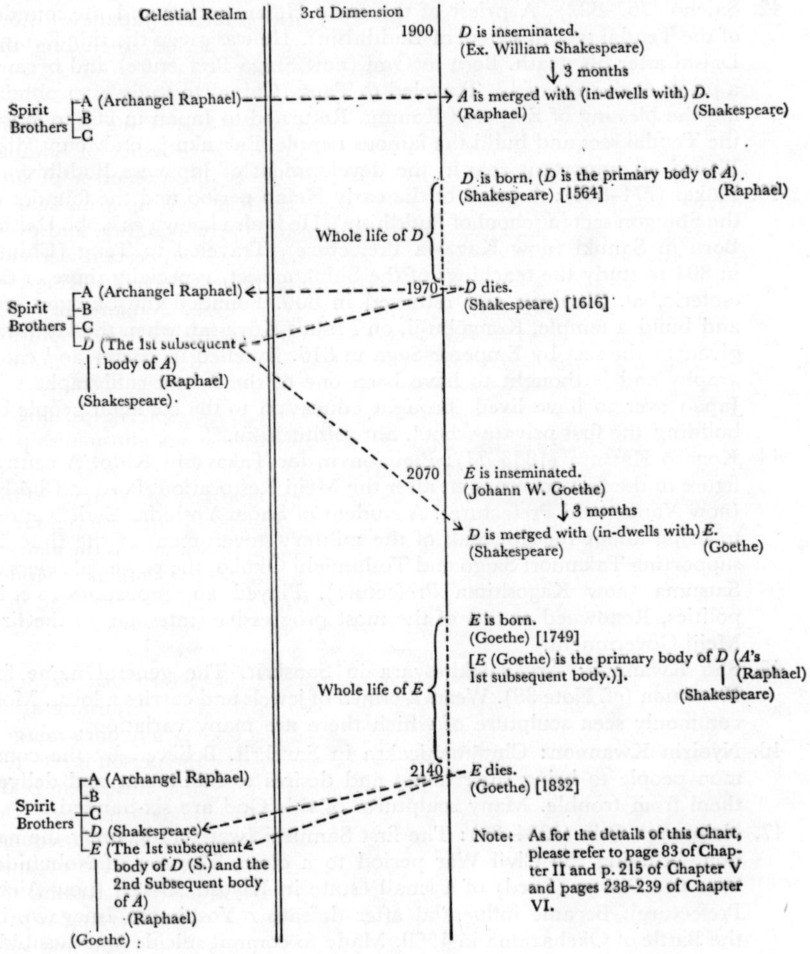

41. Chuang (Sanzo): A title of respect for a priest who is well-versed in the Chuang (the Sutra, the Canons, and the Teachings). Genjyo (or known as Sanzo-Hōshi), 600/602–664, in the era of Tang, China, is, perhaps, the most well-known or these priests.

42. Saichō (767–822): A priest of the early Heian period and the founder of the Tendai sect (a school of Buddhism). He was given the title Dengyō Daishi after his death. Born in Ōmi (now Shiga Prefecture) and became a priest at the age of 12. Traveled to Tang (China) to study after obtaining the blessing of Emperor Kanmu. Returned to Japan in 805 to found the Tendai sect and build the famous temple, Enryaku-ji, on Mount Hiei. Played an important role in the development of Japanese Buddhism.

43. Kūkai (774–835): A priest of the early Heian period and the founder of the Shingon sect (a school of Buddhism). He is also known as Kōbō Daishi. Born in Sanuki (now Kagawa Prefecture). Traveled to Tang (China) in 804 to study the teachings of the Shingon sect, especially those of the esoteric, at Changan and returned in 806. Founded the Shingon sect and build a temple, Kongōbu-ji, on Mount Kōya-san when the land was given to the sect by Emperor Saga in 816. Excelled in poetry and calligraphy and is thought to have been one of the 3 best calligraphers in Japan ever to have lived. Brought education to the common people by building the first private school, Shugeishuchi-in.

44. Kogorō Katsura (1833–77): Pseudonym for Takayoshi Kido. A central figure in the first government after the Meiji Restoration. Born in Chōshū (now Yamaguchi Prefecture). A student of Shōin Yoshida. Endeavoured to bring about the downfall of the military government of the time by supporting Takamori Saigō and Toshimichi Ōkubo, the powerful rulers of Satsuma (now Kagoshima Prefecture). Played an important role in politics. Renowned as one of the most progressive statesman of the first Meiji Government.

45. Shō Kwannon: Āryāvalokiteśvara in Sanskrit. The general name for Kwannon (cf. Note 38). Wears a crown of jewels and carries a lotus. Most commonly seen sculpture of which there are many variations.

46. Nyoirin Kwannon: Cintāmaṇicakra in Sanskrit. Believed by the common people to bring their hopes and desires to fulfillment and deliver them from trouble. Many sculptures of this God are six-handed.

47. Nobunaga Oda (1534–82): The first Samurai (warrior) to unify the nation, bringing the Civil War period to a close. The son of Nobuhide. Was the *Daimyo* (Lord) of a small estate in Kiyosu, Owari (now Aichi Prefecture). Became influential after defeating Yoshimoto Imagawa in the Battle of Okehazama in 1560. Made to commit suicide by Mitsuhide Akechi (*cf.* Note 52) at Honnō-ji in Kyōto in 1582, known as the "Disturbance at Honnō-ji." Contributed to unified rule by abolishing the border posts in his territory, setting up the *Raku-ichi/Raku-za* system

which permitted free commerce, surveying of country, and forbidding those not of Samurai rank to bear arms.

48. Ikkyū (1394–1481): A priest of the Rinzai sect (a school of Zen) in the middle of the Muromachi period. Was a priest at Daitoku-ji, a temple in Kyōto. Excelled in poetry, painting, and calligraphy. Traveled the length and breadth of the country and was notorious for his peculiar behaviour. Author of a collection of poems *Kyōun-shu (The Mad Clouds)*. Immortalized by *Ikkyū Shokoku Banashi (Ikkyū's Stories of the Countryside)* and has since been the subject of many novels and plays.

49. Susanoo-no-mikoto: The son of Izanagi-no-mikoto and Izanami-no-mikoto. The brother of Amaterasu Ōmikami (the Great Sun Goddess). Was supposedly of a ferocious disposition and was sent to kill Yamata-no-orochi, the eight-headed dragon. Was also supposed to have traveled to Shiragi (Korea). He returned with wood for ship-building and was also believed to have taught forestry. (One of the hero in the Japanese mythology.)

50. Sun Wen (1866–1925): Revolutionary and statesman of the late Ching period. Called the Father of the Chinese Revolution. The first President of the Republic of China. Born in Canton. Studied medicine in Hong Kong and started a business in Macao. Led the life of a revolutionary without success and fled to Japan. While in Japan he formulated the Three Principles of the People and after the Chinese Revolution of 1911 became the Provisional President of the Republic of China. Came again to Japan when exiled by Yuan Shih-Kai, returning to China in 1916. In 1919 formed the Chinese National Party. Died at Peking in 1925.

51. Yoshitsune Minamoto (1159–89): A Samurai (warrior) of the late Heian period. Was active in destroying the power of the Heike family. The son of Yoshitomo Minamoto and Tokiwa. A half-brother of Yoritomo Minamoto (*cf.* Note 54). Brought up at the Kurama Temple in Kyōto, under guardianship of Hidehira Fujiwara of Hiraizumi. On hearing of the raising of an army by his half-brother joined him and attacked the forces of Yoshinaka Kiso and destroyed the Heike clan at the Battles of Ichi-no-Tani, Ya-shima, and Dan-no-Ura in 1185. Was warmly received by Emperor Goshirakawa which engendered the envy of his half-brother's who forced him to return to his guardian, Hidehira. After the death of Hidehira committed suicide when defeated by Hidehira's son Yasuhira at the Koromo River.

52. Mitsuhide Akechi (1528–82): A Samurai (warrior) of the Azuchi-Momoyama period. Successfully served under Yoshikage Asakura and Nobunaga Oda. Forced Nobunaga (*cf.* Note 47) to commit suicide when Nobunaga was on his way to attack the Mōri clan in 1582. Killed in a battle with Hideyoshi (*cf.* Note 55) at Yamazaki.

53. Toshizō Hijikata (1835–69): A famous swordsman and supporter of the

last Edo Military Government. Joined the *Shinsengumi* (the Newly Elected Group) in 1863 and guarded the City of Kyōto with Isamu Kondō. After losing the Battle of Toba-Fushimi, opposed the national army. Joined the army of Takeaki Enomoto and died at Hakodate *Goryōkaku*.

54. Yoritomo Minamoto (1147–99): The Samurai (warrior) who founded the Kamakura Military Government. The first *Shōgun*. Lost the Battle of Heiji in 1159 and was exiled to Hiruga Island in Izu where he was under the supervision of the Hōjō family (the retainer of the Heike clan), but was protected by them and married their daughter, Masako. In 1180 raised an army to attack the Heike clan. Subjugated the country from his base at Kamakura. Became *Shōgun* in 1192 and kept the nation under military rule.

55. Hideyoshi Toyotomi (1536–98): A Samurai (warrior) of the Civil War period who unified the nation. The son of a farmer at Nakamura, Owari (now Aichi Prefecture). Became the page of Kahēnotsuna Matsushita at 15, later served under Nobunaga (*cf.* Note 47). Killed Akechi (*cf.* Note 52) after the "Disturbance at Honnō-ji." Unified the nation. Attacked Korea twice with the aim of conquering Ming (China), but died during the last campaign.

56. Sōseki Natsume (1867–1916): A well-known literary man of the Meiji-Taishō period. Born in Tokyo. Became famous on publication of *Wagahai wa Neko de Aru (I am a Cat)* published in 1905. Was also a Haiku poet influenced by Shiki Masaoka who he had met during his days as an English literature major at Tokyo University. Was critical of Naturalism which had a large following at that time. Was one of a group of intellectual writers with Ōgai Mori (*cf.* Note 57) and Shōyō Tsubouchi. Led the modern literature movement.

57. Ōgai Mori (1862–1922): Literary man and physician of the Meiji-Taishō period. Born in Shimane Prefecture. After studying medicine at Tokyo University, went to Germany to study. On his return published a collection of translated poems called *Omokage (Images)*. Endeavoured to introduce western literature especially German literature. Was active in the various fields of criticism, writing, and teaching modern drama.

58. Kanzō Uchimura (1861–1930): Christian philosopher of the late Meiji and early Taishō periods. As a Christian was opposed to the Russo-Japanese War. Born in Tokyo. Converted to Christianity after graduating from Sapporo Nō-Gakko (Sapporo Agricultural School). Went to the U.S.A. to study. Founded the "*Seisho no Kenkyū* (The Study of the Bible)" and proposed Non-Sectarianism. Endeavoured to establish an independent form of Japanese Christianity. Accepted as one of the greatest religeous man of Japan in modern times.

59. Sōshi Okita: The most popular member of the Shinsengumi (the Newly Elected Group *cf.* Note 53).

60. Sei-shōnagon: Essayist and Tanka-poetess of the Heian period. The authoress of *Makura-no-Sōshi (The Pillow Book)*. Of the Kiyohara family, a wellknown family of poets. Known to have been the confident of Sadako one of the wives of Emperor Ichijō. Influence at court ceased on the death of Sadako. Was a wellknown intellectual of the time. Her work, *The Pillow Book* is a collection of essays concerning everyday events in the palace and other observations.

61. Murasaki-shikibu (978–1016): A representative writer and poetess of the Heian period. The daughter of Tametoki Fujiwara. Was brilliant from childhood and excelled in *Tanka* poems and literary creations in general. After the death of her husband, Nobutaka Fujiwara entered the service of Akiko, one of the wives of Emperor Ichijō. Wrote *The Tale of Genji* during this period. With Sei-shōnagon (*cf.* Note 60) is a representative women writer of the middle of the Heian period.

62. Kanjizai-bosatsu is the Buddhist savior (Avalokiteśvara). He remains the savior of all the created things and is filled with the quality of compassion, which is of the essence of Bodhisattva or Saint. *Kanjizai* is identical with the capacity of free perception and apprehension of the truths in every phaze of all the existing rules and laws, or salvation of all the created things in the universe upon observation and immediate apprehension of the truths. Because of the compassion, the Bodhisattva is made known to assume the various forms in which he appears for the salvation of beings in the phenomenal world.

63. *Hannya-shingyo:* Among the chiefs of the Buddhist sutras in Sanskrit are the so-called Prajñāpāramitā-hṛdaya-sūtra. Hṛdaya means "heart" or "essence," thus "center." The *Hannya-shingyo* sutras were introduced to Japan through China. This particular sutra is the briefest, with less than 300 words, of all the other enormously paged *Hannya-shingyo* sutras, describing the central thought and philosophy of Buddha's teachings to his disciples in conversational style. It is loved and chanted daily by many of the Buddhists in Japan.

64. Karma (Karman) or *Gō* (in Japanese) is derived from the verbal root *kr* (to make or act). Therefore, karma means action; karma is the universal "seed" of which all action is the fruit. An action does not occur without a cause. And once the action is caused, it brings about a result. This chain of inevitability is called generically "karman" or "karma." Karma, therefore, the real factor in all that we see, feel, experience, hear, speak, and will, is the apparent creator of the phenomenal world. The totality of phenomenal existence, thus manifold in its manifestations, in its constitution and process of continuous becoming, is one. Thereby has come the philosophy of "transmigration" or the rebirth of the soul into a new life.

65. Darani is dha=rani which means "to keep" or "something to keep." Dha=rani implies that ascetics are able to keep remembering Buddhist

doctrines. It also implies the phrases which protect ascetics from disasters. Especially, the concept of dha=rani is represented by the mystic Shingon sect (the esoteric religion) because its central principle culminated in the doctrine that Bodhisattva understands and realizes the essence of dha=rani, the power of eliminating disasters, and that he enlightens the public.

66. Shintoism: Shinto means the divine way. It is originated in the native religion of Japan, related to the Japanese mythology. When Buddhism was introduced from China in the middle of the sixth century, there was no religious controversy between Shintoism and Buddhism because Shintoism was concerned with the present world, whereas Buddhism was concerned with the world after death. The religious belief (though there is a clear distinction between religion and morality) in terms of the combination of Shintoism and Buddhism became a slogan for establishing a religious government or for uniting Japanese small clans into a single political organization. Thus, Shintoism coupled with Buddhism, Confucianism has been preserved as the moral imperative of the people.

67. Yuima Koji (the retired scholar Yuima): Yuima is the name of the hero, Vimalakīrti (in Sanskrit) in the Vimala-kirtinirdeśa whose Sanskrit textbooks are lost. We can only refer to their Chinese translation by Kumarajiva. The three-volumed sutras are composed of the fable of the dialogues in the form of catechism between Vimalakīrti, a millionaire in the city of Vaiśālī, allegedly a layman Bodhisattva who has exhausted the mystery of Mahāyāna Buddhism, and Buddha's disciples. The catechism was ended amusingly with the exceeding victory on the side of the hero.

68. *Shinnyo* is bhūtatathatā, fundamental reality which exists in the universe and all beings. The syllable "*shin*" means the truth that is distinguished from an illusion. The syllable "*nyo*" means eternal reality.

69. *Zenjo* is dhyāna. The difference of the method between the Indian and the Chinese Buddhist teachers is that of between "Tathāgata Dhyāna" and "Patriarchal Dhyāna." The former one is the mode of contemplation, where the latter one intruded by Bodhidharma and developed by Hui neng, is not the mode of contemplation but the aquisition of prajñā (wisdom) without contemplation. For instance, when you concentrate yourself on one thing, there is no possibility of other things being involved. Thus, the aquisition of prajñā by contemplation is not the right way. This line of patriarchal dhyāna is continued to this day in the Zen schools of Japan.